Harry Northwood
The Wheeling Years
1901-1925

William Heacock
James Measell
Berry Wiggins

PB ISBN# 0-915410-74-5

HB ISBN# 0-915410-75-3

TABLE OF CONTENTS

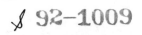

Publisher's Introduction

Take I-94 out of Chicago until you come to Route 12, then follow that until you break out of the deep woods. You'll see a little town with a Best Western Motel and a thirty foot orange moose. You can't miss it." These were the directions which Bill Heacock gave to my photographer and me in 1987 when we were heading out for what we hoped would be our final photo session for the Northwood carnival book. Photography had extended over three years, and we had traveled almost three thousand miles pursuing the finest collections of Northwood carnival to illustrate this book. We took trips to upstate New York and Pennsylvania, and now we were headed to Wisconsin.

When we finally arrived there, it was just like he said – the deep woods stopped and suddenly we were in a valley with a little town and a horizon dominated by a big orange moose. (Bill took the snapshot shown here. I don't know the name of the moose, but the woman is Deana Wynn, our photographer and the old guy is the publisher.)

We worked hard that trip, but we had a lot of fun. It was on that trip that Bill found his jade and black Martha Washington powder box – an item he had hunted for several years (for the

whole story, see *Glass Collector's Digest,* volume II, number 3, page 15.) It was also on that trip that I saw Bill totally speechless. It happened when he walked into the room and saw the collection we came to photograph!

The book you hold in your hand is the culmination of thousands of hours of work, including more than a few of my own, but these were some of the most enjoyable hours I've ever worked. It was my good fortune to be directly involved with all the photo shoots which gave me the opportunity to see some fabulous carnival glass and which ultimately led me to become a collector of carnival glass in general and Northwood carnival in particular.

As I sit here in my office on this cold blustery November day, five years later, my mind is swirling with a hundred thoughts regarding this book and my friend Bill. As most of you readers know by now, "Bill" refers to William Heacock, the man who started this book and who passed away in August 1988. Beginning with *Fenton Glass: The Third Twenty-Five Years,* the first book to be published after Bill's death, a publisher's introduction has been added to each book. This was done partly to memorialize Bill (i.e., to be sure that every reader would know the story behind the story) and partly to share with all of

iv

you some of the "backstage" drama involved in getting a book into print.

For those readers who do not have *Harry Northwood: The Early Years,* and thus may not know what led up to the publication of this book, a section of the publisher's introduction from the first book is reproduced below.

Bill began his Encyclopedia of Victorian Pattern Glass series in 1974 and by the time the sixth book came out in 1981, he had confided in me what his "grand plan" was. The last three books in the series would be his crowning achievement, a trilogy on Harry Northwood. Bill's research and writings on Mr. Northwood would be the accomplishment of his life, for which he wished everyone to remember him.

As the years rolled by, Bill spent a lot of time accumulating information on Northwood. His computer and manila file folders bulged with tidbits of information. As he was researching and writing his other books, every time he came across something pertinent to Harry Northwood or a Northwood pattern, he would add it to his data banks. When he started to publish his journals – *The Glass Collector* and later, *Collection Glass* – he was so excited about some of the Northwood information he had found that he decided to share it with his readers in short articles instead of waiting until the trilogy was completed.

In early 1986, Bill began to have health problems which greatly reduced his strength and his ability to write. A deadly debilitating disease was already at work. He was having great difficulty meeting his deadlines and public appearances. By the spring of 1987, Bill's illness was wrecking havoc with his ability to concentrate and to organize data. Each time he would sit down at his computer to work on the book, his thoughts would be so jumbled that he could never get much accomplished. None of us knew it at the time, but Bill would have a little more than twelve months to live, during which time he was unable to do anything on his manuscripts.

Shortly before he passed away, Bill finally realized that he was unable to finish this series. He asked me what was going to happen to his incomplete manuscripts. I told him that I would do whatever was necessary to see that they were completed and published and that they would be under his name as author. At that time, he was working on *Fenton Glass: The Third Twenty-Five Years, More Stained Glass from A to Z* (Book 8 in the Encyclopedia Series), and the trilogy on Northwood.

He passed away on August 14, 1988.

We began to complete his unfinished projects in the same sequence in which he had been working on them. First came the third Fenton book, which was published in the spring of 1989. But when we turned our attention to the proposed book on stained glass, we discovered that it was not as well developed as Bill's work on Harry Northwood, so we decided to do the Northwood series next. The first book was released in 1990, and then we began working on the second.

(The "we" to whom I refer in the above paragraph is Dr. James Measell, noted glass historian and author, Berry Wiggins, glass researcher and my staff here at Antique Publications.) After another eighteen months of hard work, this second book was finally completed and published. I feel a great deal of pride and satisfaction in seeing this book in print. I hope that you, the reader and collector, enjoy the color reproductions of Northwood's extraordinary carnival pieces which we have tried to bring to you as accurately and beautifully as possible. As you read and use this book, remember Harry Northwood and his glass, but also remember the man who wanted the world to know and appreciate Mr. Northwood, my late friend, Bill Heacock.

David E. Richardson, Publisher

INTRODUCTION AND ACKNOWLEDGEMENTS

This is the second of two volumes devoted to the career of Harry Northwood (1860-1919), an Englishman who emigrated to the United States and became a highly-successful glassmaker and businessman. The first volume, *Harry Northwood: The Early Years, 1881-1900,* was published in 1990. Like its predecessor, this book draws upon many sources, both public and private, and these are listed in the Bibliography. Within each chapter, sources are cited as they are used, so that readers can readily understand both the reasoning and the evidence for each statement.

Many people contributed their advice, expertise and support to this project. David Richardson, president of Antique Publications, remains firmly committed to the highest standards of excellence in both print production and glass history. His desire to see the research begun by the late William Heacock brought to fruition made this book possible. Photographers Deana Tullius Wynn and Becky VanBrackel contributed their talents, as did Ronda Ludwig, who supervised this book's layout and design.

Miss Elizabeth Northwood Robb, the granddaughter of Harry Northwood, was gracious in allowing access to family scrapbooks and heirlooms, and she shared her memories of family and events. Others in the Northwood family supported this project: Robert and Doris Hamilton; Brian McKinley; David and Mary McKinley; Karen McKinley; and Ken Northwood.

Two noteworthy Carnival glass collections, assembled by Harold Ludeman and by Rose Schleede and her late husband Carleton Schleede, were the basis for most of the photos of this remarkable glass. Mrs. Schleede and long-time Carnival glass researchers and writers John and Lucile Britt were always ready to answer inquiries, and the Britts double-checked all of the color plates of Carnival glass as well as the captions. Don Moore, Raymond Notley, Ed Radcliff and Ruth Schinestuhl also provided help in this area.

Pattern glass collector/dealer William Gamble was instrumental in obtaining important items from collectors to be photographed for this book. Others brought pieces to Marietta, sent photos, or offered other assistance. Among those contributing in one or more of these ways were the following: Bud Ashmore; Kerry Bachler; Arthur Beedham; Jack Burk; Bill Carney; Orville and Leona Crouch; Bob and Sherry Czya; Seeley and Loretta Disorda; Ernest and Althea Dugan; Frank M. Fenton; Lloyd Georges; Bob Hefner; Sarah Jenkins; Tom Klopp; Tom and Betty Laney; Larry Loxterman; Al and Ann McBride; Joan McGee; Paul Miller; Ken Northwood; William Olejniczak; Floyd Schramm; Jabe Tarter; Roger Thorngate; Edwin and Jocelyn White; Berry Wiggins; and Otto, Marion and Kurt Zwicker.

The cooperation of the Corning Museum of Glass, particularly Librarian Norma Jenkins, was most welcome. Both the Fenton Museum and the Oglebay Institute loaned objects and photographs, and the Rockwell Museum provided a photo of an article in its collection of Carder material. Royal Brierley Crystal, Ltd., allowed quotations from private diaries in the firm's possession, and Mr. Charles R. Hajdamach of the Broadfield House Glass Museum in Stourbridge, England, provided a number of useful notes.

Frank M. Fenton answered numerous questions on glassmaking technology and color chemistry, and he also allowed access to the voluminous records and papers of the National Association of Manufacturers of Pressed and Blown Glassware. The American Flint Glass Workers Union provided copies of material at its national headquarters in Toledo.

The records relating to the receivership proceedings of the Northwood firm and the lawsuit between Macbeth-Evans and Northwood were obtained from the National Archives Mid-Atlantic Regional Center in Philadelphia. The Center for Research Libraries loaned trade journals for much-needed photography, and the University of Wyoming's American Heritage Center permitted interlibrary loan of its Montgomery Wards catalogs on microfilm. The Minnesota Historical Society provided access to numerous G. Sommers & Co. catalogs.

Perhaps the greatest debt is that owed to the late William Heacock, who began to research the glassmaking career of Harry Northwood well over a decade ago. It is hoped that this book, like its predecessor, will be a large part of Bill's legacy to collectors of American glass, both present and future.

James Measell
Marietta, Ohio
July, 1991

A Dandelion tumbler, ice blue Carnival glass

B Dandelion pitcher, ice blue Carnival glass

C Peacock at the Fountain orange bowl, aqua opalescent Carnival glass

D Grape and Cable banana boat, blue Carnival glass

E Peacocks on the Fence ruffled bowl, iridescent blue marble glass

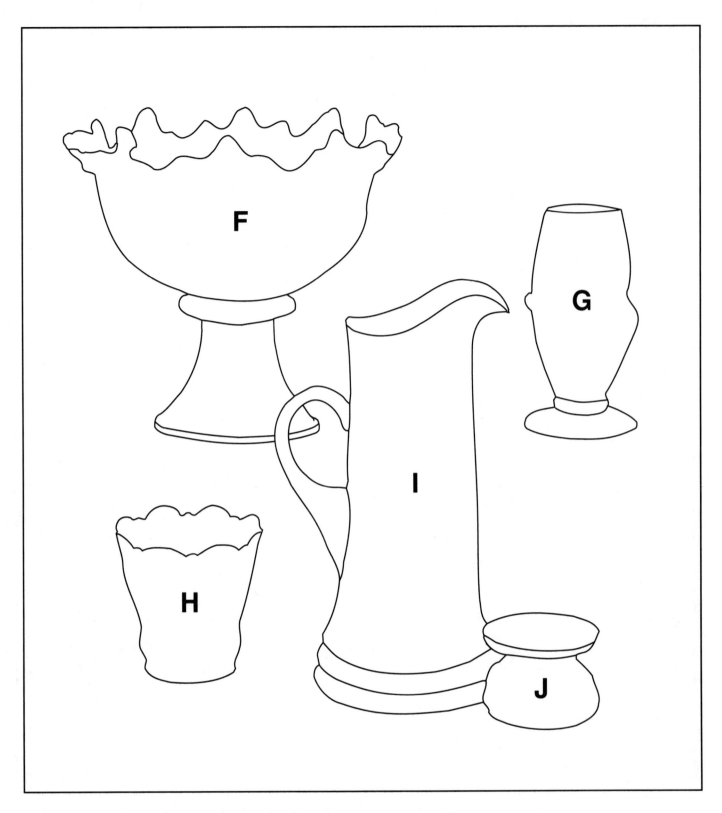

F Peacock at the Fountain two-piece punch bowl, aqua opalescent Carnival glass

G Corn Husk vase, purple Carnival glass

H Plums and Cherries, purple Carnival glass

I Daffodils pitcher, ruby (cranberry) opalescent glass

J Grape and Cable spittoon, purple Carnival glass

CHAPTER ONE
HARRY NORTHWOOD: THE EARLY YEARS

Although Harry Northwood's glassmaking career 1881-1900 has been covered in a previous volume, this overview of that time period will serve to introduce the new reader to Northwood as well as to reorient those familiar with the Northwood story. The summary given here lacks the documentation present in the earlier volume, of course.

Harry Northwood (1860-1919) was the eldest son of John Northwood (1836-1902), a famous English cameo glass carver and glassmaker who was associated with the Stevens & Williams firm in Stourbridge for most of his working life. Young Harry was educated at government design schools and was probably also tutored by his father, who was then a partner in a glass ornamenting firm called J. & J. Northwood. Despite seemingly unlimited opportunities in England, Harry Northwood immigrated to the United States in November, 1881, not long after he had turned 21. He left behind his fiance, Clara Elizabeth Beaumont.

His first job in the United States was at the Hobbs, Brockunier firm in Wheeling, West Virginia. He is listed as a "glass etcher" in city directories from 1882-83, as is his cousin, Thomas E. A. Dugan, who had immigrated about the same time. Both Northwood and Dugan may have been encouraged to come to America by their maternal uncle, Thomas Dugan, who had a hotel in Pittsburgh and was later instrumental in the founding and development of Ellwood City, Pennsylvania, in the early 1890s.

After working at the Hobbs, Brockunier plant for several years, where he probably observed the Leightons and other glass chemists, Northwood was hired as an engraver by the La Belle Glass Co. of Bridgeport, Ohio. He soon established himself as a glassmaker of some repute, although his career at the La Belle was interrupted by strikes and floods which shut down the plant periodically. During part of this time, Northwood apparently had an independent business, offering both glass decorating and general artistic services.

There is also good evidence that Northwood spent over a year at the Phoenix Glass Co. in West Bridgewater (now Monaca), Pennsylvania, in close contact with Joseph Webb, another glassmaker who had come from England. Northwood was lured to the Buckeye Glass Company in nearby Martins Ferry in April, 1887, but his tenure lasted just a week until the La Belle hired him back at a higher salary. Northwood continued at the La Belle until it was destroyed by fire in September 1887.

GLASS WORKS OF J.H.HOBBS, BROCKUNIER & CO.
COR. OF 36TH & MCCULLOCH STS, WHEELING, WEST VA.
JOHN H. HOBBS.   JOHN L. HOBBS.   WM LEIGHTON JR.   CHARLES W. BROCKUNIER

From Hayes' Atlas (1877). **Courtesy of the Fenton Museum, Williamstown, WV.**

1

From Hayes' **Atlas *(1877). Courtesy of the Fenton Museum, Williamstown, WV.***

By this time, Harry Northwood had a young family. Clara Elizabeth Beaumont came to the United States in May, 1882, and she and Harry were married within a few days of her arrival. Her brother, Percy J. Beaumont, was also a glassmaker, and he was associated with Harry from time to time during the 1880s. Harry Northwood probably had known Clara Elizabeth Beaumont for a number of years, for several glass articles, one of which bears an 1879 date, remain among the family heirlooms. The Northwoods had two children, Harry Clarence, who was born in 1883, and Mabel Virginia, who was born in 1884.

This letterhead was used when Harry Northwood maintained a freelance glass decorating business from his rented home on Wheeling Island. The "Wm. Hare and Son" firm was a large plumbing contractor in Wheeling. **Courtesy of Roger Thorngate.**

Ad from Crockery and Glass Journal *(March, 1886-April, 1887).*

In November, 1887, wealthy investors from nearby Martins Ferry joined with Harry, who was then 28, to form the Northwood Glass Company. The firm was located in a renovated glass factory which had been erected some years earlier by the Union Flint Glass Co. From 1888 through 1892, the relatively small Northwood firm made its presence felt in the American glass tableware industry. Its products were, almost exclusively, blown glass tableware articles in such patterns as Pillar, Aurora, Leaf Umbrella, Jewel, Royal Ivy, Royal Oak, and Leaf Mold. These are today's collectors' names for the patterns, of course; originally, they were designated only by numbers—No. 245, No. 263, etc.. The Northwood plant made a specialty of ruby glass, but a number of other hues were made, including blue, yellow, and a variety of cased glass "spatter" colors. Two particulalrly interesting colors were called "Royal Silver" and "Royal Art." Royal Silver articles have an opal (milk) body containing rosy pink streaks and minute silver flakes.

Glass cross and book, probably engraved and cut by Harry Northwood. **Courtesy of Miss Robb.**

Harry Northwood and Clara Elizabeth Beaumont Northwood with their children, Harry Clarence (b. March 13, 1883) and Mabel Virginia (b. September 3, 1884). **Courtesy of Miss Robb.**

3

Opalescent glass, made by using spot moulds and reheating articles before or after finishing, was also popular. Among the skilled employees at the Northwood plant were several members of the Dugan family, including Thomas E. A. Dugan and his father, Samuel Dugan. All of the Dugans were to work in Northwood enterprises for the next decade.

Harry Northwood provided considerable copy for the columns of the glass trade journals. Many of his activities—from introducing a new glass color or pattern to building a home in Martins Ferry, going to England or taking his prize-winning English setters to a dog show—were grist for the mill in *Crockery and Glass Journal, Pottery and Glassware Reporter* or *China, Glass and Lamps*. Northwood was outspoken and sometimes blunt, but he was cooperative and always quotable.

In 1892, the Northwood firm moved to Ellwood City, Pa., where Harry Northwood's uncle, Thomas Dugan, had built a hotel and was working closely with real estate developers to create a modern, carefully planned municipality. A new glass factory, much larger than the old plant at Martins Ferry, was constructed especially for the Northwood Glass Company. Glassmaking began in October, 1892. Unlike the earlier concentration on tableware, the plant at Ellwood City made many condiment sets—salt and pepper shakers, syrup jugs and the like. Northwood developed new colors, called "neutral tints," in various shades of opaque green and blue. Some opal (opaque white) glass was manufacturered, as was ruby and opalescent glass. Among the patterns made at Ellwood city are Cactus, Flat Flower and Bow and Tassel. The firm mentioned shades and lamps

Courtesy of Miss Robb.

in its advertising, but the nature of these products remains a mystery.

The Ellwood City plant was not a success. The general hard times and competition in the glass

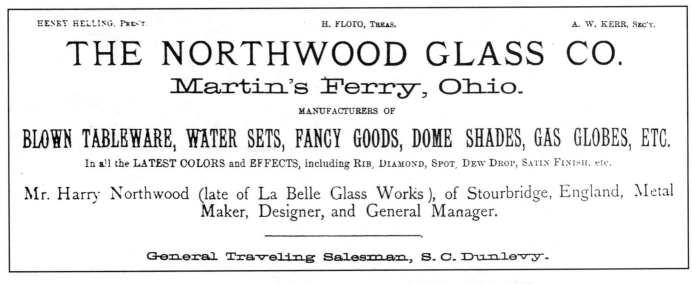

Ad from **Crockery and Glass Journal** *(January, 1888-September, 1888).*

4

Ad from China, Glass and Lamps *(July 27, 1892).*

Ad from China, Glass and Lamps *(April 15, 1896).*

Ad from Crockery and Glass Journal *(December 6, 1894).*

PAGODA OPAL 4-PIECE SET.

A handsomely decorated opal set, richly decorated in oil colors, with elaborate gold work. Very neat and taking and will prove a winner wherever shown. Each set contains a large footed and covered butter dish, spooner, fancy handled creamer and covered sugar. Try one set for a sample and you will easily sell a dozen.

Price per set, $1.50.

Pagoda table set from G. Sommers and Co. wholesale catalog (October 25, 1900).

tableware industry, coupled with internal difficulties among the investors, sealed its doom. In early 1896, Harry Northwood resigned abruptly and went to Indiana, Pa., where he supervised the refurbishing of a glass plant which had been shut for several years. The next four years in Indiana were, without doubt, the most successful of Northwood's early years.

Like the earlier plant at Ellwood City, Northwood's factory at Indiana was financed in part by his uncle, Thomas Dugan. The Indiana factory also received considerable support from local investors, including Judge Harry White, whose son was employed in the office of the new enterprise. White and others had been investors in the ill-fated Indiana Glass Company, which opened in 1892 and closed shortly thereafter. They sought somone to revive their factory. They found Harry Northwood, and he did just that.

The first pattern made at Indiana by the Northwood factory was called Apple Blossom. It was a decorated line in blown opal (milk) glass.

Other opal lines, such as Netted Oak and Panelled Sprig, were also produced, but Apple Blossom was the first and probably the most popular.

Northwood introduced Ivory (custard) glass in 1897 with a pressed glass pattern dubbed Louis XV. This opaque color was popular for the next several years, and new pressed patterns were added once or twice per year. Among the noteworthy patterns were Intaglio, Geneva, Pagoda, Nautilus, and Inverted Fan and Feather.

Northwood also produced two extraordinarily successful colored glass patterns, Klondyke and Alaska, in opalescent hues called "Pearl Yellow" and "Pearl Blue." Novelty items, such as candleholders and card receivers, were made, and the best known of such items today is the distinctive Pump and Trough.

In early 1899, the success of the Northwood concern attracted the attention of the newly-formed National Glass Company, a combine which ultimately embraced nineteen glass tableware factories. Soon after the Northwood Glass Co. became part of the combine in September,1899, Harry Northwood was appointed to the position

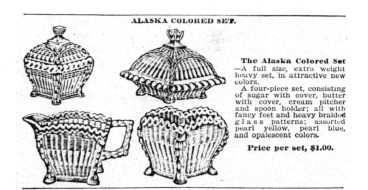

ALASKA COLORED SET.

The Alaska Colored Set—A full size, extra weight heavy set, in attractive new colors.

A four-piece set, consisting of sugar with cover, butter with cover, cream pitcher and spoon holder; all with fancy feet and heavy braided glass patterns; assorted pearl yellow, pearl blue, and opalescent colors.

Price per set, $1.00.

Alaska table set from G. Sommers and Co. wholesale catalog (April 6, 1898).

Ad from China, Glass and Pottery Review *(February, 1898).*

of London sales representative for the National. Northwood and his younger brother Carl, who had immigrated to the United States in 1892, returned with their families to England in December, 1899. The Northwoods' cousin, Thomas E. A. Dugan, was among the experienced glassworkers who remained with the plant in Indiana.

The period between 1881 and 1900 marked a time of rapid growth for Harry Northwood the glassmaker. His training as a glassetcher and designer was soon supplemented by other decorating techniques as well as by acquired knowledge of the chemistry of glassmaking. Northwood patented several moulds for making opalescent glass, and he improved a crimping device patented in 1885 by his father, John Northwood. Northwood's Ivory glass was unique in its time, and his pattern designs and decorating treatments were especially suited to the innovative color. Moreover, the Northwood name was ever-present in the editorial columns of the glass tableware industry's journals. Whatever Harry Northwood said or did made news in the trade.

Perhaps it was inevitable that Harry Northwood would return to America to begin anew his glassmaking career. Indeed, he had had more than a decade of notoriety in the glass tableware trade publications, where his every move in the 1890s made news. He was certainly a highly competent glass manufacturer, and his knowledge extended from glass color chemistry to great familiarity with decorating techniques. The success of his Indiana, Pa., factory in the late 1890s was due to both manufacturing and marketing, and much of the credit must go to Harry Northwood himself, for he was the key: an experienced glassman at the head of a well-run business. The sale of the Northwood plant to the National Glass Company changed the nature of operations at the factory. No longer would decisions be made by the local plant management. The National Glass Company, from its Pittsburgh headquarters, tried to unite 19 heretofore competitive enterprises. Most had been headed by individual entrepreneurs with considerable glassmaking expertise and strong personalities. Typically, these men accepted stock in the National Glass Company and persuaded their respective boards of directors to sell the individual plants to the National for, as the various sale deeds indicate, a dollar and "other diverse considerations," namely, the promising economic future of the National Glass Company. But it was not to be.

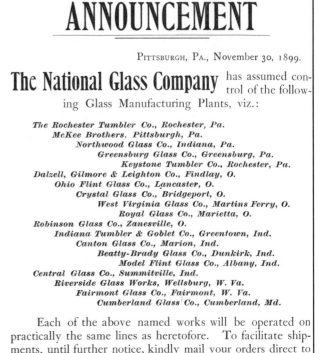

ANNOUNCEMENT

PITTSBURGH, PA., November 30, 1899.

The National Glass Company has assumed control of the following Glass Manufacturing Plants, viz.:

The Rochester Tumbler Co., Rochester, Pa.
McKee Brothers, Pittsburgh, Pa.
Northwood Glass Co., Indiana, Pa.
Greensburg Glass Co., Greensburg, Pa.
Keystone Tumbler Co., Rochester, Pa.
Dalzell, Gilmore & Leighton Co., Findlay, O.
Ohio Flint Glass Co., Lancaster, O.
Crystal Glass Co., Bridgeport, O.
West Virginia Glass Co., Martins Ferry, O.
Royal Glass Co., Marietta, O.
Robinson Glass Co., Zanesville, O.
Indiana Tumbler & Goblet Co., Greentown, Ind.
Canton Glass Co., Marion, Ind.
Beatty-Brady Glass Co., Dunkirk, Ind.
Model Flint Glass Co., Albany, Ind.
Central Glass Co., Summitville, Ind.
Riverside Glass Works, Wellsburg, W. Va.
Fairmont Glass Co., Fairmont, W. Va.
Cumberland Glass Co., Cumberland, Md.

Each of the above named works will be operated on practically the same lines as heretofore. To facilitate shipments, until further notice, kindly mail your orders direct to the works from which the goods are to be shipped.

We assure you that all orders entrusted to us shall have our prompt and careful attention.

COMMERCIAL DEPARTMENT
WESTINGHOUSE BUILDING
Penn Avenue and Ninth Street

SALES OFFICES
HARPER BUILDING
723-725 Liberty Avenue, corner Eighth Street

This announcement appeared in **Housefurnisher: China, Glass and Pottery Review** *when the National Glass Company was first formed.*

The National Comes Undone

Despite the initial fanfare surrounding the merger in 1899, the National Glass Company soon experienced problems. A central salesroom in Pittsburgh's Heeren Building was created, and some of the experienced road salesmen were let go. The National sought to maximize its profits by eliminating some of the representatives who sold the glassware of various firms on commission through showrooms in major cities. Buyers were used to visiting these outlets on a regular basis, however, and the National soon had the added expense of establishing its own showrooms in these cities. In 1899-1900, the National Glass Company undertook an extensive and expensive advertising campaign in the glass trade publications in an effort to focus attention upon its products.

Rumors soon abounded that the National Glass Company intended to close its "western"

plants, those in the Ohio-Indiana gas belt where supplies of natural gas were becoming increasingly undependable. In the first half of 1900, plants in Zanesville, Ohio, and Summitville, Indiana, were indeed closed, and D. C. Jenkins, Jr., left the National's Greentown, Indiana, plant to start a competing firm at nearby Kokomo. In February, 1900, one of the National's most efficient and modern facilities, the Rochester Tumbler Company, burned down. It had been the brainchild of Henry Clay Fry, a longtime glassman who was then serving as president of the National Glass Company. Fry and A. Hart McKee of McKee and Brothers in Jeannette, Pa., had been the major forces in effecting the merger of glass plants.

The National's board of directors decided not to rebuild in Rochester and looked toward Cambridge, Ohio, as the site for a new, modern factory. The Union Trust of Pittsburgh underwrote a bond issue of $2 million for the National's ambitious plans. Fry resigned his post and set out to rebuild the Rochester plant, adding yet another competitor to the National's marketing woes. He retained his National Glass Company stock, however, and his son, George H. Fry, remained part of the National's sales force. The March, 1901 issue of *Housefurnisher: China, Glass and Pottery Review* reported that George Fry was "in London now drumming up orders" for the National Glass Company. One wonders why he was needed there, for Harry and Carl Northwood had been manning a large showroom for over a year.

In March, 1901, the National lost another key executive when W. A. B. Dalzell resigned to assume the presidency of the Fostoria Glass Company in Moundsville, West Virginia. Clearly, all was not well within the National Glass Company. The internal problems came to a head on August 13, 1901, when the company's annual meeting was held in Pittsburgh. According to an account in the *National Glass Budget* (August 17, 1901), "a spirited contest was had over the election of a board of directors." Harry Northwood was nominated for a director's position by a group of stockholders led by Henry Clay Fry.

Presumably, Northwood and C. P. Walker, another directorship candidate backed by the group, were allied with Fry and shared his views on the future of the National. The Fry coalition was unsuccessful in its nomination of Northwood and Walker, and the National Glass Company's "present management ... elected their ticket" (*National Glass Budget,* August 17, 1901). A few months later, Harry Northwood was back in the United States, seeking financial backing and looking for a building site or a glass factory to purchase.

Back Home Again

Apparently, Northwood made Indiana, Pennsylvania, his destination when he decided to return from England. His ties there with investors, such as Judge Harry White and his son Harry White, Jr., went back to the mid-1890s, when Northwood was at the forefront of the re-opening of the defunct Indiana Glass Company. His cousin Thomas Dugan was factory manager of the Indiana-based plant in 1901, and "Uncle Tommie" Dugan, who had provided much of Northwood's financial wherewithal in the 1890s, lived in Ellwood City, Pa. Miss Elizabeth Northwood Robb, Harry Northwood's granddaughter, recalls family conversations which related that Harry

Birdseye view of Wheeling, c. 1903-04. **Courtesy of the Oglebay Institute, Wheeling, WV.**

Northwood returned to the United States by himself, leaving his family as well as that of his brother Carl in England.

The first direct information concerning Northwood's desire to leave the National and to get back into the glassmaking business in the United States can be found in the November 23, 1901, issue of *China, Glass and Lamps* under the headline "Harry Northwood's Plans": "Another glass factory on colored pressed ware and lamps is proposed, and Harry Northwood, who has just returned from England, is back of it. He is talking of leasing the factory at Washington, Pa., which was sold this week and which was operated a few years ago by the Washington Glass Manufacturing Co. Mr. Northwood has had charge of the National Glass Co.'s London branch, which was lately turned over to local parties there, so he has returned here to again enter the glass business as a manufacturer, having severed his connection with the National. He made a great success of the Northwood Glass Works, at Indiana, Pa., now operated by the National Glass Co. Mr. Northwood may follow along the same lines as formerly, with the exception of adding lamps, and is expected to announce his intentions in a few weeks."

Crockery and Glass Journal (November 28, 1901) reported this same information, but the November 30, 1901 issue of *China, Glass and Lamps* linked Northwood with Harry White, who had been associated with Northwood in the late 1890s: "Latest reports are to the effect that Harry Northwood and Harry White, formerly of the Northwood Glass Works, Indiana, Pa., will form a partnership and engage in the manufacture of glassware. There is a probability that they will lease or buy the plant formerly operated by the Washington Glass & Manufacturing Company at Washington, Pa."

A month later, all speculation about Northwood's possible affiliation with interests in the Washington, Pa., area had disappeared. Under the bold headline A NORTHWOOD RUMOR, *China, Glass and Lamps* (January 4, 1902) broke the story that Harry Northwood's attention was focused on Wheeling and vice versa: "It is rumored that Wheeling, W. Va., is trying to induce Harry Northwood to locate his proposed glass factory there. Although his deal with the National Glass Co. is not yet off, still indications are that the National will not hold him if he breaks the present agreement."

This was not the first time that rumors had circulated regarding the resurrection of the old Hobbs plant, which had been abandoned by the United States Glass Company in 1894. About five years later, *Crockery and Glass Journal* reported that Senator N. B. Scott, who had been associated with the Central Glass Company in Wheeling, was at the forefront of a movement "to secure control of the old Hobbs-Brockunier glass plant" and that "all that is wanting now is the lowest cash price the United States [Glass] Co. will take..." (October 5, 1899). A month later, *Crockery and Glass Journal* said that Scott had been quoted a price of $52,500 and that "the effort is now being made to capitalize the company for the purchase and operation of the plant" (November 9, 1899). The *Journal* added that some potential investors considered the price "too high," although the writer remained optimistic that "the project will go through."

Scott's effort was, however, unsuccessful, and the plant remained idle until Northwood was able to put together a deal to take over the plant. Although not mentioned by name, Northwood may have been involved in the efforts mentioned in this brief report of rumors from Wheeling in the October 26, 1901, issue of *China, Glass and Lamps*: "Prospects at Wheeling, W. Va., are said to be bright for the erection of two new glass factories and a company is reported as forming to buy and operate the old Hobbs tableware plant of the U.S. Glass Co. there."

In mid-January, 1902, *China, Glass and Lamps* (January 18, 1902) had a long, revealing account under the headline WATCH HARRY NORTHWOOD. This story provides the details of Northwood's contract with the National Glass Company: "Harry Northwood, the former Indiana, Pa., colored tableware manufacturer, who lately returned from England, where he represented the National Glass Co., has been released by that company and is now arranging to get back into the manufacturing end on his own hook. He had a three-year contract to remain out of the manufacturing of glass, and it would not expire until next November, contingent upon him being paid a salary for three years. Mr. Northwood agreed to release the National Glass Co. from the salary end if they would concede the part of restraining him from again becoming a manufacturer of glass. He will now, no doubt, immediately complete his arrangements to re-enter the field and will soon be either leasing or building a plant."

By early February, 1902, Harry Northwood was nearing agreement with the United States Glass Company for purchase of the old Hobbs, Brockunier works in Wheeling where, ironically,

Birdseye view of Wheeling, c. 1903-04. **Courtesy of the Oglebay Institute, Wheeling, WV.**

he had begun his career in 1881 as a glass etcher. *China, Glass and Lamps* had this to say: "Harry Northwood will soon be in the field at the head of a new glass manufacturing company and promises to repeat his record of success made at Indiana, Pa. He has an option on the old Hobbs plant of the United States Glass Co., at Wheeling, W. Va., and will either get that plant or build another at or near Wheeling. It is said the Hobbs option is for $40,000, but that can hardly be correct, as the plant has long been a veritable ruin."

Just as the pieces of this deal were about to fall into place in February, 1902, Harry Northwood received word that his father, John Northwood I, had passed away. He left for England, and all the plans for Wheeling were left unfinished. According to a notebook kept by Harry Northwood, he sailed on the S. S. St. Paul. Passage across the Atlantic Ocean took several days, so he arrived after the funeral. *China, Glass and Lamps* reported in its March 8, 1902, issue that "the plan to buy the old Hobbs flint glass factory at Wheeling, W. Va., and have it operated by the

Northwood Glass Company on colored glassware and novelties, is dragging now, as Mr. Northwood is in England. His return will soon settle the plan one way or the other."

Death of John Northwood

John Northwood, Sr., the patriarch of the Northwood family, died on Thursday, February 13, 1902. An obituary in the *County Express,* a local newspaper, indicated that Northwood had undergone an operation for eye cataracts in May, 1901. The surgery was successfully performed by Dr. Lloyd Owen, but John Northwood's general health was never again the same.

According to the biography *John Northwood: His Contribution to the Stourbridge Glass Industry,* written by John Northwood II, the elder Northwood's health declined steadily after he had the operation. Nonetheless, he remained as active as possible in the affairs of the Stevens and Williams glass firm: "... although very ill he persisted in coming to the works and eventually had a seat made for him to sit by the furnace in

This bronze and wood plaque, which is dated 1893, depicts John Northwood and bears the distinctive signature of Frederick Carder. **Courtesy of the Rockwell Museum, Corning, NY. Gift of Gillett Welles.**

Portrait of John Northwood, painted by John Northwood II in 1895. **Courtesy of the Broadfield House Glass Museum, Stourbridge, England.**

This photo of the Northwood family tomb was probably taken at the burial of Harry Northwood's mother, Elizabeth Duggin Northwood, in January, 1908. Three names are clearly visible: John Northwood's and those of a sister, Minnie Northwood, and a brother, William Northwood. Note the replica of the Portland vase atop the tomb. **Courtesy of Miss Robb.**

the glass house on a Monday, when the glass house was not occupied by the glass makers. ... Whilst sitting there he would receive reports and enquiries and give advice. At last he became too weak to leave his bed and there, sinking into a coma, he passed quietly away."

John Northwood's funeral occurred Monday, February 17, 1902, and several newspaper clippings about it were kept by the Northwood family. As one might expect, many of those in attendance came from the glass industry. One account (preserved as an unattributed newspaper clipping dated February 22) detailed a "bitterly cold" day on which "many hundreds" assembled to pay their respects. Another English newspaper, *The Advertiser* (February 22, 1902), listed many Stevens and Williams employees. Among the mourners was "F. Carder," a protege of John Northwood I, who soon emigrated to America, establishing himself in Corning, New York (see Paul Gardner's excellent book, *The Glass of Frederick Carder*, pp. 5-28).

Burial was in the church cemetery at Holy Trinity in Wordsley. A large stone tomb there contains a replica of the Portland vase atop it. Mr. Charles Hajdamach of the Broadfield House Glass Museum visited the Northwood tomb and provided some notes regarding its inscriptions for this book. Three children of John and Elizabeth Northwood are also interred there: "Minnie Northwood who died [in] 1868 aged 3 1/2 years [and] Ada and John who died in Infancy." John Northwood's parents, Frederick Northwood (d.

1881) and Maria Northwood (d. 1884) are buried there, as are four of his sisters—Elizabeth, Maria, Eliza and Mary Ann—and one of his brothers, William Northwood (d. 1867). When John Northwood's wife, the former Elizabeth Duggin, died in 1908, she was also buried in this tomb.

John Northwood I had joined the Stevens & Williams firm about April 24, 1882, as "artist manager etc.," according to the diary of Samuel Cox Williams (quoted here courtesy of Lt. Col. R. S. Williams-Thomas of Royal Brierley Crystal, Ltd., the modern successor to Stevens & Williams). By this time, Northwood had attained considerable fame as the artisan who carved a replica of the ancient Portland Vase, but the Stevens & Williams firm was probably more interested in his methods for the commercial production of cameo glass as well as several innovative machines and glass cutting and etching processes which he developed.

Harry Northwood and a brother-in-law, David Campbell, were named executors of John Northwood's estate. His will, which had been written in 1898, provided shares in the estate to John and Elizabeth Northwood's six daughters— Amy, Ethel, Eva, Ina, Mabel and Winifred—at least five of whom had married by 1902. Son Fred Northwood also shared in the estate, but Carl Northwood was not mentioned in the will. John Northwood II, born in 1870, was a child fathered by John Northwood with Margaret Lawley, an office employee at Stevens and Williams. He was excluded from the estate, because, as

Medal from the Prince of Wales presented to John Northwood "for glass ornamentation." **Courtesy of Miss Robb.**

Northwood's will stated, "I have otherwise provided for [him] in my lifetime." Northwood remained in England for several weeks to settle his father's estate before returning to the United States on the S. S. Teutonia. His half-brother, John Northwood II, soon succeeded his father at Stevens and Williams, Ltd., where he remained for many years before retiring in 1946. John Northwood II died in 1960, aged 90.

This wagon must have been a real attention-getter around Wheeling for the Grand Opera House. **Courtesy of the Oglebay Institute, Wheeling, WV.**

It's A Deal in Wheeling

As one might expect, Harry Northwood's return to England, albeit understandably occasioned by his father's death, was cause for worry in Wheeling. Although *China, Glass and Lamps* (March 15, 1902) noted that "the option on the old Hobbs tableware factory ... has been extended," it also reported that "there are some doubts as to the success of the plan, but much will depend on the enthusiasm Mr. Northwood can arouse on his return."

The concern may have grown stronger when *China, Glass and Lamps* (March 29, 1902) later reported that "there is a rumor here [in Martins Ferry] that Harry Northwood would like to get possession of the Beaumont glass factory after it is given up by the present company next summer. He was the first manager of that plant and made it a success. Martins Ferry people would be glad to see him in the harness again." The April 26, 1902, issue of *China, Glass and Lamps,* under the headline NORTHWOOD'S PROPOSITION, published the most definitive statement thus far,

quoting a letter from Northwood to Wheeling interests:

"Since the return of Harry Northwood from England, the negotiations with Wheeling, W. Va. to locate there and revive the old Hobbs glass factory, has been taken up again, and last week the following letter was addressed to the board of trade there:

Wheeling, W. Va., April 19, 1902.
Wheeling Board of Trade,
Gentlemen—The draft of the agreement which has been prepared to be executed by your company and myself, with respect to the purchase and operation of the Hobbs glass works, has been seen and carefully examined by me. The agreement is in satisfactory form, and if you shall be prepared by the third day of May of this year, the day on which the agreement bears date, to pay me the ten thousand dollars provided for in the agreement, I will sign the agreement as prepared and will proceed at once to carry it out to the best of my ability.
Yours truly, HARRY NORTHWOOD.

Market Street in downtown Wheeling, c.1903-04. Courtesy of the Oglebay Institute, Wheeling, WV.

The subscription committee immediately renewed its efforts at securing subscriptions and expects to be able to satisfy the request of Mr. Northwood by May 3."

On April 24, 1902, the United States Glass Company's Board of Directors met at Pittsburgh and approved the sale of its Wheeling property, Factory H—the old Hobbs, Brockunier plant—to Harry Northwood and Thomas Dugan. The consideration was $40,000, but the United States Glass Company agreed to hold a mortgage for $20,000. The remaining $20,000 was, apparently, paid by Northwood and Dugan, although $10,000 of that was derived from the subscriptions of the Wheeling Board of Trade.

Shortly thereafter, such headlines as HOPES FOR NORTHWOOD DEAL and NORTHWOOD DEAL ASSURED appeared in the glass tableware periodicals, but the final word did not reach the trade until a short notice in the May 10, 1902, issue of the *National Glass Budget*; the article reveals that the $10,000 from the Board of Trade was contingent upon Northwood's agreement "to operate the plant with not less than 250 hands for a period of not less than three years." The May 17, 1902, issue of *China, Glass and Lamps* had a similar story, plus praise for Harry Northwood,

under the headline "NORTHWOOD DEAL A FACT": "This week the last details were closed of the deal to have the old Hobbs factory at Wheeling, W. Va., started by Harry Northwood. The town raised $10,000 towards the plan and now Mr. Northwood and his associates, under the style of H. Northwood & Co. will at once put the famous old plant in shape for an early start on a fine line of colored glassware and novelties. Mr. Northwood is one of the most successful glass men in the business, and the record he made at his Indiana (Pa.) plant is well known to all dealers. He is said

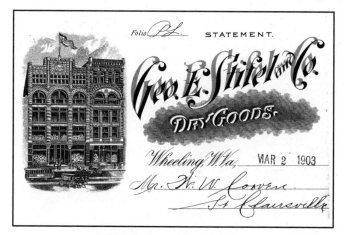

Billhead from Wheeling firm.

to have some ideas ready to work out in his new factory that will create a sensation in the way of fine ware at most attractive prices."

Two weeks later, the new firm, which was to be called H. Northwood and Co. throughout its existence, placed an introductory advertisement in *China, Glass and Lamps*. The company's products were listed as "Crystal, Colored and Opalescent Glassware—Plain and Decorated." A familiar name appeared in the upper right hand corner of the ad: "Thos. Dugan of Ellwood City, Pa." This was, of course, "Uncle Tommie," the

Billhead from Wheeling firm.

brother of Harry Northwood's mother, who had been involved financially with Northwood's glassmaking plants at Ellwood City and Indiana, Pa., during the early years. The ad also listed Frank M. Miller of New York as Northwood's sales representative, a capacity he had also fulfilled in 1898-1900 for the Indiana plant. The ad concluded with this brief letter describing some products to prospective customers:

Dear Sir:

You will make no mistake in awaiting our new lines. We shall be on time with NEW GOODS for FALL TRADE. Two new lines of Decorated Tableware - many new shapes and decorations in LEMONADE SETS - lots of pretty NOVELTIES -everything new - no old chestnuts. Ample capacity to fill orders promptly. Wait for us, we are sure to please you.

Yours very respectfully,

H. NORTHWOOD & CO."

An article in the June 7, 1902 issue of *China, Glass and Lamps* provided the details of Northwood's arrangements with the Wheeling Board of Trade: "The H. Northwood & Co. are pushing to get things in shape as fast as possible at the old Hobbs factory, Wheeling, W. Va. The company also filed a mortgage there last week giving to the seller, the U. S. Glass Co., first mortgage on the property of $20,000. A second mortgage is given to the Board of Trade, Wheeling, for $10,000, to secure it for two years during which time the glass company agrees to operate the plant and employ not fewer than 200 persons. The operation of the plant to be subject to strikes or other causes, over which they may have no control. Failing in the agreement he shall refund the $10,000. There is hardly much doubt but that the company will meet all the requirements if Mr. Northwood keeps up the reputation he established at Indiana (Pa.) plant several years ago."

The role of the Wheeling Board of Trade in attracting Northwood to Wheeling cannot be underestimated. The board, which was founded on October 2, 1900, was interested in the bettering the economic climate of Wheeling, and it linked Wheeling's real estate, banking and financial interests with those of potential businesses and investors. Among the board's directors in 1900-01 were George E. House and Stephen Hipkins. House later became affiliated with the Northwood firm upon its incorporation in 1905, as did Hipkins' son George. Director William Mann, who lived in Martins Ferry,

Wheeling's downtown area, viewed from the "new bridge," c. 1903-04. The visible surname "House" at left (on a sign for House and Hermann) is that of George E. House, who was an influential member of Wheeling's Board of Trade in 1902. He later became president of H. Northwood and Co. **Courtesy of the Oglebay Institute, Wheeling, WV.**

The center entrance on the left side of this building led to the offices of Wheeling's Board of Trade. The entrance between the columns on the right corner of the building led to the Court Theatre. **Courtesy of the Oglebay Institute, Wheeling, WV.**

certainly knew Northwood from his glassmaking ventures in that city during the 1890s, and director George W. Lutz, who was president of Trimble and Lutz Plumbers' Supplies in Wheeling, became a Northwood family friend. Harry Northwood is listed among the members of the Wheeling Board of Trade from 1908 through 1919. In a section of its 1907 *Year Book* entitled "A Few Things the Board of Trade Has Done for Wheeling," the board took credit for reopening "the old Hobbs Glass Works on the south side, giving employment to several hundred people."

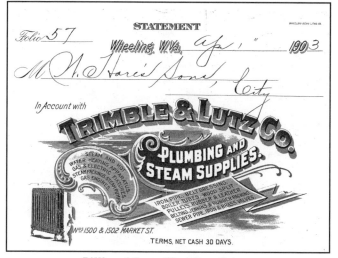

Billhead from Wheeling firm.
Courtesy of Roger Thorngate.

Production Begins

Harry Northwood quickly contracted with the Hipkins Novelty Mold Company in Martins Ferry for his new firm's first moulds. Several mould drawings survive which show a two-part iron mould jug (pitcher). One drawing (dated May 2, 1902 by Northwood), adds this note: "Please substitute this Jug for the one of similar shape sent you on April 30th. You will notice that I have changed the bottom so as to hold our snaps."

The spring and summer of 1902 were punctuated regularly with progress reports in the various glass trade periodicals as workmen labored to ready the facility for glassmaking. The company's office force gained an employee when S. G. Robinson, "chief clerk of the West Virginia Glass Works at Martins Ferry ... resigned to go with H. Northwood & Co." (*China, Glass and Lamps*, June 14, 1902). By mid-July, the furnace had been fired, and the glassworkers at the new H. Northwood & Co. were making samples for the fall trade. Carl Northwood was one of the firm's travelling salesmen, and the August 9, 1902 issue of *China, Glass and Lamps* noted that he was already on the road, this time in Grand Rapids, Michigan.

As the massive renovation project neared its conclusion, the glass trade periodicals lauded Harry Northwood. This note, from the August,

1902, issue of *Housefurnisher: China, Glass and Pottery Review,* is representative:

"Harry Northwood is again to the front with the Grecian and Roman patterns in a full line of tableware and specialties, which we predict will take as well as or better than anything he has ever placed on the market. He has a herculean task placing the old Hobbs factory in shape, but has accomplished wonders, and will soon have the factory in fine fettle."

Wheeling's local newspapers were quick to cover events at the new Northwood plant, of course, but most reports were simply records of day-to-day events involving workers. The August 24, 1902, issue of the Wheeling *Intelligencer,* however, provided a detailed story:

"Among the foremost industries of Wheeling is the Northwood Glass Company's plant, an independent concern. It is located at the head of Thirty-sixth Street, Plunkett & Miller as operators. In April 1845, it passed into the hands of James B. Barnes and John L. Hobbs, who came to Wheeling from Massachusetts. In 1849 and in 1856 there were changes in the firm that did not have any effect on the operation of the plant. In 1861, when the civil war began, the fires in the furnace were out for six months, many of the men enlisting in the army. In 1863 the firm of Hobbs, Brockunier & Co. was formed, which, with slight changes, operated the plant until about nine years ago, when it passed into the possession of the United States Company, who put out the fires and closed the plant. It remained in this quiescent attitude until a few months ago, when, owing to the exertions of the board of trade of Wheeling, the plant was taken in hand by Mr. Harry Northwood, an experienced glass man, remodeled and equipped with the most modern machinery and started upon a new career."

The Northwood plant apparently had no formal opening, but other events at the glass house certainly made for colorful news. The October 23, 1902, issue of *Crockery and Glass Journal* carried this account of an incident at the factory:

"An incipient riot was precipitated near the Northwood factory the latter part of last week which had its origin in the discharge of one boy. The boy had deliberately dashed a tool to pieces in a fit of temper, and the management discharged him at once. To even up matters the boy persuaded the other boys to strike for more money the next day. Their demand was refused and they quit work. When the foremen of the various departments left for home in the evening,

the boys started in to do battle, and stones and other missiles were flying through the air at a lively rate for a time. Two boys and one of the foremen were quite badly hurt. The matter got before the local courts, and one man and four boys were fined for their part in the melee. In the meantime, the factory resumed, leaving out all the boys who had been offensively troublesome."

The first references to specific Northwood products appeared during the fall of 1902. The October 10, 1902, issue of *China, Glass and Lamps* mentioned a tableware pattern and described it as "most ornate." About a month later, *China, Glass and Lamps* had these details in its November 15, 1902, issue:

"There is a real novelty in a lemonade set shown here from the Northwood factory. This set and some new molasses cans are among the newest things on the display tables of Frank Miller, the New York representative of H. Northwood & Co. The lemonade set referred to has a jug of graceful shape, but it is the decoration which at once attracts the eye. Its flowers and foliage seem to stick right out, although the relief is not high. The effect is secured by the opalescent tint of the relief, which upon the various backgrounds of canary, flint,

Opalescent blue Poinsettia syrup. These were originally called "molasses cans."

*Northwood's Poinsettia pitcher with swirl and coinspot
motif pitchers in Lyon Brothers catalog (1906).*

blue and pink, is most striking. It is certainly a
novelty and shows that Mr. Northwood knows
how to produce original effects. Still, he usually
did do that. The molasses cans have nothing new
in the shapes, but they are revivals of one of the
best selling shapes we ever had, and, made as the
Northwood factory is making them, in dainty
colors, why shouldn't they sell better than ever
they did?"

The colors and the descriptions suggest that
this is Northwood's Poinsettia motif in opalescent
glass. The water sets are known in a variety of
opalescent colors—flint, blue, canary, green, and
ruby. More information about this line, and the
similar Daffodils motif, is given in the next
chapter.

Miss Elizabeth Northwood Robb, the
granddaughter of Harry Northwood, recalls her
grandmother's mention that the Northwood
family lived at the McLure House hotel in
Wheeling for a time until they purchased a house
on Wheeling Island (the home stands today at 310
South Front). Wheeling Island is in the Ohio River,
of course, and Northwood reached the city, which
could be viewed from his backyard, via a steel
bridge. The Northwood factory, with its tall,
funnel-shaped stacks, was some distance away at
36th and Wetzel Streets.

The deal in Wheeling was destined for
prosperity. Northwood was in firm control of the
last glass factory which bore his name, and the
future was bright indeed. The next five years
witnessed a series of innovations and
considerable success and recognition.

*Poinsettia and Coinspot pitchers from the 1906
Northwood catalog.* **Courtesy of Steve Jennings.**

Between 1903 and 1907, Harry Northwood and the firm which bore his name became established as one of the premier glass tableware plants in the United States. During this time, Northwood revived glassmaking designs and techniques from his past and also broke new ground with innovative patterns and decorating treatments. As one might suspect, Northwood at first returned to the sources of his earlier successes—pressed wares in colored and opalescent glass—but he also experimented with some unusual colors. This chapter will deal with the plant's history and production from the beginning of 1903 through the end of 1907, and it will also discuss some tableware patterns for which production dates cannot be established.

A number of sources document this important period in the Northwood plant's history. Foremost among these is an original Northwood catalog from the fall of 1906, which was found and reprinted by Steve Jennings (see Bibliography). In addition to the usual advertising and the typical quotes in trade journal editorial columns, research for this chapter has been greatly aided by the existence of other primary sources—ranging from over one hundred Butler Brothers and G. Sommers Co. catalogs to original records of correspondence between the Northwood company and the National Association of Manufacturers of Pressed and Blown Glassware.

The National Association, formed in 1893 to negotiate with workmen in the American Flint Glass Workers Union, also acted as a clearinghouse for manufacturers seeking information relating to wages and working conditions, particularly on new products. The National Association's files contain many original letterheads from the Northwood plant, as well as sketches of glass items made by Harry Northwood. Some of these will be used as illustrations in this book.

Despite the sources available, some Northwood patterns (even a few with the N-in-a-circle mark) cannot be dated for certain. Most are included in this chapter because the 1903-1907 period was Northwood's most prolific era in pressed pattern lines and novelties, especially those in opalescent colors or in emerald green decorated with gold. From 1908 to about 1914, the Northwood firm was heavily involved in the production of iridescent ware (popularly known as Carnival glass today) and, beginning in 1912, Luna lighting glassware. Trade journal coverage

of the iridescent and Luna lines was extensive, but, unfortunately for today's collectors, Northwood's few pressed pattern lines from 1908-1914 received minimal notice at best.

Carnelian, Mosaic and Opalescent Novelties

Since the Northwood plant was not fully operational until well into 1902, one would expect a rather abbreviated offering at the annual exhibition in January, 1903, in Pittsburgh. The January 1, 1903, issue of *China, Glass and Lamps* noted that "H. Northwood & Co. will be a new exhibitor this year with a line of colored and crystal novelties, tableware and decorated lemonade sets."

A brief account of the Northwood's earliest line was carried in the monthly publication *Housefurnisher: China, Glass and Pottery Review.* This story details the first product lines from Northwood's Wheeling plant: "An exceptionally beautiful exhibit of ware, from the H. Northwood & Co.'s plant, at Wheeling, W. Va., is shown by their representative, Mr. Frank M. Miller, 25 West Broadway. The corporation is now putting on the market a set of Carnelian table ware. These goods

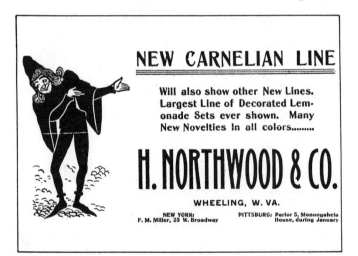

NEW CARNELIAN LINE

Will also show other New Lines. Largest Line of Decorated Lemonade Sets ever shown. Many New Novelties in all colors.........

H. NORTHWOOD & CO.

WHEELING, W. VA.

NEW YORK: F. M. Miller, 25 W. Broadway   PITTSBURG: Parlor 5, Monongahela House, during January

are made of ivory and are decorated with gold. ... The set presents a remarkably beautiful appearance." The term "carnelian" generally denotes a milky-colored quartz substance, so the relationship to Northwood's Ivory glass is apparent. There is a formula labelled Carnelian among the early records (c. 1884) of Percy Beaumont.

Northwood's Carnelian line graced the front cover of *China, Glass and Lamps* for January 3, 1903; two weeks later, a reporter penned a story in which the Northwoods' past was recalled:

"In Room 5 at the Monongahela House, H. Northwood & Co., of Wheeling, W. Va., represented by Carl Northwood, make an attractive display of lemonade sets, tableware and novelties. The Northwoods were the originators of colored lemonade sets and are so acknowledged by the trade. Although the Wheeling firm has been in business less than six months they are adding to their output right along and are getting their share of the trade. They are now operating the old and famous Hobbs-Brockunier plant at Wheeling.

"In their present exhibit the firm shows a very great variety, the Carnelian line in ivory and gold decorations and their line of fancy tableware in opalescent colors being especially attractive, while the display of lemonade sets is large and varied, both in color and design. In their novelties are shown many things entirely new in imitation of tortoise shell.

"Northwood colors and Northwood designs have always borne an excellent reputation in the trade and the company has good reason for feeling gratified over the many handsome and original lines included in their exhibit. Mr. Northwood says business has been more than up to their expectations, and anticipates a most prosperous season's run" (*China, Glass and Lamps*, January 17, 1903).

Clearly, Harry Northwood had reached back into his past at Indiana, Pa., to recreate Ivory and opalescent glasses. Some of his Ivory lines (called Louis XV, Intaglio, Pagoda and Nautilus) had been among the most successful, and the National Glass Company continued to make this color at Indiana after Northwood had left for England. The colored opalescent lines (called "pearl blue" and "pearl yellow") in the Klondyke and Alaska patterns had been the foundation of the Indiana plant's prosperity in 1897-98.

A Butler Brothers catalog from May, 1903, contains two assortments from Northwood's Wheeling plant. The "Opalescent" grouping of a dozen items, includes the creamer and compote in Carnelian. The articles were offered in "blue, canary and flint [crystal] opalescent." Today's collectors know the Carnelian line as the "Everglades" pattern, and articles in all three opalescent colors—flint, blue and canary—have been documented; most are decorated with gold trim (Figs. 13-28 and 145-150). The Ivory pieces are decorated with green and gold (Figs. 2-12). The Carnelian line consisted of berry set, table set and water set as well as cruet, jelly compote and salt/pepper shakers. The shakers are also known in amethyst, and other Carnelian items may turn up in this hue.

In addition to the Carnelian pattern pieces (2 and 4), the May, 1903, Butler Brothers group also includes these novelty items in opalescent glass: (1) Spool crimped top compote; (3) Hobnail bowl, another one of which (7) has been crimped and

Our "OPALESCENT" Novelty Assortment.

Nothing Better Ever Shown to Retail at 10c.

C593—All fancy shaped pieces and all extra large sizes, equally assorted in blue, canary and flint opalescent. Each piece being richly finished and fire polished. It is your loss if you do not sample this assortment.

Assortment Comprises 1-2 doz. Each of the Following:

7¾-in. Fancy Shape Dish—Rich scalloped crimped edge.
High Footed Deep Fancy Dish—Extra heavy and brilliant. Diameter 4½-in.
6½-in. High Footed Card Tray—Useful also for many other purposes.
7¾-in. Fancy Shape Dish or Card Receptacle—Of beautiful design, 3 dainty feet.
Large Milk or Cream Pitcher—Footed with fancy handle and wide top.
7½-in. Fancy Shape Basket—Large Handle and fancy scalloped edge.
Tall Flaring Flower Vase—Rich crimped edge. Height 6½-in.
Extra Large and Extra Deep Open Sugar Bowl—Diameter 5½-in. Beautiful dew drop pattern.
Extra Large Fancy Shape Bonbon Receptacle—Footed, rustic design. Diameter 5½-in.
6½-in. Extra Large Rustic Vase—Of beautiful design.
5¼-in. High Footed Receptacle or Jelly Dish—Fancy embossed pattern, with scalloped edge.
8¼-in. Footed Tray or Receptacle—Heavy dew drop pattern, fancy crimped edge.

(Total 6 doz. in barrel. Barrel 35c.)   Per dozen, **79c**

flared; (5) Ocean Shell vase; (6) Ring-Handled Basket; (8) Spool of Threads compote; (9) Beads and Bark vase; (10) Beaded Cable rose bowl which has been crimped and flared; (11) Floralore crimped and flared bowl; and (12) a jack-in-the-pulpit vase. A similar opalescent group, in which the Carnelian creamer is shown, appears in a spring, 1904, Butler Brothers catalog. Eight of these twelve items also appear in the spring, 1904 catalog, and the other four are variations of the same Pearl Flowers piece. Some of these novelties were also made later in iridescent glass.

Some of the items shown in the opalescent group also appear in yet another Butler Brothers assortment from the May, 1903, catalog, this time in "Mosaic" glass. The term mosaic refers to glass called "purple slag" by collectors today. Harry Northwood is not known to have made any such glass during his earlier career, but it was surely well-known to him, for it has a long tradition in England and was also made at Tarentum, Pa., in the 1880s.

Correspondence between the Northwood firm and the National Association of Manufacturers of Pressed and Blown Glassware reveals some of the problems in manufacturing mosaic glass. On March 31, 1903, National Association secretary

John Kunzler invited the members to a meeting at which "disputes" between the workers and various member companies would be considered, among them one "at H. Northwood & Co. over cracked wares made from mosaic glass." The minutes from this meeting (April 7, 1903) contain the following statements: "... it was admitted by both sides that when the wares were first made there was an excive [sic] breakage, but for the last several weeks the breakage was no greater than that on crystal glass. The dispute being settled by adopting the following suggestion: Excessive breakage must be reported by the workmen to the management; the management to investigate the cause; if found to be no fault of the shop, then the shop is to be paid for said breakage."

The mosaic glass matter did not come to rest, however. At the annual conference of the National Association and the AFGWU representatives in August, 1904, the parties in the Pressed Ware branch considered a proposition that "onyx or mosaic or mixed glass pay turn work [a set wage like an hourly rate]." The motion was amended to refer to "the method used by H. Northwood & Co." and, in turn, further refined to include glass made "by throwing cold glass into pot or tank ...." The technique mentioned may reflect the Northwood firm's unique procedure for making the "purple slag" mosaic glass—introducing opal cullet into the melted amethyst batch prior to

OUR NEW "OPALESCENT" NOVELTY ASSORTMENT.

Nothing better ever shown for a special 10c sale.

C593—All fancy shaped pieces and extra large sizes, equally assorted in blue, canary and flint opalescent. Each piece richly fire polished. Your loss if you do not sample this assortment.
Assortment comprises ¼ doz. each of the following:

7¾ in. Fancy Shape Dish, scalloped crimped edge.	Large Footed Rose Bowl.
8 in. Fancy Salad Dish.	Fancy Bonbon Receptacle, footed, rustic design. Diam. 5¾ in.
6½ in. High Footed Card Tray.	6½ in. Extra Large Rustic Vase.
7¾ in. Fancy Dish or Card Receptacle, 3 feet.	5¼ in. High Footed Receptacle or Jelly Dish.
Large Milk or Cream Pitcher.	8¼ in. Footed Tray or Receptacle, dew drop pattern.
6½ in. Deep Nut Bowl.	
9½ in. Crimped Salad Dish.	
Total 6 doz. in barrel. (Bbl. 35c.)	Per dozen, **79c**

Butler Brothers catalog, spring, 1904.

gathering and pressing. Such glass is usually made by mixing hot opal glass with hot amethyst, so it is not surprising that Northwood encountered problems.

The Mosaic assortment in the 1903 Butler Brothers catalog includes three pieces in the pattern called Scroll with Acanthus. This was surely a more extensive tableware line, probably offered in a range of colors, for today's collectors know of pieces in the typical opalescent hues (flint, blue and canary) as well as green opalescent, crystal, blue and a light green described by Heacock as "apple green" (H2, p. 23); occasionally, pieces are enamel decorated. Among the items known are the berry set, table set and water set as well as cruet, jelly compote, toothpick holder and salt/pepper shakers (Figs. 60-67).

The Mosaic assortment also includes a Carnelian (Everglades) creamer (Fig. 39) as well as some novelties-Beads and Bark vase, Ocean Shell vase, crimped bowls in both Floralore and Hobnail, Beaded Cable rose bowl, Spool of Threads compote, Ring-Handled Basket, an unnamed rose bowl with vertical panels and a blown vase. Heacock also attributed the Grapevine Cluster vase (H2, 503) to Northwood because of its purple slag color; the vase is also known in flint and blue opalescent.

Heacock (CGl, pp. 7-8) spent some effort attempting to differentiate between Northwood's Floralore and a similar pattern by the Jefferson Glass Co. of Steubenville, Ohio, which appeared in Butler Brothers assortments in 1905. There is no doubt that Northwood bought some moulds from Jefferson (see p. 157), but the extent of these transactions is difficult to determine.

Trade journal reports during the latter half of 1903 are rather general, but a clear picture of the Northwood's growing success emerges. The June

Scroll with Acanthus creamer in Mosaic glass.

20, 1903, issue of *China, Glass and Lamps* reported the Northwood to be "enjoying a good run" and noted that the men were working "double turn," an indication that demand for products was strong. In late July, *China, Glass and Lamps* (July 25, 1903) mentioned that the Northwood firm "have distributed a catalogue, made by the Rawsthorne Engraving & Printing Co., of Pittsburgh," but no specifics about patterns were given, save that the catalog illustrated "their new set." A note several months later in another publication, however, called attention to the "Regent" line, so it must have been the pattern introduced in mid-1903 (*Housefurnisher: China, Glass and Pottery Review*, October, 1903).

In its September 12, 1903, issue, *China, Glass and Lamps* mentioned "nearly a dozen new things in 10-cent novelties" as well as a "new, elongated

vase" from the Northwood firm, calling the latter "a low priced article ...[but] one of the best recently on the market." This surely refers to a so-called "swung" vase, made by snapping up a newly-pressed vase and swinging it in an arc or circle, allowing centrifugal force to lengthen and narrow the body of the vase. The dime novelties were probably the opalescent articles discussed above.

The popularity of Northwood's products in the marketplace extended to some plant workers who obtained glassware illegally. Under the bold headline WARE STOLEN AT THE NORTHWOOD, the October 10, 1903, issue of *China, Glass and Lamps* had the details: "Wholesale robbery has been going at the H. Northwood & Co. plant, Wheeling, W. Va., and the loss became so great that Mr. Northwood secured the services of two detectives to investigate the matter, and as a result on Tuesday last eight boys were arrested and warrants were issued for four others. The value of the ware stolen amounted to nearly $500. It was all fancy decorated ware, nothing but the best taking the eye of the boys. The boys were called into the office and questioned by the officers. One little fellow on being asked if he had got all the glass he wanted, answered, "No sir; I need two more salts to fill my set out." The patrol wagon came down and the boys got their first ride in it, and it is to be hoped that this will be a lesson to them and other boys as to the bad results of stealing."

Early Lemonade Sets

Among the first products of the Northwood firm at Wheeling were lemonade sets—pitchers accompanied by six matching tumblers and a white metal tray. In its November 15, 1902, issue, *China, Glass and Lamps* mentioned "a real novelty in a lemonade set shown here from the Northwood factory" and went on to describe it as "a jug of graceful shape ... [with] decoration which at once attracts the eye. Its flowers and foliage seem to stick right out, although the relief is not high. The effect is secured by the opalescent tint of the relief, which upon the various backgrounds of canary, flint, blue and pink, is most striking."

In their book *Cranberry Glass from A to Z*, Heacock and Gamble concluded that the jug described above was probably Northwood's opalescent Poinsettia (also known as Big Daisy), but it could also be opalescent Daffodils. The Poinsettia water set occurs in several opalescent hues—flint, blue, canary, green and ruby (cranberry)—and the syrup and sugar shaker

28   31   26

21   27   30

have been reported in all except ruby (cranberry). Heacock and Gamble pictured a large crimped bowl in rubina opalescent, too. The procedure used to make opalescent wares (a spot mould plus a shape mould) means that the poinsettia flowers will be found in somewhat different positions on two separate pitchers of the same shape.

The Poinsettia pitcher is known in several different shapes (Figs. 50, 52, 55, 226 and 240). Two Poinsettia pitchers (Figs. 50 and 55) match shapes illustrated on the front cover of the January 10, 1903, issue of *China, Glass and Lamps*. All of the shapes and decorations have been compared to the few extant Butler Brothers catalogs from 1903-1905, but no definite Northwood products were found. The trade journal quote also indicates clearly that lemonade sets were being made in four opalescent hues: flint (clear), canary, blue, and pink (ruby). None of the Butler Brothers groupings, however, mentions ruby glass.

Incidentally, it is not surprising to find both opalescent ware and decorated ware in the same Northwood shapes, simply because of the economy of using the moulds over and over. Opalescent ware also required an initial spot mould, of course, but it is not particularly expensive to make. Decorated ware was a long-time Northwood staple, and both Harry and Carl Northwood were familiar with various decorating techniques and motifs.

The water set is known in Northwood's Daffodils (see Figs. 224, 233, 284 and 294) in these opalescent colors— flint, blue, canary, green and ruby (cranberry).

Lemonade sets remained an important aspect of Northwood's glass production for a number of years. An illustrated ad appeared in the September 26, 1903, issue of *China, Glass and Lamps,* and the January, 1904, issue of *Glass and Pottery World* mentioned "125 lemonade sets ..., arranged in a most effective way for catching the eye easily," but no other details about patterns or colors were provided. Fortunately, the 1906 Northwood catalog reprinted by Jennings will make possible the identification of some Northwood products later in this book.

New Lines in 1904-1906
During this period of approximately three years, the Northwood company introduced a wide variety of pattern lines in pressed ware. Many were decorated with gold, and some were also decorated with ruby stain. Emerald green was

These lemonade set assortments are from Butler Brothers catalogs issued in 1906.

obviously a favorite color, but Northwood also made blue and canary, especially in opalescent ware, as well some articles in dark amethyst.

As was mentioned above, the Regent (Leaf Medallion) pattern had been introduced by October, 1903, although its first showing in Pittsburgh would have been in January, 1904. The January 16, 1904, issue of *China, Glass and Lamps* mentioned that it was "a line of amethyst, green and blue with decorations in plain gold." Crystal pieces, usually decorated with gold, are also known. The typical Regent (Leaf Medallion) colors are rather dark, and some mention of each of them is made in Northwood's notebooks. One entry recounts the batch for a "Rich Royal Blue made in pressed ware at Wheeling in [the] fall of 1903" and adds that it was a "very fine blue to decorate with gold." A "Rich Dark Green" is also credited to the fall of 1903, and Northwood added "Regent" in the margin. A batch for amethyst glass is not dated, but Northwood used it "for pressing and decorating with gold."

Regent (Leaf Medallion) is popular today in all three colors, and collectors seek pieces with the outstanding gold decoration in mint condition (Figs. 70-99). An ad from 1904 shows the table set, water set, berry set, a jelly compote and an interesting condiment set consisting of salt/pepper shakers, cruet and tray.

A writer for *Glass and Pottery World* visited the Northwood exhibition in January, 1904, and he began his report with a resume of Northwood's glassmaking ventures before turning to the new pattern lines:

"The name of the Northwood is synonymous with high-grade colored glass to everyone in the trade. When Mr. Harry Northwood sold out his Indiana, Pa. plant to the National Glass Co., about two years ago, he went abroad, and the leisure afforded to a man of such artistic tastes, retentive memory and original ideas meant added capital of the richest kind for the new plant, which he opened in Wheeling, W. Va., in May, 1902.

"He bought the old Barnes & Co. site, where glassmaking was in vogue in 1830. The new buildings and additions are modern; equipped with the best appliances for his special lines. Good sites in Wheeling are not plentiful. High water on one side and precipitous hills on the other, make it difficult to locate satisfactory buildings for a new industry. Everything in the Northwood display is practically new. There are about 125 lemonade sets alone, arranged in a most effective way for catching the eye easily. The chief feature of the room is several complete

lines of tableware, radically different in design and finish from anything in the house. One of these, the Mikado, in frosted glass with transparent colored enamel flowers artistically trimmed in gold, is novel, almost too novel, but it grows in favor the more it is inspected. The Encore and the Regent are regal looking patterns, in several solid colors, rich in heavy gold trimmings."

Mikado (also called Flower and Bud or Blooms and Blossoms) is among the most elaborate of Northwood's decorated lines. Crystal pieces are decorated with ruby stain and gold, and each of the flowers is carefully shaded with red, yellow-green and either blue or light purple. The table set, water set, berry set, salt/pepper shakers and cruet are known to collectors, but all are rather scarce (Figs. 114-119). A few pieces, such as a handled nappy, have been seen in blue as well as blue opalescent. The 1906 Northwood catalog shows a "square olive dish" with handle in Mikado, and it was available in three opalescent hues: flint, blue and green.

The account by the reporter from *Glass and Pottery World* (January, 1904) concluded with some observations regarding Carl Northwood and Harry Northwood's son, Harry Clarence, who went by "Clarence" alone to avoid confusion with his father. These lines are among the first to refer to these two men in regard to their roles in glassmaking: "The display is in charge of Mr. Carl Northwood, who, although twelve years younger than Mr. Harry Northwood, might be taken for his twin. Mr. Harry Northwood comes up about once a week, and his son, Clarence Harry, spends the week's end at the exhibit. This young man, about 21 years of age, is also an enthusiastic factor in the general sales department. He devotes all of his leisure time to studying, utilizing hours when on the trains in perfecting himself in chemistry." Carl Northwood also figured prominently in a lengthy article in the January 16, 1904, issue of *China, Glass and Lamps,* and this publication also offered a fulsome report on the Northwood's products:

"Carl Northwood, representing H. Northwood & Co., of Wheeling, W. Va., suggested that I adopt a popular advertisement in speaking of his stock and put the words "Nuf Ced" in large capitals after his name. I assure him that I would, but passing by his open door several days later the glass and the salesman shone so alluringly that I couldn't resist the temptation to have a look. I don't know the name of the obliging gentleman who was holding forth at that time, but he was tall and wore glasses and spoke the truth about Wheeling.

"The prettiest thing in the display, the man and I thought, was the Reliance line of crystal tableware, but there are stacks of colored goods that will probably be more popular. The Reliance, which is made of a high grade of glass, comes in a general line of high and flat-footed pressed tableware, and sparkles brilliantly. The Mikado is the name of another line which is sort of Japanese in its effect. The line which, by the way, is the most expensive of the several new ones, comes in tea, lemonade and berry sets, oil and salt bottles and several other pieces. It is of crystal frosted glass with decorations of pansies and crooked stems (you will understand what I mean by crooked stems when you see them) done in four transparent colors and gold.

"I wish all good things to the Northwood Company for calling everything by names. They have a decided talent in this direction and are likely to spring four upon you at one blow. "Encore" is the name of the new line of opalescent tableware. The line comes in canary, blue and flint opalescent undecorated and in the three colors decorated in ruby and gold. A rather queer effect is produced by the gold and ruby decoration on blue and canary opalescent. Another name, the Regent, applies to a line of amethyst, green and blue with decorations in plain gold. There are twenty-five new lemonade sets in fine colors, some of which are fearfully and wonderfully loud. The whole display is most interesting as showing what can be done in color

This blue opalescent creamer must be a variant of Northwood's Encore (Jewel and Flower) line; compare with Figs. 132, 136 and 155, which have a different design on the lower one-third of the creamer. Courtesy of Edwin and Jocelyn White.

work. There are also some novelties in opalescent ware. Here's thank you to the man who showed me."

The Encore (Jewel and Flower) line is decorated with ruby stain and gold, but the aesthetic effect may be somewhat less dramatic on opalescent glass. The table set, water set, berry set, salt/pepper shakers and cruet are known in Northwood's usual opalescent shades— flint, blue and canary (Figs. 120-136 and 151-155). The creamer is part of a large opalescent assortment in the Chicago-based Lyon Brothers wholesale catalog issued for the spring and summer of 1906. The Reliance line has yet to be identified.

Little news appeared about the Northwood plant during the rest of 1904, but a brief note in October indicated that all was well with the growing and successful concern:

"At the H. Northwood Glass Company October has been a banner month. About a thousand barrels a week represent shipments from some time past. Mr. Northwood is always searching for the best men. Glass workers, if men of artistic taste and competent, can usually find employment at this large plant. Every call here impresses the writer that in no other plant is there a closer watch kept on every detail of manufacture by the owners. Glass making has been the profession of the Northwood for several generations and the artistic shapes and decorations put out here find ready appreciation whenever shown. Besides the characteristic creations in colored glass Mr. Northwood is making a full line of tumblers, also electric globes. The catalogue from this company should be on every glass buyer's desk" (October, 1904, *Glass and Pottery World*).

A year-end review, quoted from the January 7, 1905, issue of *China, Glass and Lamps*, contains similar sentiments: "The Northwood Glass Company, one of the representative plants of the city, claims the year 1904 as one of the most successful yet enjoyed by the company. During the past year the force of the concern, about 300 in number, has been without work for no length of time whatever. General Superintendent Northwood speaks very favorably of conditions, and, from a financial standpoint, thinks the business transacted was greater in results than that of almost any year previous. An enormous amount of stock has been placed on the market, the finished product being noted for the excellence of design and quality. Prospects for 1905 are unusually bright, and everything points to a most prosperous season."

The outset of 1905 saw some changes in the Northwood's staff. Carl Northwood took charge of the important decorating department at the factory, and Harry White, Jr., a long-time Northwood friend who had worked in the office of Northwood's Indiana, Pa. plant, was a salesman for the firm. He was mentioned prominently in this report from the January 14, 1905, issue of *China, Glass and Lamps*:

"Some grand function or other would appear to be on the eve of accomplishment, from a glimpse through the door of the H. Northwood and Company's exhibit presided over by Mr. White. The crash covered floors, the bright lights, the glass reflecting mirrors and the artistic arrangement of the samples are productive of a cheerful glow in the heart of the onlooker, and were I a wealthy merchant I should buy whole rafts of glass there even though I didn't want it, just because the exhibition and its environment were so attractive. There is a remarkable thing about the new Diadem line of glassware which is the principal feature of the exhibit. On the 15th of October, Mr. White told me, not a single piece belonging to the line, let alone the design, was in existence. Now it is being shown in full and exciting general enthusiasm on account of its brilliancy, design and finish. The line is in imitation cut in a combination design with the bottoms cut and polished on the flat pieces. A tall tankard and flat jug are interesting features of the line. The W. B. line—Woggle Bug it means, Mr. White says, is short and varied, crystal, blue, green and amethyst being some of the guises in which it may appear. Another short line comes in three varieties of opalescent, and still another short line known as the "Magic" is decorated in gold and rich enamel. Also the staples in the pressed bar goods line have been considerably added to, as well as wine and liquor sets. There are 42 new decorations in colors on the water sets and more things than it is possible to mention."

A nappie in Diadem (Sunburst on Shield) was illustrated in the January 14, 1905, issue of *China, Glass and Lamps*, and the line was called a "new crystal imitation cut pattern." The clear glass examples do indeed resemble cut ware, but Diadem is best known in opalescent glass (flint, blue, and canary). In addition to the typical table set, water set and berry set, the Diadem line also included a small creamer and matching spooner or open sugar (these are sometimes called a "breakfast set"), as well as salt shakers, a handled nappy, a celery or relish tray and a cruet, which is

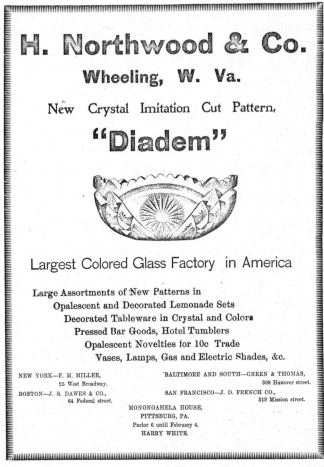

This ad in China, Glass and Lamps *(January 14, 1905) introduced Northwood's new Diadem (Sunburst on Shield) line; note the other products described.*

quite scarce in any hue (Figs. 164-180). The small creamer and spooner or open sugar were part of an opalescent assortment in the Lyon Brothers wholesale catalog for spring and summer, 1906 (see p. 33).

The "short line ... in three varieties of opalescent" could be one of several Northwood patterns. Perhaps it is Frosted Leaf and Basketweave, which Heacock attributed to Northwood based upon the basketweave motif's similarity to the Carnival glass "Rose Show" pattern (H2, p. 20). Frosted Leaf and Basketweave comes in both blue and canary opalescent, and some flint opalescent pieces were reported to Heacock. The four-piece table set is known (Figs. 106-113), and a rose bowl and a crimped piece called Woven Wonder by Heacock (H2, pp. 73, 84 and 86) may be part of this same line.

Another possibility is the attractive opalescent line called Northwood's Drapery. The water set, table set and berry set are known in both flint and blue opalescent, and they may be decorated with heavy gold on the vertical ribs as well as the rims of bowls (Figs. 156-163). Some moulds were apparently used later for production in iridescent glass. Unlike Frosted Leaf and Basketweave, Northwood's Drapery items usually have the N-in-a-circle mark. A Drapery swung vase appears with other Northwood vases in an April, 1906, Butler Brothers catalog (see p. 29), so the Drapery line may have been introduced prior to this time, although no firm evidence is at hand.

The delightfully-named Woggle Bug line is probably Northwood's Teardrop Flower pattern, which occurs in all the colors listed by the reporter—amethyst, blue, green and crystal. Like some of the other Northwood patterns from this period, Teardrop Flower occurs in table sets, water sets, and berry sets as well as salt/pepper shakers and the cruet (Figs. 53, 58-59 and 181-186). The various sets were offered in barrel lots in the Lyon Brothers wholesale catalog for spring and summer, 1906.

Teardrop Flower assortment from Lyon Brothers catalog (1906).

Many of the pattern lines already discussed—Regent (Leaf Medallion); Mikado (Flower and Bud); Encore (Jewel and Flower); Diadem (Sunburst on Shield); and Teardrop Flower—share an interesting characteristic—the stoppers for the cruets are identical. Sharp-eyed collectors will also contrast this short-shanked, pyramid-shaped stopper from the Wheeling era with the longer version developed earlier by Northwood at Martins Ferry, Ellwood City and Indiana in the 1890s, which has a faceted, spherical head (see *The Early Years,* pp. 140 and 143). A stopper similar to this was used by Northwood in the Carnelian line about 1903 (Figs. 12, 17, and 27), so the pyramid-shaped stopper may have been developed shortly thereafter. In any case, the pyramid-shaped stopper was in use from 1904 until the Regal line was introduced for the 1907 season, as will be discussed below. With one exception (see Fig. 70), the cruets shown in color in this book have the correct stoppers, an important concern to serious collectors, who place no little value on having the proper stopper to complete a cruet!

Yet another salesman, George Mortimer, joined the firm in January, 1905. Mortimer, like Harry White, Jr., had been affiliated with Northwood's Indiana, Pa., operation, but his role there was much more significant. Advertisements from 1897-99 list Mortimer as Northwood's travelling salesman for the East, Carl Northwood having had responsibility for the West. Mortimer left the Indiana, Pa., factory in late 1900 to become vice president of the new Jefferson Glass Company at Steubenville, Ohio, which was headed by Harry Bastow. The Northwood firm apparently attached some importance to Mortimer's abilities, for the firm placed notices in the glass trade publications during January, 1905, to announce that he had joined the firm. In late 1905, Mortimer left the Northwood firm to establish his own decorating operation at Toronto, Ohio, according to the December 2, 1905, issue of *China, Glass and Lamps.* By November, 1906, there were rumors that Mortimer would also manufacture glass on his own, but the January, 1908, issue of *Glass and Pottery World* links him with the Fenton Art Glass Co.

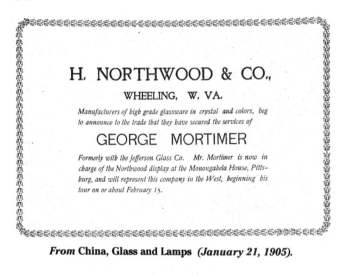

From China, Glass and Lamps *(January 21, 1905).*

In addition to White and Mortimer joining the sales staff and Carl Northwood assuming control of the decorating department, another major change took place in the Northwood firm in 1905. The factory, it will be recalled, was jointly owned by Harry Northwood and his uncle, Thomas Dugan of Ellwood City, Pa. Mortgages were held by the United States Glass Company and the Wheeling Board of Trade, which had a three-year contract (commencing about May, 1902) with Harry Northwood. On June 17, 1905, Harry Northwood and four other men—George E. House, George R. Hipkins, Matthew H. McNabb, and John R. Mendel—completed a Certificate of Incorporation which was approved by C. W.

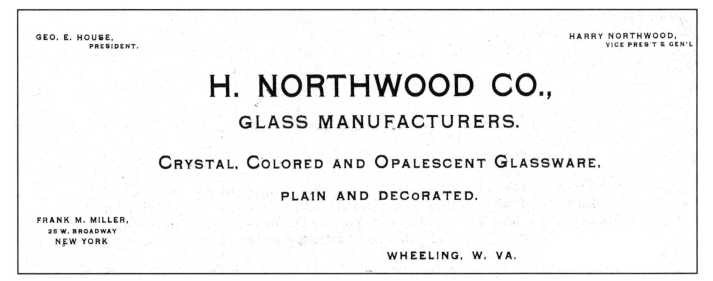

This letterhead was used in 1905.

Swisher, Secretary of State for West Virginia (Ohio County Corporation Book 6, p. 423).

House, who was president of both House and Hermann Home Furnishings in Wheeling and the W. H. Keech Co. of Pittsburgh, had been a key figure on the Wheeling Board of Trade in 1901-02, when Harry Northwood decided to locate in Wheeling. George Hipkins was the son of Stephen Hipkins, proprietor of the Novelty Mould Works in Martins Ferry and another director of the Board of Trade. Matthew H. McNabb, who passed away shortly after the Northwood firm was formed, was manager of the Lyceum Advertising Bureau. John R. Mendel was a principal in the Mendel Brothers Pearl Laundry.

According to the incorporation papers, Northwood held two shares of stock, as did House, who was to be president of the firm during its entire corporate life, eventually presiding over its receivership in the 1920s. The other men held one share each. House purchased Thomas Dugan's interest in the real estate on June 24, 1905 (Ohio County, WV, Deed Records, vol. 119, p. 50). House was listed as president on the company's earliest letterhead stationery, and Northwood's name was followed by the designation he was to hold throughout: "Vice-Pres't & Gen'l Mgr."

House was also associated with the little-known Wheeling Glass Letter and Novelty Company, which was founded in 1902. An undated mould drawing for a vase or pitcher found in the Fenton Museum archives has the note "Glass Letter Co." as well as "Northwood Glass Co.," so the two firms may have shared some moulds. The history of the Wheeling Glass Letter and Novelty

Letterhead from 1906.

30

Co. is sketchy at best, but the Welkers' comprehensive *Pressed Glass in America* reports that the firm was still operating in 1912 (p. 57).

The July 1, 1905, issue of *China, Glass and Lamps* reported the Northwood firm's incorporation to the glass trade, fixing the capital stock at $150,000 [1500 shares at $100 each]. Thomas Dugan of Ellwood City, Pa., was no longer financially involved with the company, of course, although his name had appeared prominently in advertising when the old Hobbs, Brockunier plant was first purchased and undergoing renovation. The newly-constituted H. Northwood Co. moved quickly to divest itself of some real estate. On July 13-14, several lots were sold to R. J. McCullagh and the Schmulbach Brewing Co. for $15,000 and $1700, respectively (Ohio County, WV, Deed Records, vol. 119, pp. 51-54; 70-71).

In the late fall of 1905, the Northwood firm was having moulds made for a new pressed glass tableware line. A pencil drawing in the Fenton Museum archives, dated November 21, 1905, shows the details for a nappy mould labeled only "line #31." This was rather plain ware, and it was intended to be decorated. The line was a short one, consisting of water set, table set and berry set, and it was in production in June, 1906, when a photographer visited the Northwood plant, for

Portrait of Harry Northwood, c. 1906.

Northwood's No. 32 was called "Gold Band Pattern" in the 1906 catalog; several floral motifs were also available (see Figs. 187-190). The decoration on this covered sugar bowl is similar to a line of kerosene lamps in 1906 (see Chapter Five).

articles are visible in several photos (see pp. 34-40). Heacock named this pattern Belladonna in a column for the weekly *Antique Trader* in 1975.

An assortment of Belladonna items in crystal and green, called "quite a favorite," is in the fall, 1906, Northwood catalog, which reveals that the #31 designation was reserved for a floral decoration and that #32 was a somewhat less expensive treatment called only "Gold Band." The complete assortment comprised four-piece table sets in both crystal and green as well as seven-piece berry sets and water sets in both hues. Belladonna articles are also known in blue (Figs. 187-190), and most bear the Northwood N-in-a-circle mark, although it is often difficult to see, especially on the crystal pieces.

The year 1906 opened on an auspicious note for the Northwood firm, as its namesake's portrait appeared on the cover of the January, 1906, issue of *Glass and Pottery World*. The accompanying editorial comment was brief and positive: "Mr. Harry Northwood, of Wheeling, W. Va., needs no introduction. The Green Book has had past occasion to speak of his early days and a notable business record. A descendant from glass makers of genius and fame, Mr. Northwood has ever been foremost in creating new forms and colorings. As a progressive and resourceful manufacturer, he has steadily built up a remarkable business in colored and opal goods. His crystal lines in table ware this season are noticeable for unique beauty and the wide profit margin left for dealers."

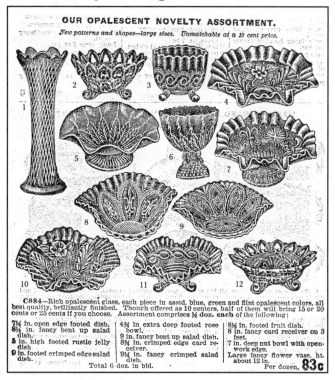

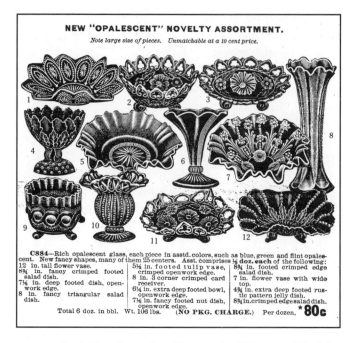

A Butler Brothers catalog from April, 1906, shows a nice array of Northwood's opalescent novelties. The Beaded Cable mould (3 and 11) dates from 1903-04, but the other patterns were probably new to the Northwood line in mid-1905 or shortly thereafter: (1) Diamond Point vase; (2 and 12) Shell and Wild Rose, which is also known as Wild Rose; (4 and 10) Blossoms and Palms; (5) Leaf and Beads; (6) Hilltop Vines; (7) Sir Lancelot; (8) Diamond Point and Fleur-De-Lis; and (9) Spokes and Wheels. Most of these are known with the N-in-a-circle mark. The Diamond Point vase is shown elsewhere in the same catalog with two other vases—Tree Trunk and Drapery (the latter made by swinging out a spooner).

Yet another opalescent assortment from Butler Brothers (mid-spring, 1906) adds to our knowledge of Northwood articles in production at this time. Most of these motifs have been mentioned earlier—Spokes and Wheels (1); Shell and Wild Rose (2, 3 and 11); Hilltop Vines (4); Pearl Flowers (7); and Beaded Cable (8)—but several appear in Butler Brothers for the first time. The crimped bowl (5) appears to bear no pattern. The smaller vase (6) is in Northwood's fall, 1906, catalog, where it is called the No. 185 Tulip Vase. The taller vase (8) appears to be the

one called Feathers by Heacock (H2, pp. 66, 87). The Beads and Curly-Cues item (10) was also named by Heacock, who pictured a slightly different shape (H2, p. 85), so this piece occurs in at least two variations. The Leaf and Beads open bowl (12) has three openwork feet, unlike the item shown in the April, 1906, Butler Brothers catalog, which has a typical footed base.

Two assortments of opalescent novelties in a catalog issued by the Lyon Brothers of Chicago for spring/summer, 1906, also show many of these novelties. A few odd pieces in earlier patterns, such as Scroll with Acanthus, Encore (Jewel and Flower) and Diadem (Sunburst on Shield), are within the assortments, but at least two

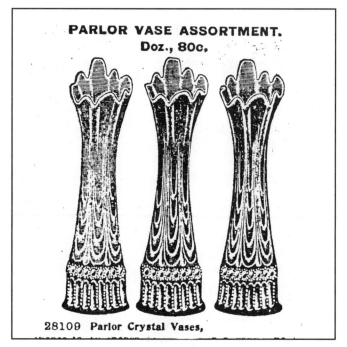

Lyon Brothers catalog (1906).

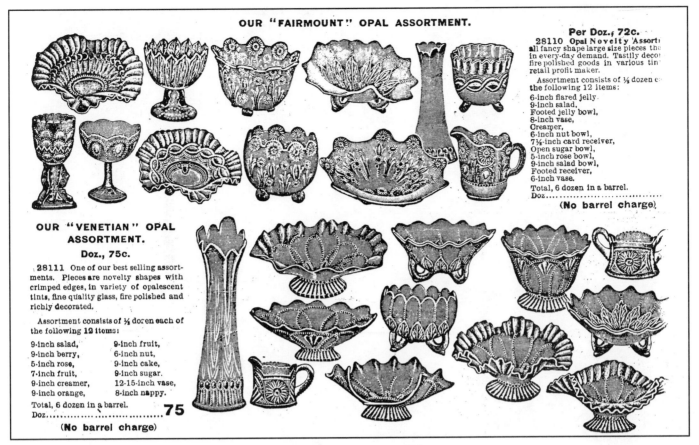

Lyon Brothers catalog (1906).

OUR "FAIRMOUNT" OPAL ASSORTMENT.

Per Doz., 72c.

28110 Opal Novelty Assort,
all fancy shape large size pieces tha
in every-day demand. Tastily deco
fire polished goods in various tin
retail profit maker.

Assortment consists of ⅓ dozen e
the following 12 items:

6-inch flared jelly,
9-inch salad,
Footed jelly bowl,
8-inch vase,
Creamer,
6-inch nut bowl,
7½-inch card receiver,
Open sugar bowl,
5-inch rose bowl,
9-inch salad bowl,
Footed receiver,
6-inch vase.

Total, 6 dozen in a barrel.
Doz. . . . .

(No barrel charge)

OUR "VENETIAN" OPAL ASSORTMENT.

Doz., 75c.

28111 One of our best selling assortments. Pieces are novelty shapes with
crimped edges, in variety of opalescent
tints, fine quality glass, fire polished and
richly decorated.

Assortment consists of ⅓ dozen each of
the following 12 items:

9-inch salad,	9-inch fruit,
9-inch berry,	6-inch nut,
5-inch rose,	9-inch cake,
7-inch fruit,	9-inch sugar.
9-inch creamer,	12-15-inch vase,
9-inch orange,	8-inch nappy.

Total, 6 dozen in a barrel.
Doz. **75**

(No barrel charge)

heretofore unseen items are shown. The vase bears a slight resemblance to Heacock's Jewels and Drapery (H2, p. 87), but the area near the base is not quite the same. The vase was offered in crystal in this same Lyons catalog, a fact which may be significant when one considers that the fall, 1906, Northwood catalog shows an assortment of crystal vases. Furthermore, a vase identical to Jewels and Drapery, coincidentally dubbed "Venetian Opalescent," is shown in a Baltimore Bargain House catalog dated February-March, 1907.

Also among the pieces in the Lyons' Venetian assortment are six different articles made from a single mould in a design known as Roulette (H2, p. 85). Heacock noted its similarity to Diamond Point and Fleur-de-lis, which also occurs in a number of crimped and flared pieces. It is unfortunate that the Lyons catalog's text does not mention the specific colors of these opalescent wares, referring only to "various tints" and the like.

No. 12 "Semi Cut"

One of the Northwood firm's most ambitious early pattern lines was an imitation cut glass motif called simply No. 12. It was first introduced in 1906, and a newly-pressed jug (pitcher)

appears in a photograph taken inside the Northwood plant in June, 1906. The January 13, 1906, issue of *China, Glass and Lamps* mentioned No. 12 prominently in its review of the Northwood display: "They are using all numbers this year and have discarded names, so that I will have to refer to them in that way. Take their No. 12 line. This comes in crystal and also in gold decorated and is

No. 12 pitcher and tumbler.

33

Photo, (June, 1906) of Northwood workers. Note No. 12 pitcher near the mould. Courtesy of Ken Northwood.

Decorating room at H. Northwood and Co. in June, 1906. The No. 12 pattern is being ruby-stained, and many plain tumblers are ready for decoration. Foreman Carl Northwood, wearing a light shirt and a cap high on his head, is standing in the rear of the photo, between a woman in a dark dress and a support post. The man near the support post on the right appears to be holding a wine decanter with his left hand. Courtesy of Ken Northwood.

all to the good. They have some peculiarly shaped baskets in this line that are the only kind you will find on the market. They show originality, and as I have said and reiterate again, originality is what the buyers want. The pattern is also shown in ruby and gold and green and gold, and is pretty."

The No. 12 line is profusely illustrated in the fall, 1906, Northwood catalog. Over 30 different articles appear in a listing of "open stock" items, ranging from the four-piece table set and several pitchers to a 14" punch bowl and four different sizes of handled baskets. The catalog described the line as "one of the very best Press Cut Patterns ever made," and asserted that it had great success overseas: "It is really the very closest imitation of rich cut glass ever made and we are exporting quantities of it even to Germany, which is like selling coals to Newcastle."

The fall, 1906, catalog mentions only gold decorated crystal ware in the No. 12 line, but the several other treatments known to collectors today were surely Northwood's own decorations. Various bowls have been seen with a pale ruby (some prefer the term "cranberry") stain on smooth elements of the pattern, and, rarely, some are stained with a pale green in these same areas. Darker ruby-stained items are scarce, as Heacock indicated in his *Ruby-Stained Glass from A to Z* (p. 161). A photo of the Northwood decorating shop in June, 1906, shows No. 12 bowls. The No. 12 table set is also known in emerald green, and these pieces are usually decorated with gold (Figs. 202-205).

When Northwood's iridescent (Carnival) glass went on the market in 1908, some items in the No. 12 line—such as tumblers, goblets and water pitchers—were probably among the earliest offerings. These are generally called "Northwood's Near Cut" by carnival glass collectors today.

Northwood's No. 12 line was offered in several wholesale catalogs. An ad for a 72-piece assortment (dubbed "Electric Cut") in a single barrel was a fixture throughout 1906 in catalogs issued by the G. Sommers Co., a St. Paul, Minnesota-based firm which sold to customers in the northern Great Plains. Small groups of baskets and bowls in the No. 12 line appeared in Butler Brothers catalogs as early as April, 1906, and an assortment dubbed "Crystal Gem" was featured in the Mid-Spring, 1906, offerings of this firm.

In February, 1906, Clarence Northwood married "one of Bridgeport's most popular young ladies," to quote *China, Glass and Lamps*

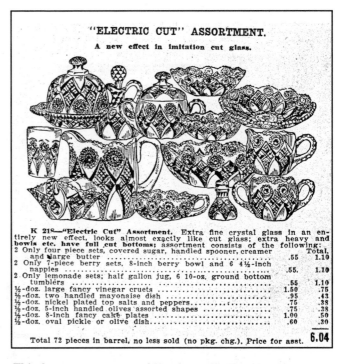

This large assortment of Northwood's No. 12 pattern was offered by G. Sommers & Co. of St. Paul in their 1906 catalogs. Courtesy of the Minnesota Historical Society.

(February 24, 1906), which carried a full report: "Clarence Northwood, of Wheeling, W. Va., and Miss Rae Cook, daughter of Mr. & Mrs. L. Cook, Jr., of Bridgeport, O., were united in marriage on Monday evening at the Presbyterian church in the last named place at 6 o'clock. The ceremony was witnessed by only the immediate families of the young people, the Rev. J. A. Donahey officiating. Immediately after the wedding the happy couple boarded a Pennsylvania train for an eastern wedding trip of two weeks." Clarence Northwood's father-in-law, Louis Cook, may have been a stockholder in the old La Belle Glass Company of Bridgeport, where Harry Northwood was employed between early 1884 and September, 1887. Perhaps the young Northwood and his bride were childhood friends.

The Verre D'or and Intaglio Lines

In July, 1906, the Northwood firm took the unusual step of introducing a line of glassware in mid-year. This may have been done to gain some competitive advantage over those manufacturers who traditionally unveiled their new lines at the outset of the year, or perhaps the Northwood concern had not been able to ready its products earlier.

The Northwood's new line was called Verre D'or, a French phrase which translates as "glass of gold." Almost two years earlier in September, 1904, Northwood had obtained a patent (U. S. Patent #770,867) for a "process of decorating

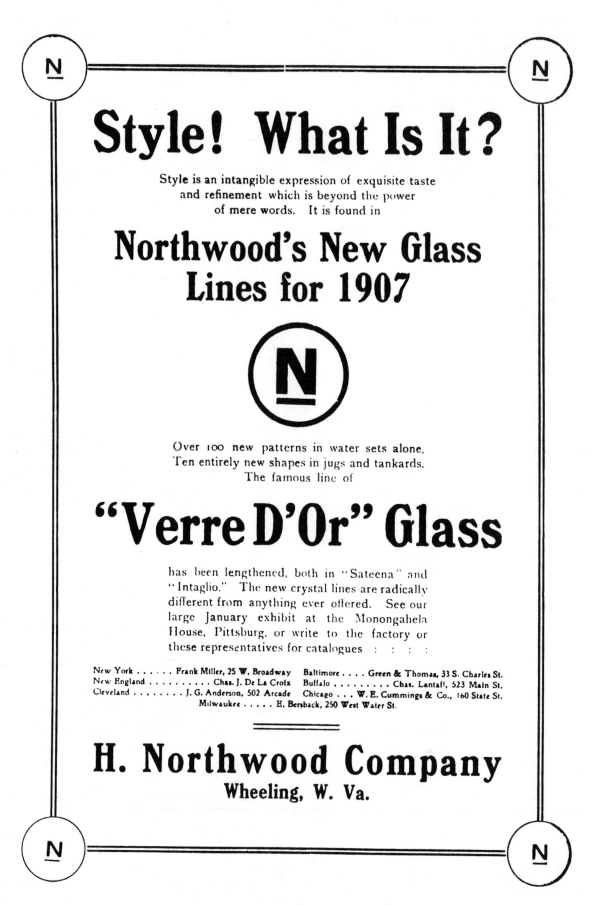

Style! What Is It?

Style is an intangible expression of exquisite taste
and refinement which is beyond the power
of mere words. It is found in

Northwood's New Glass Lines for 1907

Over 100 new patterns in water sets alone.
Ten entirely new shapes in jugs and tankards.
The famous line of

"Verre D'Or" Glass

has been lengthened, both in "Sateena" and
"Intaglio." The new crystal lines are radically
different from anything ever offered. See our
large January exhibit at the Monongahela
House, Pittsburg, or write to the factory or
these representatives for catalogues :   :   :   :

New York . . . . . Frank Miller, 25 W. Broadway   Baltimore . . . . Green & Thomas, 33 S. Charles St.
New England . . . . Chas. J. De La Croix   Buffalo . . . . Chas. Lantaff, 523 Main St.
Cleveland . . . . J. G. Anderson, 502 Arcade   Chicago . . . W. E. Cummings & Co., 160 State St.
Milwaukee . . . . . E. Bersback, 250 West Water St.

H. Northwood Company
Wheeling, W. Va.

Ad in **Glass and Pottery World** *(January 20, 1907).*

The grinding room at the Northwood plant, June, 1906. The women are removing excess glass from the bottoms of tumblers. The man nearest the stove is Jack McCarthy, "an old Stourbridge boy" who was foreman of the grinding shop at the time. **Courtesy of Ken Northwood.**

glassware with liquid gold," and this method was probably utilized for the Regent line. His application was prepared by Wheeling patent attorney H. E. Dunlap and officially filed in May, 1904, but a typescript draft of the patent specifications is dated March 12, 1903. The Verre D'or line's characteristically heavy gold decoration may be the culmination of Northwood's patent.

The July, 1906, issue of *Glass and Pottery World* had an article which spotlighted the new line: "The H. Northwood Company, Wheeling, are putting on the market their new line, Verre D'Or, which is a startling novelty in decorated glass, and is likely to take the trade by storm .... The name Glass of Gold pretty well describes the ware, but it is dull gold, massive and elegant, with no tinsel or bronze effect to cheapen its appearance." A month later, this same publication again mentioned the Verre D'or line and revealed the startling notion that it had been inspired by "the decorations in the Court Theater, Wheeling" (*Glass and Pottery World,* August, 1906).

By September, 1906, the Verre D'or line was well-established, and an article in *Housefurnisher:*

China, Glass and Pottery Review noted the glassware's "massive richness and peculiar elegance" and added that "it has scored an instant success ...." Verre D'or was later described as the "latest novelty in three colors—royal blue, amethyst and emerald green. The designs stand out in bold relief on the glass and are decorated with the richest gold in polished and matt effects, making a beautiful contrast."

A year-end article in the December 29, 1906, issue of *China, Glass and Lamps* both summarized the Northwood's fortunes and revealed the complete range of colors used for the Verre D'or line: "The name of Northwood has for some years been synonymous with leadership in the colored glassware industry of America. This has been on account of the ability to work colors which Harry Northwood is known to possess as few others do. It is said that there is not a color in glass that he has ever tried to make but what he has succeeded. This year the Northwood line is better and more extensive than ever and my readers will say that this a pretty broad statement, but I am willing to stand for it and let them go and see for themselves if it is not so. A visit to the Northwood rooms will bear me out. The Verre D'or line is, as its name suggests, a very rich production. It is made with an ivory body and gold decorations, and also in blue, green and Royal amethyst body and gold decorations. It has been a great seller and promises to continue to be so."

Ivory articles in the Verre D'or patterns have rather light gold decor, and a few of these known today seem to have a faint iridescent sheen. These articles pre-date Northwood's entry into Carnival glass production by about a year.

Northwood's fall, 1906 catalog shows eight different Verre D'or items, numbered individually and accompanied by explanatory prose. Unfortunately, there is some confusion within the numbering of the items, so modern names, albeit arbitrary, are preferable to sorting out the original numbers. Hartung identified three motifs in her *Northwood Pattern Glass*, naming them Grape Frieze, Shasta Daisy, and Southern Gardens (Figs. 207, 210 and 215 as well as 208-209).

Hartung (1, p. 48-49) named yet another design Star of David and Bows, but the similar Verre D'or articles actually have an eight-pointed central star created by overlapping two squares (Figs. 213-214), while a Star of David, of course, has six points. Presznick (book 3 pl. 77) named the design Golden Star of David. A footed bowl in Carnival glass has a six pointed Star of David, created by overlapping two triangles, on its interior, so this is not simply a reissue of an item from the Verre D'or line. Neither Hartung's nor Presznick's name is accurate for this Verre D'or piece, so the name Ribbons and Overlapping Squares is used here (Figs. 213-214) .

Two other Verre D'or pieces (Ribbon Star and Bows and Beaded Star and Mums) are mentioned by Presznick (4, pl. 166 and 3, pl. 7, respectively), but only the latter is known today (Figs. 211 and 219). In his *Pattern Glass Preview* (4, p. 10),

Shasta Daisy 10" fruit in iridescent Ivory (custard) glass. Courtesy of Jabe Tarter and Paul Miller.

Heacock named yet another article Violet Bouquet (Fig. 217). Another Verre D'or motif is named here—Iceland Poppy—by collector Bud Ashmore, who loaned most of the Verre D'or articles photographed for this book (Fig. 216).

The 1906 Northwood catalog lists five different Verre D'or articles—10" fruits, 8" fruits, 6"

Grape Frieze 6" handled bon bon.

Ribbons and Overlapping Squares 6" sweet.

comports, 6" handled bon bons (both heart-shaped and round) and 6" sweets. The fruits in both sizes are, of course, simply shallow plates, and the larger size has three scrolled feet, a design strongly reminiscent of Northwood's Klondyke pattern from Indiana, Pa. The 8" fruits were available in the typical round shape or in several crimped versions—one termed "3 corner" and another called "square." The comports feature a relatively plain stem with an octagonal base. The 6" sweet was transformed into a bon-bon by an applied, round handle. Most of the articles in the Verre D'or line carry the North-wood N-in-a-circle mark except the stemmed comports, which are often unmarked. The mark is generally found on the center of the base of the larger items, but it appears well off center on the comports as well as the 6" sweets and bon-bons which have had the marie ground off.

Another line of glassware being made in 1906 was an array of flat plates and footed comports called Intaglio. Neither this line nor the similarly-named Ivory glass line made by Northwood at Indiana, Pennsylvania, in 1898 is true "intaglio," an ingenious cutting process developed by John Northwood I in the 1890s at Stourbridge (see *John*

Iceland Poppy motif.

Northwood, pp. 114-127). Harry Northwood's Intaglio ware at Wheeling was pressed ware with red/gold decoration in patterns moulded in deep relief on the outside of the crystal articles. These articles are generally included in the "goofus"

The mouldmakers at H. Northwood and Co. in June, 1906. A plaster Intaglio bowl is visible behind the vise at left. The man wearing the light shirt, suspenders and hat is factory manager James Haden. **Courtesy of Ken Northwood.**

glass category by collectors today, although no such designation existed at the time.

The July, 1906, issue of *Glass and Pottery World*, which contained the first account of Northwood's Verre D'or, also mentioned the Intaglio line, albeit briefly, as a form of glassware "which the Northwood and several other houses are still making," an indication that the line had been on the market for a time. The August, 1906 issue of this same publication also made reference to Northwood's Intaglio, noting that it was "originally brought out by the Dugan Glass Company ...."

Intaglio was first advertised in three motifs—Strawberry, Apple and Pears, and Scroll and Poppy. The Strawberry and the Apple and Pears renderings were made in 10" round fruit dishes as well as 4 1/2" nappies and an 11" cake plate. These items are quite heavy, and the edges are decorated with bright gold which has been fired in a decorating lehr, so it will not wear off readily. The red/gold decor on the pattern is not fired, however, and pieces in collections today are apt to show chipping and flaking. A Cherries motif was added to this selection of heavy ware, and the three occur together in Butler Brothers assortments. The Cherries line is occasionally found in iridescent glass (Figs. 429-430).

The Scroll and Poppy items in the Intaglio line are thinner and lighter in weight (Figs. 889, 893). The fall, 1906, Northwood catalog shows comports with scalloped edges and ruffled edges,

All three of Northwood's Intaglio motifs are illustrated in this selection from a Fall, 1908, Butler Brothers catalog.

and these have stems with an octagonal base. The edges are bright, fired gold.

The Verre D'or and Intaglio lines must have made considerable contributions to the Northwood's economic success in 1906. The October issue of *Glass and Pottery World* noted sales "averaging from $1,000 to $2,000 a day," and the November 17, 1906, issue of *China, Glass and Lamps* reported "two furnaces are in full operation with about 18 shops making 11 turns per week." Factory manager James Haden was quoted to the effect that "the firm's traveling representative has been off the road for over a month, the firm having more orders booked than can be filled this year."

Northwood's "Goofus" Glass

The popularity of Verre D'or and Intaglio seems to have overshadowed several new lines introduced by Northwood in late 1906. Called Sateena and Khedive, these two lines are among the multitude of glassware articles called "goofus" by collectors today. Not all goofus glass was made by Northwood, of course, and much research remains to be done in this area. At present, unfortunately, the term goofus has wide meaning, being applied to virtually any glassware decorated with gold or gold and red paint to

Assortment of Northwood's red/gold decorated Intaglio line in a Butler Brothers catalog, 1909. The Strawberry and the Apples and Pears motifs are illustrated, but the description also mentions the "cherries" design.

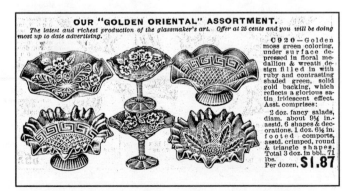

A splendid assortment of Northwood's "goofus" ware from a 1909 Butler Brothers catalog. These articles are in green glass with red flowers and gold covering the underside of the glass.

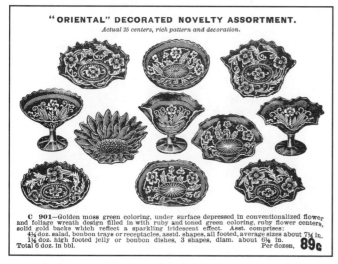

Northwood "goofus" in a Fall, 1908, Butler Brothers catalog.

items with elaborate painted decorations in several colors. Carolyn McKinley's *Goofus Glass* identifies a few marked Northwood pieces.

An ad in *Glass and Pottery World* (January 20, 1907) which features Verre D'or and Intaglio also mentions a "Sateena" line. The term sateena refers to "satin-like," and this may be the line dubbed "Golden Oriental" by Butler Brothers in a Fall, 1908, offering, for their catalog cut mentions "a glorious satin iridescent effect" produced by the gold-decorated back of the green glass when seen from the opposite side. The flowers are decorated with red paint. The articles in the fall, 1908, Butler Brothers catalog include Blossoms and Palms, Greek Key and Scales, and Netted Roses. A few pages later in this same Butler Brothers catalog (fall, 1908), an "Oriental" assortment includes pieces in various "poppy" motifs (see McKinley's *Goofus Glass*, pp. 95-96).

These, like the stemmed compotes in the other assortment, bear some resemblance to Northwood's Mikado (Flower and Bud) pattern.

The December 29, 1906, issue of *China, Glass and Lamps* had a full account of the Northwood display at the Monongahela House exhibition, discussing Verre D'or and Intaglio, among others, and concluding with a reference to the Khedive line:

"The name of Northwood has for some years been synonymous with leadership in the colored glassware industry of America. This has been on account of the ability to work colors which Harry Northwood is known to possess as few others do. It is said that there is not a color in glass that he has ever tried to make but what he has succeeded. This year the Northwood line is better and more extensive than ever and my readers will say that this a pretty broad statement, but I am willing to stand for it and let them go and see for themselves if it is not so. A visit to the Northwood rooms will bear me out. The Verre D'or line is, as its name suggests, a very rich production. It is made with an ivory body and gold decorations, and also in blue, green and Royal amethyst body and gold decorations. It has been a great seller and promises to continue to be so.

"The Intaglio line which is made in the heavier pieces, is reproduced from the Baccarat cuttings, and is very massive in appearance. This line is in plain and decorated and has also gained royal favor with the buying public. Their lemonade sets that have always created a furor are still there in all their glory, but several new designs and colors are shown on this occasion. Their new lemonade

Strawberries "goofus" bowl (note Basketweave exterior).

"Goofus" crimped bowl, green glass with red/gold on underside.

Carl Northwood (light shirt) was foreman of the decorating room at H. Northwood and Co. when this photo was taken in June, 1906. A number of decorated tumblers can be seen as well as pieces of the No. 31-32 line. The second woman from left, wearing a long apron, is holding a No. 12 bowl with both hands. **Courtesy of Ken Northwood.**

sets are sure to make a strong bid for permanent popularity. In tableware there are several new creations that are worthy of the attention of every buyer. There are two green and gold sets, another in three colors, green, blue and crystal, a block colonial set in opalescent and blue and gold and a block colonial in plain opalescent. The No. 12 line is a big one and comes plain and also decorated in ruby and gold. The one thing for the buyer to see is a distinctly new line with a punty and panel pattern and gold and ruby decoration. Its there; see if you can pick out. If you don't see it you'll miss a lot.

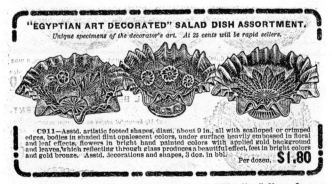

This could be Northwood's mysterious "Khedive" line; from a Butler Brothers catalog, April, 1906.

"Another thing. Ask Clarence Northwood about the Khedive line. He's more eloquent on it than I am, but it speaks for itself in more convincing terms than either he or I could do. They say that when an artist puts his name to a picture he's really proud of it. Northwood & Co. are proud of their glass and on each piece will be found their trade mark, the circle N."

The term Khedive designates "viceroys of Egypt," and an array of Northwood glass was advertised as "Egyptian Art Decorated" in the Butler Brothers April, 1906, catalog. If the Butler Brothers copy is accurate, the Khedive line consisted of opalescent articles decorated with painted gold on the underside. There is no doubt that the three pieces shown are Northwood products, since all bear the Northwood N-in-a-circle mark. Two of the patterns are familiar (Netted Roses and Leaf and Beads), and the other is probably Blossoms and Web.

The Northwood Mark
The first evidence regarding the well-known Northwood N-in-a-circle mark comes from late in 1905. An advertisement for Northwood's pattern

No. 12, appearing in the December 30, 1905, issue of *China, Glass and Lamps* features the distinctive mark at each corner. No mention is made in the editorial columns of the trade press until later.

Interestingly, Northwood's fall, 1906 catalog (reprinted by Jennings) makes no special note of the mark, but it does appear in an illustration in which a display card accompanies a box of six pattern No. 12 concave tumblers (Jennings, p. 24). The mark is also known on other items pictured in the catalog, such as the No. 31 and 32 decorated articles (Belladonna) and pieces in the Verre D'or line discussed earlier in this chapter.

In the December 29, 1906, issue of *China, Glass and Lamps,* the long review of the products of H. Northwood & Co. quoted above concludes with these words: "They say that when an artist puts his name to a picture he's really proud of it. Northwood & Co. are proud of their glass and on each piece will be found their trade mark, the circle N." The term "trade mark" may be a bit misleading, for the N-in-a-circle was never officially registered by the Northwood firm. Like the Dugan Glass Company's "D-in-Diamond" mark, Northwood's N-in-a-circle is not mentioned in Dr. Arthur Peterson's definitive work, *400 Trademarks on Glass.*

Some writers have attempted to distinguish among various so-called "Northwood" marks, ranging from a simple N or an N with a line under it, to the underlined N-in-a-circle to an underlined N within two concentric circles. In fact, the only mark of these types actually used by Northwood seems to be the underlined N-in-a-circle. Freeman's *Iridescent Glass* mistakenly dates one mark as 1901, well before Northwood was even in business at Wheeling! Pullin's *Glass Signatures, Trademarks and Trade Names* erroneously attributes the mark to Martens [sic] Ferry, Ohio, and further notes, quite illogically, that the mark was "used until 1910" and can be found "molded in [the] bottom of depression glass dish."

On some small items, such as the colonial-style No. 21 (Flute) sherbets, the mechanics of pressing or the characteristics of the glass itself may have rendered the circle and/or the underline virtually invisible to the unaided eye; often, powerful magnification reveals the missing elements. The appearance of one or two circles is not another trademark, as the circle is necessary

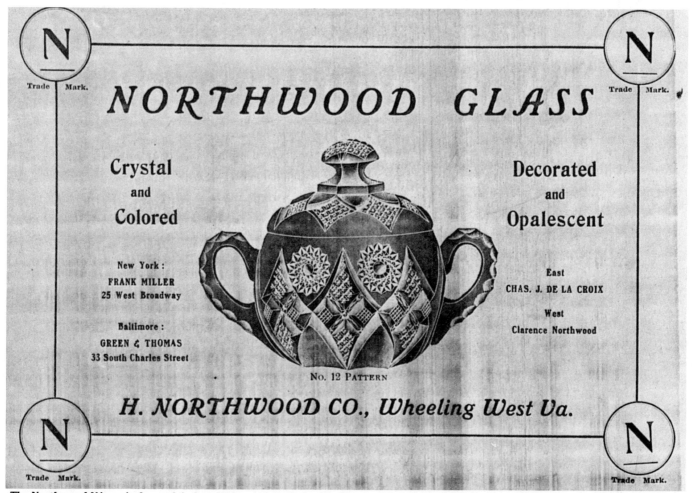

The Northwood N-in-a-circle mark is featured prominently in this Glass and Pottery World *(February, 1906) ad for the firm's No. 12 line.*

This letterhead was used from late 1906 through 1915.

for successfully pressing flat-bottomed items in iron moulds, particularly large plates or bowls, for it eliminates the tendency of the plunger to "suck" as it is being withdrawn from the mould. Some Northwood patterns, such as Grape and Gothic Arches, have a circle on the inside of the base for this reason, not to designate them as Northwood-made. Grape and Gothic Arches occurs in emerald green (Figs. 280-283) and crystal (Fig. 298) but its production in Carnival and, later, Ivory glass overshadows this transparent hue. A plain pitcher and tumbler in deep blue with gold decoration strongly follow the general proportions of Grape and Gothic Arches (Figs. 299-300).

The Northwood underlined N-in-a-circle mark is found on a great number of the patterns and items discussed in this chapter. The patterns, listed in alphabetical order, are as follows: Atlas, Belladonna, Diadem (Sunburst on Shield), Drapery, Encore (Jewel and Flower), No. 21 (Flute), Gold Rose, Lustre Flute, Memphis, Mikado (Flower and Bud), No. 12 (Nearcut), Panelled Holly, Peach (often called Northwood's Peach), Posies and Pods, and Regal. The mark is also found on most of the pieces in the Verre D'or line. For information on later patterns, see the chapter on Carnival glass and consult the Index under individual pattern names.

Collectors should bear in mind that not all pieces in every pattern will carry the mark, and that a four-piece table set may contain some items with the mark and others without it. Most of the time (and always on marked tumblers) the underlined N-in-a-circle is on the inside (i. e., interior) of the base of the item. In addition to the N-in-a-circle mark, some Northwood-made tumblers in crystal or transparent colors may have another letter (E, F, G, H, O or P) on the inside of the bottom, not far from the N-in-a-circle.

Shops making tumblers worked in close proximity to one another, and the same lehrs were used to anneal the ware, so these letters might have served to keep track of an individual shop's output and verify that production quotas were being met by each shop.

When did the use of the Northwood mark cease? Northwood letterhead stationery may offer the best evidence. Those sheets in the National Association files bearing dates between 1907 and 1915, without exception, have the underlined N-in-a-circle as part of the letterhead design. As the Luna line of lighting fixtures became increasingly popular, the firm changed its letterhead. The new rendering mentions Luna by name, and the underlined N-in-a-circle is no longer present. The earliest Luna letterhead which has turned up in the National Association's files is dated 1915, so this may be the time when the Northwood N-in-a-circle was being phased out.

The 1906 Northwood Catalog

Mention has already been made of the Northwood catalog, dated fall, 1906, which was discovered and reprinted by Steve Jennings. This catalog is used throughout this book to document the Northwood products under discussion, but this section will deal with products not discussed elsewhere.

Two numbered patterns are of some interest. A 7 1/2" nappy in pattern No. 14 was modified to form at least five other articles—ranging from cupped and flared versions to a crimped square bowl and a flat cake plate, all of which were offered as an assortment for 80 cents per dozen in five dozen lots. Elsewhere, the No. 14 berry set was combined with berry sets in Diadem (Sunburst on Shield) and No. 12 in a "Massive Berry Set Assortment." No other items are shown

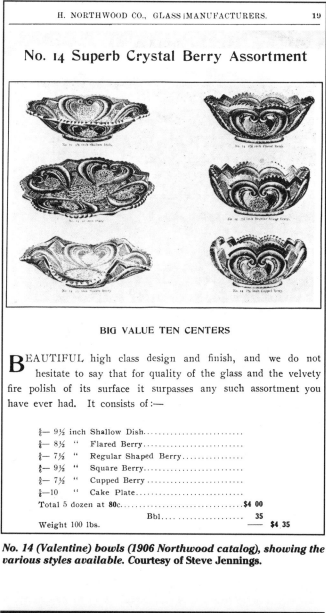

No. 14 Superb Crystal Berry Assortment

BIG VALUE TEN CENTERS

BEAUTIFUL high class design and finish, and we do not hesitate to say that for quality of the glass and the velvety fire polish of its surface it surpasses any such assortment you have ever had. It consists of:—

⅚— 9½ inch	Shallow Dish	....	
⅚— 8½ "	Flared Berry	....	
⅚— 7½ "	Regular Shaped Berry	....	
⅚— 9½ "	Square Berry	....	
⅚— 7½ "	Cupped Berry	....	
⅚—10 "	Cake Plate	....	
Total 5 dozen at 80c	....		$4 00
		Bbl.................	35
Weight 100 lbs.			— $4 35

No. 14 (Valentine) bowls (1906 Northwood catalog), showing the various styles available. Courtesy of Steve Jennings.

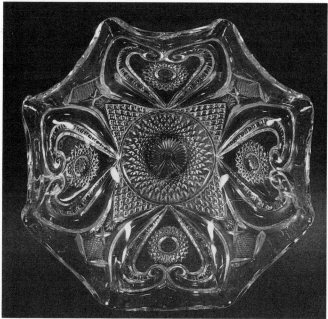

No. 14 (Valentine) crimped bowl.

in No. 14, which Hartung called "Valentine" in her *Northwood Pattern Glass* (p. 27). She reported bowls only (in various sizes) in clear glass, and a fine crimped example is shown on the book's second color page.

A pitcher and tumbler are shown in a pattern designated No. 5 in the Northwood catalog. The tumbler is relatively plain, but the pitcher has egg-shaped protrusions near the base, much like the Northwood's Plums and Cherries pattern discussed below and the Two Fruits spooner shown elsewhere in Carnival glass. A few other No. 5 items are known—a sauce dish and a sugar bowl base—so it seems likely that the berry set and table set were part of original production.

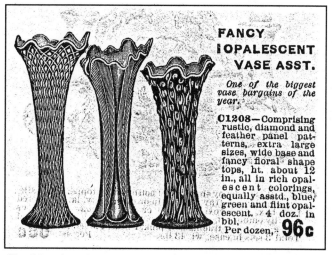

Northwood opalescent vases (Butler Bros., April, 1906, catalog).

The opalescent assortments shown in the fall, 1906 Northwood catalog are much like those in the Lyon Brothers spring-summer, 1906, wholesale catalog, for many of the same novelties are pictured (see p. 33). Flint, green and blue opalescent are the only colors mentioned. Some opalescent vases are also shown, and it is significant that these were also mentioned in crystal with ruby-stained top. Northwood's opinion of these qualified: "Looks like real Ruby Glass, but it is not, it is cold-stained, and we do not guarantee it to wear."

Among the more spectacular pieces in the 1906 catalog is an assortment of wine sets and an 18" tall epergne, dubbed No. 305 Flower Stand. The wine sets—listed in crystal, blue and green—consist of blown decanters with applied handles and a set of six wine glasses. All are decorated in what Hartung called the "Cara Nome" fashion, which consists of delicately shaded floral motifs with stylized leaves nearby. Sometimes, elaborate designs of enameled white dots accompany the flowers and leaves. The Cara Nome decoration

Decorated Wine Sets

"RICH" WINE SET ASSORTMENT

HERE we show nine beautiful sets. The Decanters are large and showy. Each set consists of Decanter and 6 Wines with Glass Tray. The Decanters are Blown with genuine stuck handles and together with the Glasses are beautifully Decorated in Enameled Colors and Gold. All the pieces have Gold Edges except the Trays, which are always of Crystal Glass as Colored Glass Trays are not popular.

Packs nine sets to the bbl., 3 Crystal, 3 Blue, 3 Green.

Price for the Assortment...........................$7 15
Pkge................. 35
Weight 85 lbs.   —— $7 50

Don't Over-look the Glass Trays

Wine sets (1906 Northwood catalog). Courtesy of Steve Jennings.

Decorated tumbler in a typical Northwood style.

No. 305 Flower Stand

18 Inches High

VERY handsome, consisting of the large 12 inch Dish with pretty fluted edge, large Center Flower Tube and three Side Tubes, connected with a metal fitting, which is completely hidden by a glass block or fitting which holds the tubes in position. This is a very pretty stand and is made in three colors —Flint Opalescent, Blue Opalescent and Green Opalescent. We pack nine stands to the bbl.

3 Flint Opalescent
3 Blue "   The Assorted Package... .$7 50
3 Green "   Pkgs........ 50
Weight 100 lbs   —— $8 00

This stand is original with us and is a duplicate in size and construction of the very expensive Import Flower Stands.

These epergnes were available in three opalescent colors, as noted in the 1906 Northwood catalog. Courtesy of Steve Jennings. One such epergne is now on display at the Mansion Museum, Oglebay Institute, in Wheeling, WV.

can be found on plain tumblers which bear the N-in-a-circle mark and on crystal and green examples which have vertical panels inside.

The fall, 1906, Northwood catalog shows several dozen decorated lemonade sets (pitcher and six tumblers) as well as eight sets in various opalescent colors, including ruby. The lemonade sets were offered in these colors: crystal, amethyst, blue, green, and ruby. A plethora of painted decorations was offered, ranging from floral motifs to geometric designs (Figs. 191-192, 220-223, 241-242, 245-246, 252-256, 285, 287, 291-292, and 301-314). The pitchers are usually mould-blown and have applied or "stuck" handles. A few of these sets are in a Butler Brothers catalog for mid-spring, 1906.

The opalescent lemonade sets in the 1906 Northwood catalog included a mould-blown

Opalescent Lemonade Set Assortment

"BEAUTY" ASSORTMENT

IN four Opalescent Colors including two Ruby. Opalescent Glass will always be in demand and the sets shown above are the most popular of their kind we ever made.

The Assortment consists of 8 complete sets with 13 inch Embossed Trays—2 Ruby Opalescent, 2 Blue Opalescent, 2 Green Opalescent and 2 Crystal Opalescent. These necessarily are hand made—all blown—large stuck handles, and made of the very best quality glass.

Price for 8 sets with trays..	$5 15
bbl.	35
Weight 75 lbs.	$5 50

Don't over-look that two sets are Ruby.

Assortment of lemonade sets from the 1906 Northwood catalog. Courtesy of Steve Jennings.

Coinspot motif, and photographs taken inside the Northwood plant on June 9, 1906, shows Coinspot pitchers in some quantity. Heacock noted opalescent Coinspot pitchers in two distinct shapes, both of which are confirmed by the photographs and the fall, 1906, Northwood catalog. Heacock reported that both pitchers bore the N-in-a-circle, a noteworthy fact, since this distinctive mark is usually imparted by the plunger in making pressed ware (Figs. 243 and 293).

Other Northwood Lines

A number of Northwood lines are known to collectors today, largely because of the fact that they bear the N-in-a-circle mark. With the exception of the Regal line, which was introduced at the outset of the 1907 trade season, these other lines—Atlas, Cherry and Cable, No. 21 (Flute), Gold Rose, Grapevine and Cherry Sprig (Frosted Fruits), Hobnail, Lustre Flute, Peach, Plums and Cherries, Posies and Pods, and Strawberry and Cable—cannot always be dated precisely as to their respective times of initial production.

A full-page advertisement in the December 29, 1906, issue of *China, Glass and Lamps*) shows the Regal pitcher and berry bowl, but the pattern was not identified by name or number. A reporter described the line only as "a block colonial in plain opalescent." Crystal and emerald green (usually gold decorated) Regal pieces are known, but the opalescent hues—flint, blue, green—are of most interest to collectors today. Regal water sets, berry sets and table sets were featured in Butler Brothers catalogs in 1907. In addition to the celery vase, today's collectors have also

Bill Heacock named this pattern "Barbella." This pitcher is similar in shape to Grape and Gothic Arches (see Fig. 298). The pattern may have continued as Northwood's No. 301 line, which was being produced from 1920 to 1925. The berry bowl and sauce are shown in the Rainbow and Cobweb folder (see Chapter Six), and other No. 301 articles appear in The Lure of Rainbow (see Chapter Seven) and in The Rainbow Glassware (see the last color page and the five following it). See Fig. 895 for a Barbella plate.

This photo was taken in June, 1906, "at the end of #3 and 4 lehrs" in the Northwood plant. Coinspot pitchers and several tankard styles are clearly visible. Courtesy of Ken Northwood.

found cruets and salt/pepper shakers (Figs. 262, 315-321, and 334-336). "Green and flint opalescent colors" are mentioned in Butler Brothers, and all had the added attraction of "extra wide burnt in gold band decoration...." The Butler Brothers called the ware "Golden Opalescent," so the gold decor may have been made by Northwood especially for this assortment for Butler Brothers and not for general sales.

Atlas is surely a Northwood colonial-type line in the plain style, but it is difficult to find in the

This assortment of Northwood's Regal, shown in Butler Brothers Mid-Spring 1907 catalog, mentions green and flint opalescent "with extra wide burnt in gold band decorations...."

collector's market today. Crystal table sets, berry sets and water sets are known, but the most striking articles have a "maiden's blush" ruby-stained effect and are decorated with gold. All pieces seem to be marked with the N-in-a-circle (Figs. 229 and 276-279).

A new pattern for 1907 was apparently called "Golden Cherry," and the evidence for this appellation is a trade journal quote from January, 1908, concerning a new line "which replaces the Golden Cherry of last season." Hartung (*Northwood Pattern Glass*, pp. 19-20) thought that Northwood made at least three patterns utilizing a cherry motif—Cherry and Cable; Cherry Lattice; and Cherry Thumbprints (also called Cherry Thumbprint or Cherry and Thumbprints). Heacock documented yet another, Plums and Cherries, but he also noted that Cherry Thumbprints and Cherry and Cable are the same pattern, although the thumbprints are absent from some small items such as tumblers. The descriptive name Cherry and Cable probably should be retained since the pieces with thumbprints are indeed part of the original line.

The Cherry and Cable line consists of berry set, table set and water set, all of which are

Ad for Northwood wares, December 29, 1906, including the Intaglio, Verre D'or and Regal lines. See Fig. 301 for a decorated pitcher.

Atlas creamer.

Cherry and Cable two-piece punch bowl.
Courtesy of Bud Ashmore.

reminiscent of the general shape of the colonial style. The fruit is stained with color (ranging from ruby red to purple), and the gold decor is both attractive and durable (Figs. 258 and 360-364). A Cherry and Cable water set appears in the Butler Brothers fall, 1908, catalog along with sets in Memphis and Lustre Flute. Articles carry the N-in-a-circle, and a few pieces of this pattern were also made in iridescent glass.

Cherry Lattice was a probably somewhat later pattern, but the date of its inception cannot be ascertained. Nevertheless, a premium catalog issued by the Lee Manufacturing company of Chicago, Illinois, sometime after May 1, 1911, shows all of the known pieces—berry set, table set and water set. Apparently, this line was made only in decorated crystal (see Fig. 257).

Northwood's No. 21 (Flute) line is, of course, yet another in the colonial style. The pattern's

No. 21 (Flute) spooner.

number indicates a post-1908 time period, for the Memphis line, introduced in early 1908, was No. 19. In corresponding with the National Association in September, 1912, Harry Northwood needed a bit of scrap paper for a sketch, and he used the blank side of an illustrated sheet showing several pieces in pattern No. 21, which featured heavy gold decoration on rims, bases and handles. The January 16, 1913, issue of *Pottery, Glass and Brass Salesman* described "a pattern of simple and attractive design ... decorated in ruby and gold, in gold only and also undecorated." Some articles have also been found with a "maiden's blush" ruby treatment as well as in undecorated, bright crystal. Berry sets, table sets and water sets are known (see Figs. 340, 370-371 and 378). A particularly attractive set consists of blue No. 21 (Flute) pieces with an interesting silver filigree-like decoration. All bear the N-in-a-circle mark. Northwood's No. 21 (Flute) pattern was also made in iridescent glass (particularly the sherbert dish). An undated mould drawing in the Fenton Museum archives depicts the tankard-style No. 21 (Flute) pitcher.

The general outline of Northwood's Gold Rose is decidedly colonial, but the pattern's chief feature is the heavy decoration on the flowers and their stems and accompanying leaves. Hartung (*Northwood Pattern Glass*, p. 23) mistakenly assumed that a wholesaler's illustration revealed its original name. In fact,

THESE ARTISTIC GOODS HAVE QUALITY AS WELL AS BEAUTY

Cherry Lattice pieces as shown in Lee Manufacturing catalog, c. 1911.

51

PATTERN—Full Finished Pot Glass.

Cream.

No. 21. Butter and Cover.

This fragment of a page from an undated Northwood catalog shows the No. 21 (Flute) pattern in crystal glass with gold decoration.

Gold Rose assortment from Butler Brothers catalog, 1910. The wholesalers rarely used original pattern names, but this ad was likely the inspiration for Hartung's name for this pattern.

catalogs issued by Butler Brothers rarely allude to the manufacturer or pattern names or numbers, simply because the customer might be tempted to deal directly with the factory rather than to order from the wholesale catalog. Gold Rose items typically have the N-in-a-circle. Table sets, water sets and berry sets were illustrated in a fall, 1910, Butler Brothers catalog, which also mentioned the two colors made, "solid wine ruby and emerald green." The green is rather dark (Figs. 102-103). Hartung mentioned items in crystal glass, too, and these typically have ruby flashing on the flowers and some gold trim (Fig. 232).

Grapevine and Cherry Sprig, which was named by Heacock, is so unlike other Northwood patterns from 1903-07 that one might overlook it but for the N-in-a-circle (Figs. 227-228). The crystal articles—table set, water set and berry set—are relatively heavy, and some have gold decoration on the rims. The peg-like feet are

different from virtually every other known Northwood pattern. The grapes and cherries may be satin finished, probably with acid, giving rise to another name sometimes applied to this pattern—Frosted Fruits. Sharp-eyed collectors will notice some similarities in design between the grape clusters and the now-famous Northwood Grape and Cable, which was developed about 1910.

Northwood's Hobnail occurs in Mosaic glass (Figs. 32-33), of course, but the full extent of the line is not certain. Heacock had a water set photographed for this book (Figs. 234-235), and there is some indication that a Hobnail line occurs in iridescent (Carnival) glass.

The Lustre Flute line was probably a contemporary of Memphis and Cherry Thumbprints, for these three are shown together in a Butler Brothers catalog from the fall of 1908. A separate ad in this same catalog shows all the Lustre Flute items which are known in flint and blue opalescent—berry set, table set and water set. The opalescent effect is sometimes quite

No. 21 (Flute) nut set in blue with silver filigree.

Grapevine and Cherry Sprig berry bowl.

52

Lustre Flute assortment (Fall, 1908, Butler Brothers catalog).

heavy, and pieces may be trimmed in bright gold (Figs. 137-144 and 238). A small creamer and open sugar are known in emerald green (sometimes iridescent; see Figs. 396-397), as is the punch cup.

The Peach pattern, which is perhaps better known as Northwood's Peach, is well-established in Carnival glass circles, but has received less attention from pattern glass collectors. One may be surprised indeed to see the "Peach" decorated with ruby-stain (Figs. 359, 365-366), even though such pieces are quite scarce.

The Plums and Cherries pattern, which was named by Heacock, cannot be dated with certainty, but it likely comes from the same time as Cherry Thumbprints, for the decorating technique is similar. The berry set, table set and water set are known, and contemporary collectors have also found a celery vase and several sizes of covered bowls. All are marked with the N-in-a-circle, and the color-stained fruit and gold decor are distinctive. The large protrusions near the base of the water pitcher (Fig. 259) are reminiscent of Northwood's pattern No. 5, which was shown in the fall, 1906, catalog. These protrusions are not present on the tumblers, however (Fig. 358). A few pieces occur in iridescent glass and are sometimes called Two Fruits by Carnival glass collectors.

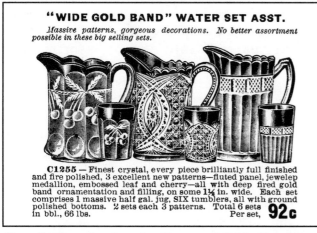

Three Northwood water sets—Cherry and Cable, Memphis and Lustre Flute—offered together by Butler Brothers in early 1909.

Some Posies and Pods items may have been produced prior to 1905, for only the large berry bowl bears the N-in-a-circle mark, despite the fact that numerous items are known— water set, berry set and table set. Crystal pieces are sometimes decorated with gold and a light ruby stain (Figs. 296-297), much like Encore (Jewel and Flower), which was made in 1904-05. Heacock, who named this pattern, also noted the similarity of its stippled background to Mikado (Flower and Bud or Blooms and Blossoms). Posies and Pods articles are also known in emerald green which is usually decorated with gold (Figs. 265-271). A few bowls are known in iridescent glass; these are known as the "Beads" pattern by Carnival glass collectors, and a crimped bowl appears in a spring, 1909, assortment offered by Butler Brothers.

The Strawberry and Cable line reminds one of Cherry and Cable, and these patterns are similar to Northwood's Grape and Cable, which was used primarily for iridescent glass and, later, for Ivory ware. Strawberry and Cable has pale ruby and gold decor, and the additional intricate pattern is a cut-type motif (Fig. 260). Hartung noted its similarity to Northwood's No. 12, the most extensive imitation cut line made at Wheeling. The table set and water set are known, and Hartung reported a goblet. There is one clue which indicates the possible time of manufacture. The November 16, 1911, issue of *Pottery, Glass and Brass Salesman* reported that Northwood's New York representative, Frank M. Miller of 25 West Broadway was showing "a strawberry and gold decoration in tableware that has all the earmarks of being a big seller. ... the decoration is in relief, the strawberry plant being the motif, with the leaves in gold and the berries in natural color."

Posies and Pods pitcher and tumbler.

A Time of Transition, 1907-1908

During this brief period, the Northwood firm moved away from the rather heavy dark blue and amethyst colors of Verre D'or and the various opalescent pattern lines and began to make tableware in emerald green with gold decoration, perhaps reflecting the success of such earlier lines as Diadem and Regal in this hue. Such Northwood patterns as Gold Rose and Posies and Pods probably originated during this time, but Memphis and Panelled Holly were the major products.

Some trade journal columns are rather general about the Northwood's activities, but others offer useful insights into the firm's products. The January, 1907, issue of *Glass and Pottery World* had this brief description of the Northwood's exhibit: "Best location in [the] house and a

"GORGEOUS" DECORATED TANKARD LEMONADE SET ASSORTMENT.
Extremely decorative design.

1C1937—All tall tankard shapes, ht. about 13 in., ½ gal. sizes, genuine stuck handles, elaborate floral leaf and enamel decorations, rich gold bands and profuse illuminations, all decorations fired, 3 crystal and 3 green. Total 6 sets in bbl., 65 lbs. Per set, **$1.00**

"PREMIUM" DECORATED LEMONADE SET ASSORTMENT.
One of the season's best things. They certainly are good.

1C1936—½ gal. stuck handle jugs, SIX tumblers, radiant green glass, allover scattered enamel and floral decorations, part with gold edges. 4 sets tall tankard, 2 low, 2 swell. Total 8 sets in bbl., 78 lbs. Per set, **69c**

Decorated lemonade sets from Butler Brothers catalogs, 1908.

display of colored lemonade and water sets, high grade heavy crystal, plain and decorated table ware and novelties far ahead of even the best ever shown by this house noted for new things and good. Carl and Clarence Northwood are the hosts while the "old man" only such by discourtesy, Mr. Harry Northwood, is occasionally to be seen."

This period of transition was marked by some changes in the factory itself. The March, 1907, issue of *Glass and Pottery World* reported that "Northwood ... have nearly completed a 75 x 75 three-story addition to their extensive plant," adding also that the factory was "crowded with large orders."

The Northwood's featured patterns for 1908 were No. 19, which is now known as Memphis, and a line called Golden Holly, which is now called simply Holly or, more often, Panelled Holly. An illustrated ad showing No. 19 appeared in the December 27, 1907, issue of *China, Glass and Lamps*. Another issue of this publication (January 11, 1908) had a report of the Northwood exhibit:

"When visitors call at rooms 7 and 8, Monongahela house, they are certain to receive a cordial greeting from Carl and Clarence Northwood, who are showing the wares of H. Northwood & Co. 'Everything new, original shapes and designs out of the ordinary,' appears to be the watchword with this well-known Wheeling concern. Three new lines of tableware, one in imitation cut [No. 19 Memphis] which comes in crystal and topaz; another in colonial design made in five different colors and the 'Golden Holly' line which replaces the 'Golden Cherry' [probably Cherry and Cable] of last season, are included in this season's elegant display. A heavy run was recorded on the last named line throughout the past year, but judging from present indications the 'Holly' line will go it one better in the matter of sales. When it comes to lemonade and wine sets the Northwood boys say they have an entirely new assortment of shapes and designs and their number is simply bewildering. Here the visitor will find the latest novelties in all colors, together with a big line of vases. Lamps, gas shades and pressed bar goods are also in evidence. New shapes and designs in the Khedive line replace last year's offerings. Last, but by no means least, comes the 'Aurora' line with handsome decorations and the Northwoods say it is a seller par excellence—a winner right from the start."

A similar, but short review appeared in *Glass and Pottery World* (January, 1908): "H. Northwood

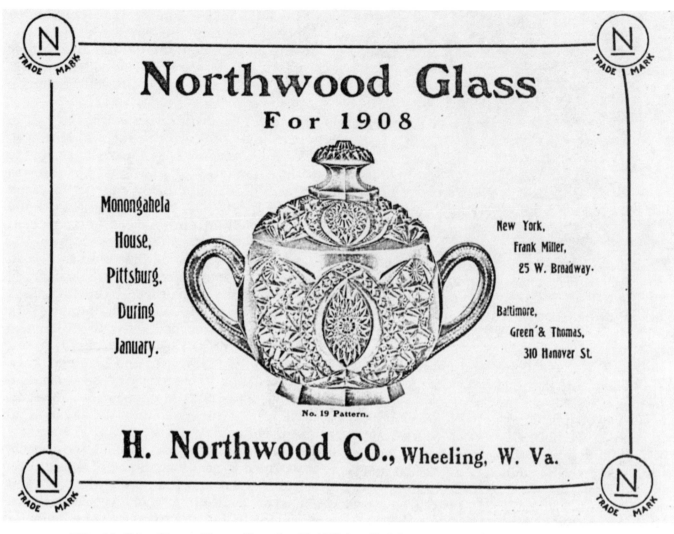

Northwood Glass
For 1908

Monongahela
House,
Pittsburg.
During
January.

New York,
Frank Miller,
25 W. Broadway.

Baltimore,
Green & Thomas,
310 Hanover St.

No. 19 Pattern.

H. Northwood Co., Wheeling, W. Va.

This ad in China, Glass and Lamps *(December 28, 1907) heralded the appearance of the No. 19 (Memphis) line.*

Co., Wheeling, W. Va., Clarence Northwood.— Colored glassware, crystal tableware, plain and decorated, including lemonade and wine sets, novelties, etc., make up an unequalled display of its kind. Ingenuity, good taste and an inherited genius for glass making have never born fruit more plentifully than in the results shown by Mr. Northwood this year. Buyers promptly recognize the exceptional selling merit of everything so seductively put before them in this exhibit. The Golden Holly, Aurora and Khedive lines are particularly noticeable."

Assuming the "imitation cut" pattern is indeed No. 19 Memphis, the use of the term "topaz" in *China, Glass and Lamps* is noteworthy. Memphis is well-known in crystal and emerald green, usually decorated with gold, and the pattern was later used for iridescent production. The Mansion Museum at Oglebay Institute in Wheeling has a topaz (canary) No. 19 Memphis spooner in its collection, one of the few pieces known in this hue. Interestingly, Memphis, like the earlier pattern No. 12, does not seem to have been made

in opalescent glass. Perhaps Northwood felt that these imitation cut glass motifs would not look well in opalescent effects.

The Memphis line probably consisted of table set, water set, and berry set at first, but a few other pieces were soon added to the line, attesting to its popularity: mustard, handled nappie, punch bowl and stand, and punch cups. The handled nappie was sometimes used as an advertising specialty item. Memphis is among the Northwood patterns in which the base (i.e., marie) is

"GOLD MEDALLION" DINING SET ASSORTMENT.
Impossible to produce richer sets than these. Quality and decoration considered the price is unusually low.

C961—Massive sets, rich new prominent raised jewel cutting, each piece with jeweled gold medallions with raised centers, solid gold feet and knobs, wide gold band edges, gold decorated handles. Sets equally asstd. in crystal and rich emerald green.

Asst. comprises:
2 only 7 pc. water sets—massive ½ gal. jug, SIX ground bottom tumblers.
2 " 7 pc. berry sets—9 in. berry bowl, SIX 4¾ in. nappies.
2 " 4 pc. table sets.
Total 6 sets in bbl., 70 lbs.

Per set, **$1.00**

Memphis assortment in the Fall, 1908, Butler Brothers catalog.

No. 19 (Memphis) handled bon bon with advertising for Pickering Furniture and Carpets.

octagonal rather than circular. Most pieces are marked with the N-in-a-circle (Figs. 264 and 343-348).

No colors were mentioned in the trade press' discussions of the Panelled Holly line, but this interesting pattern is probably best known today in a vibrant opalescent blue with heavy gold decoration on the holly leaves (Figs. 322-327 and 332-333) and in flint opalescent with red (ruby-stained) and green decoration (Figs. 328-331 and 338-339). Green items with gold decoration are known (Figs. 68-69 and 272-275), as is attractive red/gold-decorated crystal (Figs. 236-237). The Panelled Holly line included the table set and water set, as well as berry sets and salt/pepper shakers. The two-handled bon-bons were likely made from the spooner mould, a common practice in the glass industry. Like Memphis, some Panelled Holly items occur in iridescent glass.

The July, 1908, issue of *American Pottery Gazette* noted that the Northwood firm was "moving along nicely" and alluded to a "new, cheap line of tableware and specialties in good, white [crystal] glass" without providing an further information.

Heacock's handwritten notes from 1978-87 in his personal copies of the second edition of *Opalescent Glass from A to Z* make it possible to attribute a number of additional novelties to Northwood, although they cannot be dated precisely. By 1907-08, however, the Northwood plant was well into production of opalescent novelties as well as pattern lines. Most of the following pieces occur in flint blue and green opalescent; references are to figure numbers in Heacock's book on opalescent: Autumn Leaves (492); Barbells (517); Colonial Stairsteps (576); Cashews (461); Cornucopia (484); Greek Key and Rib; Jolly Bear (490); Lattice Medallions (471); Leaf and Diamonds (493); Leaf and Leaflets (491); Meander (507); Poinsettia Lattice (453); and Ruffles and Rings (512). Most do not have the N-in-a-circle mark, although Lattice Medallions is so marked, and marked items in Colonial Stairsteps were reported to Heacock, although they remain unconfirmed at this time. Some of these items (Cashews, Leaf and Diamonds and Leaf and Leaflets) are known with "goofus" gold, usually on the underside. Be sure to consult the Index for other references and illustrations in this book.

Some other patterns or items which occur in limited opalescent production are as follows: Acorn Burrs; Beaded Cable (Fig. 201); Bushel Basket; Daisy and Plume; Fine Cut and Roses; Grape and Cable (Fig. 247); Hearts and Flowers;

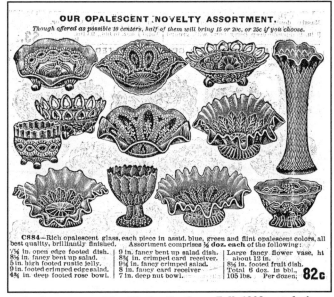

This Memphis assortment, which includes salt/pepper shakers, mustard pot and cruet, was offered as a sales premium.

OUR OPALESCENT NOVELTY ASSORTMENT.
Though offered as possible 10 centers, half of them will bring 15 or 20c, or 25c if you choose.

C884—Rich opalescent glass, each piece in asstd. blue, green and flint opalescent colors, all best quality, brilliantly finished. Assortment comprises ⅓ doz. each of the following:

7¼ in. open edge footed dish.	9 in. fancy bent up salad dish.	Large fancy flower vase, ht about 12 in.
8½ in. fancy bent up salad.	8¾ in. crimped card receiver.	
5 in. high footed rustic jelly.	9¼ in. fancy crimped salad.	8½ in. footed fruit dish.
9 in. footed crimped edge salad.	8 in. fancy card receiver	Total 6 doz. in bbl.,
4¾ in. deep footed rose bowl.	7 in. deep nut bowl.	105 lbs. Per dozen; **82c**

Opalescent novelties (Butler Brothers, Fall, 1908, catalog).

Cashews opalescent bowl.

Peacocks on the Fence; Rose Show; Singing Birds; Thistle Patch; Three Fruits and Three Fruits with Meander; and Waterlily and Cattails. Many of these patterns are discussed in the following chapter, which focuses on Northwood's Carnival glass.

The August, 1908, *American Pottery Gazette* contained a lengthy article on Harry Northwood which is quoted in full:

"WELL! Well! And whom have we here? Why yes, of course, Harry Northwood; known wherever glass is sold—and then some! When they want something in colored glass that they never had before, never heard of, that in their own hearts they don't believe exists, they mention it to Harry and then at the next annual showing at Pittsburgh there will be Harry with the goods. And he will have it with a name of his own tacked on to it, too, that will make some of them blink once or twice as well.

What a thing it is to be famous. Here we have a man who likes nothing better than to do just as he wants to do, and they make him unheard of colors in glass instead. Nevertheless and alas! to quote the novelists, Harry prospers on hard work. He comes from a famous family of glassworkers in England, his father, John Northwood, whose death occurred only a few years ago, having already been referred to in these columns as one of the men who made Stourbridge's famous glass an actuality. When Harry came over here in the early eighties, a strapping young fellow in the twenties, he started in to work in Wheeling, W. Va., in one of the old time glass factories. Of course he had to make some colored glass. Just couldn't help it. They hadn't seen before anything like the opalescent glass he made for them and his reputation was made from then on.

Harry made three or four false starts around Wheeling before he finally struck his gait in a little town in Pennsylvania. There, however, in his own factory, he made them all sit up and take notice. He surely knew the inside of colored glass making. He says himself that his father taught him all he knew and says further that what his father didn't know about the art you could put in the hollow of a hair after you had punched the pith out of it, and then that hair would rattle.

Well, anyway, this was just prior to the formation of the National Glass Co., of has-been fame. When this finally took form and shape (the stock and bondholders now insist that it took other things of theirs; things that would for example buy them cooling and luscious fruits, and drinks, in this torrid season) it just yearned for that little Pennsylvania factory of Harry's. He let it yearn till its tongue protruded fine, and when the dust had settled the National had the factory without Harry, and Harry had a wad and a job as the English representative of the National with offices in London. This, considering that Harry could build himself another factory whenever he wanted one, while the acquirement of a wad and a job take time and work, was—oh, well. What's the use? Some people who don't know any better make a practice of working for money. Those favored by the gods, why they just sit 'round and have it handed to them. Either England didn't suit the man who could make colored glass or else the National didn't have the goods. At any rate it was not long after Harry had gone over before we find one of the predecessors of the (2) Giant Turbiners, Count Them (2) sailing past the Statue of Liberty and up to the tall buildings with the returning Northwood menage aboard. And right glad was Harry to again get into the game of making the colored ware so dear to the buyer's heart; those combinations of finish and color and name that none but he could, or dared, invent. But hark! What is this noise? Aha! Others have gone into the colored field. Some of the gilt has been gnawed from the gingerbread. Does that deter the scion of the forbears who knew it from A to Z? Perish the thought ! Here's an idle factory. Harry buys it and before you can say Jack Robinson the possible factory that has already been referred to in connection with the wad and job, is an actuality. It wasn't quite as easy the next year or two as it had been but Harry has that stubborn English nature that wouldn't know it even if it was licked; he just revels in a good fight. And so, like a little man, he profited by his errors after his re-entry into the field and made good again. Today, just as if there had never been any National, when the trade wants something entirely new in glassware, there is Harry, always ready and always on the job. He has settled down these days and alternates pretty regularly between the factory and his house on Wheeling Island; the soul of good nature with a cheery word for all, a heart bluffness, fond of life's good things and with a multitude of friends. When the Ohio river floods come along they bother him very little. Downstairs carpets are taken up and with the furniture brought up into the second story. The family, with a good stock of eatables and drinkables, in common with their neighbors, then sit themselves down in patience and contentment to wait the subsidence of the floods. "But it's a devil of a messy job afterwards," says Harry.

This long article about Northwood is certainly subject to different interpretations. Writing in the *Journal* (#14, issued January, 1987) of The Carnival Glass Society, U. K., Raymond E. Notley has noted that the article has the marks of "either a pen portrait or a hatchet job." Indeed, Harry Northwood enjoyed a measure of personal popularity in the industry, especially among the reporters from the glass tableware trade press (whose periodicals often carried Northwood's paid advertising, it should not be forgotten).

Nonetheless, there was surely jealousy and acrimony in the industry, too, and those involved with the then-bankrupt (in 1908) National Glass Company probably resented Northwood's keen competition with their firm, especially in view of the fact that he had once been under contract to the National and had campaigned, albeit unsuccessfully, for a seat on its Board of Directors. But, whatever motives may have been behind this article, Harry Northwood was his own man, and his greatest successes were yet to come.

The back of this photo was captioned by Harry Northwood as follows: "Office of H. Northwood Co. Wheeling WVa June 9/06. From left to right S. G. Robinson, H. C. [Harry Clarence] Northwood, Carl Northwood, W. Green, H. Northwood, Miss Leah Noble, Miss Sarah Williams. All but Carl belong to the office force. This picture was taken on payday & the paper money together with the stack of silver dollars are on the table. Counting and putting up in envelopes ready to pay off $5000." Miss Noble was still with the firm when she died of appendicitis in 1915. **Courtesy of Ken Northwood.**

CHAPTER FOUR
NORTHWOOD'S CARNIVAL GLASS

The years 1908 to about 1915 mark the major production time of Northwood's Carnival glass wares, but, until this book, there has been no systematic attempt to provide a chronological account of this unique American glass. This chapter will use a wide variety of sources, including trade journals and wholesalers catalogs, to provide reliable dates for as many popular Carnival glass patterns and novelty items as possible.

The books on Carnival glass are many, and authors over the years have performed a remarkable service for collectors by careful comparisons of patterns and an encyclopedic listing of colors. Foremost among the early authors on Carnival glass are Marion Hartung and Rose Presznick, each of whom wrote a series of books devoted exclusively to Carnival glass. Hartung also published books devoted to opalescent glass and to Northwood glass, and her pattern names quickly met with favor among collectors. Indeed, her classifications and nomenclature remain valuable today, especially for those many patterns and items whose original names remain mysteries. Sherman Hand's work included several illustrations drawn from wholesalers' catalogs. Bill Edwards wrote frequently on Carnival glass, covering many different manufacturers, and one of his books was devoted to Northwood.

Another important contemporary writer on Carnival glass is Don Moore, who produced several books and contributes regularly to various Carnival glass newsletters. Moore is especially aware of the need to reconsider previous attributions in light of new evidence and research. Carnival glass collectors are well-organized in a variety of state, regional and national collectors clubs, and the amount of information available through their many newsletters is astounding.

The Heart of America Carnival Glass Association has published a number of color sheets showing various patterns, and this organization's recent publication, *Educational Series I*, draws together many fine articles by John and Lucile Britt which have appeared in the HOACGA newsletters. The yearly price guides by the Mordini's and the bi-monthly listings issued by *The Antique Trader* are valuable resources to keep abreast of the range of known Carnival glass colors as well as current prices.

William Heacock's early work on Carnival glass was based primarily upon a large number of glass shards from the site of the Indiana, Pennsylvania, glass plant which had been operated by Harry Northwood from 1896 through 1900 before being taken over, in turn, by the Dugan and the Diamond interests. Heacock made friends with several people in Indiana, and one of them, Del Helman, obtained the fragments on those occasions when excavations occurred at or near the factory site, which is now occupied by Indiana University of Pennsylvania. Del Helman's father, Harry A. Helman, worked for the university and was instrumental in locating and preserving shards which were sent to Heacock beginning in 1975.

In 1977, Heacock made the Carnival glass shards available to Carnival glass writer Bill Edwards, and another large group of fragments was shared several years later. Under the heading "The Northwood Story," Edwards acknowledged Heacock's generosity in his *Northwood: King of Carnival Glass* (1978); similar statements appear under the heading "The Dugan Story," in the first edition of his *Standard Encyclopedia of Carnival Glass* (1982).

The shards from Indiana were of considerable use in Heacock's *Custard Glass from A to Z* in 1976, and they formed the basis for many research reports on Carnival glass in his *Glass Collector* series and, subsequently, the three volumes of *Collecting Glass*. When he passed away in August, 1988, Heacock left many records of his determined attempts to separate Northwood Carnival glass from the similar glassware made by Dugan in Indiana and from production at the Fenton plant. Among these records is a set of Hartung's books with Heacock's updates and findings entered on appropriate pages. This chapter advances Heacock's work by utilizing dozens of wholesalers' catalogs showing important groups of Carnival glass as well as information relating to iridescent glass produced at other factories, such as Westmoreland, Cambridge, Millersburg, and the United States Glass Company.

The Nature of "Carnival" Glass
Any discussion of Carnival glass, especially Northwood's Carnival, should be prefaced by a thorough explanation of its methods of manu-

59

facture and its place in the history of glass. "Carnival" is, of course, a collector's term, derived from stories about this glassware, like others, being given away as prizes at fairs or carnivals. The association is an extraordinarily pleasant one, as most people have fond, if not fanciful, memories of such childhood occasions. To a glassmaker, however, Carnival glass is a kind of iridescent glass.

Freeman's early work, titled simply *Iridescent Glass,* differentiated between iridescent art glass produced by "in-the-mix" ingredients and that made by "an iridescent coating or spray." Carnival glass falls into the latter category. Iridescent art glass, such as the pieces credited to Louis Comfort Tiffany and Frederick Carder, predates Carnival glass by as much as twenty-five years, but it was probably the turn of the century popularity of Tiffany's and Carder's wares which spurred the development of the more economical Carnival glass.

Northwood's Carnival glass began as pressed ware (a few articles, such as pitchers are mould-blown) in crystal or a typical transparent glass color such as green, blue or amethyst. The cast iron moulds typically produce a pattern on the outside surface of the glass during pressing, but many Carnival glass articles have patterns both inside and outside. The interior patterns are created by the plunger as it forces the molten glass against the mould, which imparts the exterior pattern (or so-called "back" pattern on Carnival plates or bowls). Because some plungers were of relatively standard sizes and could be interchanged, many Northwood-made articles can be found with different interior patterns as well as various combinations of interior and exterior patterns.

After the molten glass is pressed, a worker opens the mould, and the glass is removed and "snapped-up," using a tool called a snap which holds the glass firmly in jaws which grip the "marie." Carnival glass collectors often refer to an article's "collar base;" this is what glassworkers call the marie. The marie is often circular, but it can be oval, hexagonal or any other multi-sided figure. Usually, the shape of the marie follows the general shape of the article. An important feature of this operation is that the snap holds the article firmly, with jaws of proper size and shape to avoid marring the marie, which is, of course, still hot glass. Some Carnival glass articles, such as pitchers and tumblers, will be sprayed only on one surface, the exterior. Other articles, such as plates and bowls, may be sprayed inside and out

(or inside only). The snap covers the marie during spraying, of course, so this area always remains without iridescence. Sometimes spray seeps between the joints in the jaws of the snap, and the resulting patches of pale iridescence can be discerned on the edge of the marie. The color pages in this book show the reverse sides of two items (see Figs. 586 and 719); note that the respective maries on these pieces are free from iridescence.

Once snapped-up (but before spraying), the pressed item may require reheating, called warming-in, at a glory hole prior to "finishing" by a skilled worker who may crimp or otherwise alter the shape of the piece. After finishing and possibly additional warming-in, the item is ready for the essential step in making Carnival glass— spraying the hot glass with a chemical solution which becomes a microscopically thin layer of iridescence on the surface of the glass. The article is then carried-in to the lehrs for annealing and cooling to room temperature. The iridescence is created by the ingredients in the spray (metallic salts such as iron chloride or tin chloride), not by any re-firing. Some writers, misunderstanding the chemistry of iridescent glass, have suggested that common table salt (sodium chloride) was applied to the glass!

There are, of course, some possible variations in the procedure described above. The hot glass may be sprayed more than once, with different metallic salt solutions, creating a final appearance that depends upon one layer of iridescence over another. The glass may be allowed to cool somewhat before spraying, or the spray may be applied lightly or heavily. The essential elements are always the same: the glass is blown or pressed and, if need be, finished to the desired shape; then it is sprayed. Any shaping after spraying typically creates that which collector's call "stretch" glass, an onion skin-like effect in which the thin iridescent surface displays minute breaks. Northwood made such glass, and it is discussed elsewhere in this book (see Chapter Six).

Several writers on Carnival glass have supposed that Harry Northwood's creation of iridescent glass stemmed from correspondence or direct aid from his relatives. In her *Carnival Glass,* Hallam stated that Harry Northwood, upon seeing Fenton's iridescent ware, "shipped a sample to his father, John Northwood...." The Fenton plant first made glass in 1907, and John Northwood died in February, 1902, so this story must be discounted. In his excellent *Nineteenth*

Northwood's first ad for his new iridescent glass.

Century Glass (revised ed., 1967), Revi recounts an interview with John Northwood II, suggesting that Harry Northwood contacted his half-brother (who had succeeded the late John Northwood I at Stevens and Williams), for help in the development of iridescent glass at Northwood's Wheeling plant. Harry Northwood's notebooks contain several pages of information about iridescent glass, but there is no mention of John Northwood II in conjunction with these procedures, although he is mentioned elsewhere as "Brother John." In his *Carnival Glass,* Notley suggests that iridizing techniques derived from procedures at Stevens and Williams or Webb were "taken to the United States by Harry Northwood," and this certainly could have been done either through correspondence or one of Harry's visits.

The Northwood notebooks refer clearly to some of Northwood's first iridescent products. The Golden Iris (called "marigold" today) which debuted in 1908 is mentioned by name. The iridescent effect was achieved by spraying with a solution of ferric (iron) chloride, and Northwood added these notes: "ordinary Chloride of Iron as bought at wholesale drug stores costs 3 1/2 cents lb. ... spray on glass when finished ready for lehr ... glass must be fairly hot." By February, 1909, Northwood was purchasing large containers of the solution from a firm in Philadelphia, recording that it "needs nothing at all added." The temperature of the glass was surely a variable, as this observation reveals: "Spray on the glass very hot for Matt Iridescent & not so hot for Bright

Iridescent" (Frank M. Fenton believes that "bright iridescent" is that which some Carnival collectors refer to as "radium finish" today). Northwood also noted that a solution of chloride of antimony could be "sprayed on top" of the iron chloride ("gives blue colors & is rich"). Still another entry advises that spraying iron chloride on hot glass, followed quickly by a second spraying with a tin solution "gives beautiful effects."

Other entries in Northwood's notebook indicate that he was aware of methods to produce iridescent glassware, including spraying, well before 1908. A page dated September, 1905, mentions "silver lining for open pieces," culminating with the observation that "sprayed with solution of Tin Crystals ... it gives wonderful silver metallic effects." Another record, dated March 28, 1906, recounts making glass with a metallic silver surface.

The glassworkers at the Northwood factory and other plants called their iridescent glass "dope [or doped] ware," and records of the National Association of Manufacturers of Pressed and Blown Glassware provide additional insights into production techniques. On March 22, 1909, a committee composed of members of three Local Unions of the American Flint Glass Workers Union signed an agreement regarding wages and working conditions for doped ware which was accepted by Harry Northwood. The Local Unions were from the Wheeling area (9 and 13) as well as Williamstown, West Virginia (22). Locals 9 and 13 represented workers at the Northwood firm and the Imperial Glass Company of Bellaire, Ohio, respectively, and Local Union 22 spoke for those at the Fenton Art Glass Company. The agreement was typed on the stationery of the Northwood firm and sent to the National Association.

The agreement required that shops making doped ware would have "three Snapping-Up Boys and if more help is required the shop will be provided with it." Other provisions mandated that the finisher, a skilled glassworker, "will not dope any ware, excepting large pieces, such as Punch Bowls, Pitchers etc., and then only when it is plain that the boys are unable to handle them properly." Obviously, the snapping-up boys, probably lads 12-15 years of age, were primarily responsible for spraying the dope on the hot glass.

Between 1911 and 1915, the doped ware agreement was the subject of some controversy within the National Association, as the factories making doped ware sought to standardize the basis for wages as well as working conditions.

Victor Wicke, general manager of the Imperial Glass Company, was particularly concerned about interruptions in work caused by problems with the spraying equipment as well as the fact that the management of his company was apparently not represented in the original agreement, which was accepted only by the Northwood firm, even though others were surely making doped ware in early 1909.

The question "who was first?" has come up more than once in Carnival glass circles, but the information above does not dispute the Fenton Art Glass Company's claim to be, as their early letterheads stated, "Originators of Iridescent Ware." The knowledge of procedures for making iridescent ware by spraying was probably not a tight secret, and it was likely well known at the Northwood, Fenton, Dugan, Imperial and Westmoreland factories, to mention only some of the major firms in 1905-1907.

Fenton entered the market first with its iridescent line in January, 1908, but other plants—namely Northwood, Imperial and Dugan—were not far behind. Fenton's initial success in the marketplace paved the way for others. A significant note in the December, 1908, issue of *Glass and Pottery World* acknowledges Fenton's priority and mentions the Northwood's similar line, before concluding on a rueful note: "The iridescent glass put out by the Fenton Art Glass Co., Williamstown, W. Va., and known to the manufacturers as Rubi glass, has been enjoying a great sale especially in the ten cent stores. H. Northwood & Co. have just produced a line almost identical in color with the Fenton output. It will be called Golden Iris. The number of shapes and clever application of coloring possible at this remarkable plant ensure almost a craze for the goods. It seems a pity that a glass so much like the Tiffany Favrile product, save in weight, should find the counters of the cheap stores. However, these are days when a heavy bulk production is necessary to make even a light profit, and sentiment rarely outweighs dollars when pay rolls are to be considered."

The role of the Dugan firm in Carnival glass production will be examined in a future book, *Dugan/Diamond: The Story of Indiana, Pennsylvania Glass.* There has been some speculation about a cooperative relationship between Northwood and Dugan, who were cousins and glassmaking colleagues in the 1880s and 90s. A letter written March 28, 1911, by Harry Northwood to the National Association of Manufacturers of Pressed and Blown Glassware makes clear the competition between these firms during the Carnival era (see p. 70).

Northwood's Iridescent Colors

Carnival glass collectors today have a descriptive, well-developed list of the many colors in which their favorite glass may be found. The price guide to Edwards' *Encyclopedia* (1989) mentions more than three dozen colors, and the Mordini's most recent price guide lists nearly fifty! Some terms, such as marigold, refer primarily to the color of the iridescence, while others, such as purple and green, refer to the total effect created by the color of the base glass and its iridescent finish. In theory at least, hot glass in crystal or any color could be sprayed with one or more of the chemical solutions to create iridescence. For example, the Northwood pattern called Lustre Flute may be found in crystal or in emerald green glass with marigold iridescence.

While much Carnival glass is simply iridized pressed ware made from transparent crystal, blue, green or amethyst glass (the so-called "base color"), other articles were produced using opalescent glass formulas, which have bone ash added to the basic batch. After pressing, the glass is warmed in, and the opalescent effect is achieved; then the glass is sprayed to impart the marigold effect or some other iridescent finish. Depending upon the extent of warming in, the glass may have just a bit of opalescence around the edge or rim, or there may be much opalescence throughout.

Among Carnival glass collectors today, Northwood's aqua opalescent is a very popular color, and prices for some articles have ranged into many thousands of dollars. An article in *The Carnival Pump* (September, 1987) by Don Moore devoted to this interesting color was aptly titled "Aqua Opal: A Touch of Class." As Moore noted, collectors use the phrase aqua opalescent to refer to a variety of shades, ranging from a soft pastel (Fig. 413) to a heavy marigold which produces a "butterscotch" effect (Figs. 553-554 and many of the pieces between Figs. 678 and 694).

Even opaque glasses, such as Northwood's opal (milk glass) or Ivory (custard glass) could be iridized. The Peacocks on the Fence (or Peacocks) bowl on the front cover of this book was made by applying the marigold spray over an unusual blue marble glass (see also Fig. 719); a Tree Trunk vase has also been reported in this unusual combination, which Don Moore once dubbed "sorbini." Some combinations of base glass and iridescence, of course, were more aesthetically pleasing than others, and the contemporary marketplace determined the success or failure of the various products of the iridescent glassware manufacturers. As one might suspect, individual manufacturers found a measure of success with particular iridescent finishes and tended to specialize in them. No doubt, many trials and experiments were carried out, perhaps resulting in the "one of a kind" items so prized by collectors today.

The glass tableware trade journals between 1909 and 1914 make Northwood's introduction of iridescent colors and effects reasonably clear. A full-page Northwood ad in *China, Glass and Lamps* (January 2, 1909) heralded Golden Iris, "the new iridescent glass in a hundred novelties." This was, of course, the selfsame Golden Iris mentioned in Harry Northwood's notebook entries which is known as marigold today.

The Golden Iris continued to be mentioned for several years, but other iridescent lines were soon added. The January 9, 1909, issue of *China, Glass and Lamps* covered the Northwood exhibit at Pittsburgh rather generally, and Golden Iris is mentioned with two other effects, tantalizingly described only as primrose and rainbow:

"The H. Northwood Glass Co., of Wheeling, W.Va., has a complete line of ware, it having been deemed advisable by the company to present for the inspection of buyers nothing they had seen before. ... The ware is highly colored, the principal lines being in golden iris of such tints as to make them exceedingly attractive. Other lines are in primrose and rainbow decoration, each made in a hundred different pieces and presenting a collection from which the buyer in search of this class of ware cannot with dignity retreat."

The January, 1909, issue of the *American Pottery Gazette* compared the Northwood exhibit to Tiffany's Favrile art glass: "The Northwood Co., as usual, had something for the seeker after the novel. It is a tint which while of various gradations ranges from a rich flesh pink, if one may so describe it, to the vivid peacock blues and greens seen on favrile glass. The generic name of it is "IRIS" and one may have the golden Iris, the Pomona Iris and various other Irises as he prefers." This article also mentioned other items on which the applied color is subsequently accentuated by a coating of dead white for a second background, with the result that the colors come out like a magic lantern slide." The

reference to "dead white" is curious, and one wonders if it could refer to an article like the Ruffled Rings bowl shown in this book (Fig. 714).

In September, 1909, the publication *Pottery and Glass* revealed the specific names of two new iridescent effects in the Northwood line which were on display in a showroom in New York: "Frank M. Miller, 25 West Broadway, representative of H. Northwood Co., Wheeling, W. Va.. ... points proudly to a very swell line of new Florentine and Pomona glass specialties. These are novelties for fair. The line throughout is of the dark hue style with a surface strongly suggestive of metal and bearing numerous colors, as viewed from different points. It includes large vases, epergnes, punch bowls and sets, jardinieres, etc. There is a big run on these goods and it's strictly an instance of 'the early bird catches the worm.'" The February 2, 1910, issue of *Pottery, Glass and Brass Salesman* had a similar story: "At Frank M. Miller's, 25 West Broadway, a new scalloped-edge punch bowl in the H. Northwood Co.'s three new finishes in iridescent glass—Golden Iris, Pomona and Florentine—is starting off many an order for the entire line."

Golden Iris refers to marigold, of course, but Pomona and Florentine are a bit of a puzzle. Pomona may denote a greenish color, and Florentine may designate a bluish hue. The quote from *Pottery and Glass* mentions that both were dark "with a surface strongly suggestive of metal," so Northwood's typical green and purple Carnival, both well-represented in the Grape and Cable pattern being made in 1910, may be the colors in question here.

The demand for Northwood's iridescent ware must have been quite strong. A report in *China, Glass and Lamps* (January 16, 1911) indicated that most of the glassworkers there were then engaged in making iridescent ware:

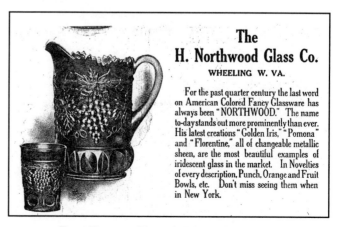

From **Pottery, Glass and Brass Salesman.**

63

"The Northwood Glass Co., Wheeling, W. Va.., are operating their plant in full with a capacity of 32 pots. Twenty-five shops are on the payroll. Twenty-two shops are turning out a fine grade of goods in iridescent ware on a general line of tableware, vases and novelties. ... The business end of this enterprising firm reports that the year just closed was one of the most successful in the history of the concern" (the Northwood receivership/bankruptcy proceedings reveal that the firm's gain for 1910 was about $40,000).

Some extraordinary photographs of New York glass showrooms appear in the August 17, 1911, issue of *Crockery and Glass Journal*. Among them is an interior view of Frank Miller's establishment at 25 W. Broadway. Many Northwood products are clearly identifiable through a magnifying lens, and this photograph provides remarkable proof of the patterns and items then being offered for sale.

Three new iridescent effects were unveiled by the Northwood firm for the 1912 season. The January 4, 1912, issue of *Pottery, Glass and Brass*

Salesman had the particulars: "New effects in iridescent glassware mark the new offerings of the H. Northwood Co., of Wheeling, W. Va. The New York representative ... has recently received samples of many new treatments in tableware lines of iridescent glass, prominent among which are three color treatments, which they call Azure, Pearl, and Emerald. These are of a softer tone than anything that has been produced heretofore in this kind of glass, and the new effects are very pleasing. As indicated by the names, the colors are light blue, pearl and green, but to say that either name fittingly described the color would be incorrect. The new goods are shown in a great variety of articles, some plain and some embellished with decorative treatments in gold. Of the last mentioned perhaps one of the most attractive is a line of the pearl tint with embossed gold decoration."

The reference to "softer tone," is noteworthy, and the three colors—Azure, Pearl and Emerald— are quite probably those called ice blue, white

This photograph appeared in the August 17, 1911, issue of Crockery and Glass Journal. *Many Northwood-made patterns and items in Carnival glass have been identified by examining the original photo with a magnifying lens. Frank Miller's showroom in New York was an important wholesale outlet for Northwood glass for a number of years.*

and ice green, respectively, by Carnival glass buffs today, who also refer to them collectively as "pastels." The gold decorated articles in Pearl are surely table sets and water sets in Northwood's Peach (see Figs. 527-534), for no other gold-decorated Carnival is known.

The glass trade journals and the *American Flint*, a monthly publication of the American Flint Glass Workers Union, mentioned iridescent ware from time to time during 1912-13, but without any specification of colors. Among the last notes is this brief report in the October 27, 1913, issue of *China, Glass and Lamps*: "The H. Northwood Co., Wheeling, W. Va.., are running their plant steadily with two furnaces of 28 pots in blast. There are 16 press shops, an iron mold and a punch tumbler shop on the payroll. The plant is busier this fall than it has been for years and there are enough orders on the books to keep it going steadily for some time to come. A big line of iridescent ware is being made which is very attractive."

Financial records from 1909-1915 may reflect the relative success of Northwood in the highly-competitive iridescent glass market. For 1909, 1910 and 1911, respectively, the Northwood firm showed profits of $43,000, $40,000 and $23,000. Both 1912 and 1913 were deficit years, with a total loss of nearly $29,000. A modest profit of about $4,800 in 1914 was followed by a loss of $3,800 in 1915 (these figures come from the House v. H. Northwood Co. case file; see Bibliography). Full accounting records are not available to reveal any extraordinary capital expenditures during this period, but the relatively lean years beginning with 1912 and extending through 1915 may have dictated the end of Northwood's emphasis on production of the iridescent ware now known as Carnival glass.

Northwood Carnival glass as shown in a catalog from Charles Broadway Rouss (February, 1912).

Northwood's Carnival Lines

This section will discuss Northwood's best known lines, especially the important patterns which were made in iridescent ware and are eagerly sought today by Carnival glass collectors. For the most part, the names coined by Hartung are retained. Many of these designs are known today in the water set, berry set and/or table set. The patterns and important motifs are arranged alphabetically, and subsequent sections deal with novelty items, other patterns which occur in a limited number of articles, and decorated Carnival glass. For ease in locating any pattern or item in the text and/or color plates, consult the Index.

Much of the information on available colors and shape variations has been derived from the excellent series of colored sheets published by the Heart of America Carnival Glass Association as well as articles from various Carnival glass organizations' newsletters and correspondence with many long-time Carnival glass collectors.

Acorn Burrs. This rugged-looking pattern was made in water sets, berry sets and table sets as well as other pieces, such as handled punch cups and a punch bowl whose rim may be crimped or fluted in several different styles. The water sets and table sets are known in three Carnival colors—amethyst, green and marigold—but the punch set occurs in the aforementioned colors plus these: ice blue, ice green, purple, white and aqua opalescent. The punch cup is also known in blue Carnival. An interesting "whimsey" item, a swung vase made from a tumbler, is shown in Edwards' *Rarities in Carnival Glass* (p. 9).

The production time of Acorn Burrs cannot be fixed precisely, but some items appear in wholesale catalogs in 1911-12. Berry sets, table

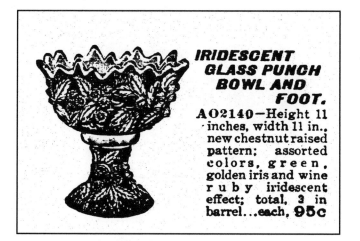

Acorn Burrs punch bowl, from a 1912 Baltimore Bargain House catalog; note the description as a "raised chestnut" pattern.

sets, and water sets are visible in the photo of Northwood products which appeared in the August 17, 1911, issue of *Crockery and Glass Journal*.

A few aqua opalescent punch cups have been found with an engraved date—1914. Most pieces carry the N-in-a-circle mark. Heacock (H2, p. 18) mentioned berry bowls in blue opalescent (not iridized), but no other such pieces have come to light. See Figs. 485-486, 505-506, 538-539, and 610-611.

Dandelion. The water set is called "sunflower" in the Butler Brothers Mid-winter, 1912 catalog, and this appellation may be botanically accurate even though Dandelion has been the popular name, following Hartung's lead (Presznick called it Sunflower). In any case, the Butler Brothers offered the set in "golden [marigold], green and dark metallic" [probably purple] along with another Northwood-made blown tankard pitcher, Oriental Poppy. These water sets reflect the very best in Northwood's Carnival production, from the graceful shape of the tall blown pitchers to the details on the tumbler (see front cover and Figs. 416-419, 491-492, and 568).

The Dandelion tumblers usually have the N-in-a-circle, but the pitchers are unmarked. Dandelion pitchers are visible in the photo of Northwood products in the August 17, 1911, issue of *Crockery and Glass Journal*. The Dandelion water set is known in these Carnival hues: amethyst, green, marigold, blue, white, ice green and ice blue. The set is also known in two transparent (not iridized) colors—blue and green—usually decorated with bright gold (see Figs. 100 and 104).

A handled mug is also called Dandelion by most Carnival collectors, and its flower is indeed a dandelion (see Figs. 692 and 790). A special version of this mug was made for a Knights Templar convention, as this note from *Crockery and Glass Journal* (May 23, 1912) reveals: "At least two glass manufacturers secured good business as a result of the Knights Templer [sic] Conclave being held in Pittsburgh this week. The Ripley Co. was given an order for two Commanderies for 10,000 goblets to be used as souvenirs, and a Wheeling firm received an order for 5,000 iridescent mugs."

Fruits and Flowers. The berry set occurs in this design as does a variety of plates and bowls and a two-handled bon-bon. The master bowl for the berry set is quite large, measuring about 10" in diameter. Northwood's Basketweave is the exterior pattern on most pieces, and all can be found in marigold, blue, green, purple, and ice green. The bon-bon, which may have either a smooth or a slightly stippled background, is also known in white, ice blue and aqua opalescent (see Fig. 694). John Britt reports rare examples in teal blue and sapphire blue. The centers of the plates and bowls may be either plain or show a group of three leaves. This pattern—which depicts apples, cherries and pears—is quite similar to Three Fruits but differs primarily in the addition of a few blossoms.

Grape Arbor. This pattern may be a close contemporary of Grape and Cable, for the water set (see Figs. 356-357, 414-415, and 487-488) is known in marigold and blue as well as ice blue,

The colors mentioned in this Butler Brothers (February, 1912) catalog ad probably refer to marigold, green and purple Carnival glass.

white and ice green—the three colors introduced in early 1912 as Azure, Pearl and Emerald. A tumbler made into a hat-shaped novelty is generally well-known (Fig. 552). Like Grape and Cable, Grape Arbor was made in Ivory glass after 1914, including some interesting pink-stained items (see Figs. 764-765). Ivory tumblers with an iridescent finish are also known. Tumblers usually have the N-in-a-circle, but the blown pitchers do not.

Like Northwood's Peacock at the Fountain, a few similar items to this motif were produced by the Dugan Glass Company in Indiana, PA, and some may mistake the water pitcher (see Fig. 523) for a Northwood product. The footed berry bowl in Dugan's Grapevine Lattice has the Inverted Fan and Feather on its exterior.

Grape and Cable (sometimes called Northwood's Grape). Without doubt, this was Northwood's most extensive Carnival glass pattern line (see Figs. 622-677). Hartung's coverage is extensive: a full-page color illustration in *Northwood Pattern Glass* and a lengthy section in the fourth book of her Carnival glass series. Likewise, Notley illustrated more than 30 items in *Journal* 12 (June, 1986) of the Carnival Glass Society (U. K.). All of the typical tableware pieces are found—berry set, table set and water set—but there are some additions and numerous variants. A tankard pitcher with larger tumblers is known (see Figs. 625-626), as are a smaller creamer with accompanying open sugar bowl (see Figs. 660-661) and a berry set consisting of a shallow, crimped plate and matching sauces (some

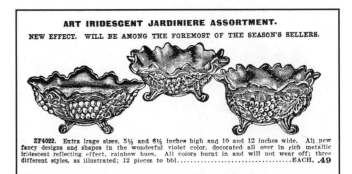

These Grape and Cable bowls were illustrated in a catalog from the firm of Charles Broadway Rouss (February, 1912).

collectors call this an ice cream set). The tumblers to the regular water set are sometimes found with a faintly stippled effect instead of the usual smooth background.

The Grape and Cable whiskey decanter comes with small shot glasses (see Figs. 651-652). Several sizes of footed round and oval bowls are known, including the "banana boat" shown on the front cover (see also Figs. 662 and 664), as well as a large stemmed compote (Fig. 631) and a two-piece punch bowl with handled cups. An attractive round bowl, usually about 9 1/4" in diameter, is called the "centerpiece" bowl by collectors (see Figs. 550, 639, and 642-649). The punch bowl comes in different sizes (see Figs. 641 and 653), the largest of which is about 17" in diameter. There are several variations in the

Grape and Cable sets from a Butler Brothers catalog.

Grape and Cable ice cream set from a Butler Brothers catalog, c. 1912.

Butler Brothers catalog (Mid-winter, 1911).

These Grape and Cable pieces, along with a Tree Trunk swung vase, were offered in a Butler Brothers catalog.

punch cups (see HOACGA's *Educational Series I,* p. 87), including one in ice blue which has been flattened out. One large fruit or orange bowl is known with a "blackberry" interior (HOACGA *Educational Series* I, p. 19), but it does not carry the N-in-a-circle. The covered cracker jar (Fig. 632) and the tobacco humidor (Fig. 633) are attractive items as is the dresser set: large and small trays, cologne bottles, hatpin holder and round powder jar (see Figs. 627-629, 655, 659, 663, and 665; for non-iridized pieces, Figs. 801, 803-804 and 807-812). Some "whimsey" items are in collections, too: a tumbler opened into a hat (Fig. 381) and a powder jar bottom fashioned into a small spittoon (see back cover and Fig. 557). Don Moore recorded examples of this spittoon in marigold, amethyst and green in his *Complete Guide to Carnival Glass Rarities* (pp. 33 - 34).

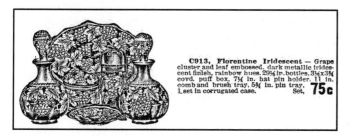

The HOACGA's *Educational Series I* discussed a "bride's basket" made by applying a large handle to a three-footed bowl. Although this item lacks the N-in-a-circle, it is likely a Northwood product (see Fig. 573). Another rare and interesting whimsey in Grape and Cable is a bowl which has been fashioned into a tri-cornered piece (Fig. 575).

Several different pieces of Grape and Cable are pictured in Frank Miller's advertising during early

From Pottery, Glass and Brass Salesman.

1910, so the pattern probably made its debut at the January, 1910, glass exhibition in Pittsburgh. Furthermore, Hartung (Book 4, p. 116) reported a 1910 souvenir item. By June, 1910, Butler Brothers catalogs were offering iridescent Grape and Cable articles in amethyst and green by the barrel—two each of the water set, table set and berry set for a total of $3.90. Two more assortments appeared in the Fall, 1910 Butler Brothers catalog. The berry set had "basket design under surface," a clear reference to the Northwood Basketweave back pattern which occurs on some Grape and Cable items as well as many other articles. The color descriptions (violet iridescent and golden sunset) suggest amethyst and marigold.

The tall tankard pitcher appears in the Midwinter, 1911 Butler Brothers catalog, and the same two colors are mentioned. A number of items are visible in the photo of Northwood products which appeared in the August 17, 1911, issue of *Crockery and Glass Journal*: table set, punch set, oval bowls and the round fernery with white liner.

Grape and Cable tankard pitcher and tall tumblers, as shown in a Butler Brothers catalog.

Grape and Cable fern dish from a Butler Brothers catalog (Mid-winter, 1911); note the reference to the "white enameled removable lining."

Two of the most popular pieces were the Grape and Cable hatpin holder and powder jar (originally called "puff box"), both of which are shown in Butler Brothers catalogs as early as Midwinter, 1911. The public acceptance of these items probably stimulated the creation of the complete dresser set—cologne bottle, two sizes of trays, hatpin holder and powder box—which was shown in Butler Brothers within a year or so. The Dugan Glass Company made a similar perfume bottle which is smaller than Northwood's cologne bottles.

Both the powder jar and the hatpin holder were the subject of disputes between the Northwood firm and its workers, and the correspondence between Harry Northwood and the National Association is revealing. The problems began when the Dugan firm made inquiry of the National Association relative to moves and wages on a similar powder jar (these Dugan products are called Vintage today, and the "cable" is not present, making them easy to

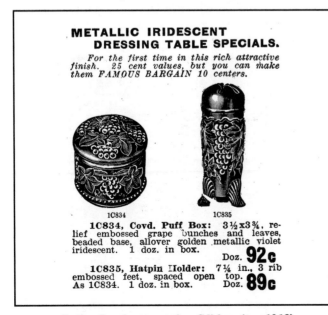

Butler Brothers catalog (Mid-spring, 1912).

differentiate from the Northwood product, which has the N-in-a-circle on both the lid and the base). The workers at the Northwood plant were making the item using somewhat different techniques, and they were required to make more of them (a greater move) than were the Dugan workers. On March 25, 1911, Harry Northwood wrote as follows: "We are in trouble over a powder box and cover: the one of which Dugan made a duplicate and sent you for information. Now these are made in Crystal, Blue, Green and Amethyst Glass, and then sprayed with the Iridescent mixture." Northwood's shops employed no finisher, but Dugan's did. The covers for Northwood's powder boxes were "warmed in on a plug by the boys and then sprayed" (April 1, 1911). Northwood ultimately gave up the dispute with his workers, and a letter makes his opinion of cousin Thomas Dugan quite clear: "In order to put you straight: Dugan evidently finished his Puff Boxes, whereas we do not. This is our affair and we do not wish to post him (being a copyist and competitor) on our methods."

The hatpin holder dispute involved the workers who finished this article by "cupping in" the large scallops at the top of the piece, which was a pressed vase before finishing. A report appeared in the November, 1910, issue of the *American Flint*: "The finishers insisted that they should have $2.00 for cupping a Hat Pin Vase, while the company would only pay $1.75. ... This article is about 7 inches high, 2 1/2 diameter and cupped in like a rose bowl." The typical Northwood Grape and Cable hatpin holder has six large scallops which are cupped in when finishing the hatpin holder. Heacock photographed a Grape and Cable hatpin holder with a Northwood paper label on the underside of the base. These hatpin holders almost always have the N-in-a-circle.

John Britt has seen a blue Carnival Grape and Cable hatpin holder with a plain band near the top, and he also reports these in marigold, too. Like the Northwood Grape and Cable vase with 17 small scallops on the rim which is shown in Don Moore's *Complete Guide to Carnival Glass Rarities* (p. 59), these were made with a different ring in the mould.

Production of Northwood's Grape and Cable pattern continued for several years, and new articles were added to the line. The June 27, 1912, issue of *Pottery, Glass and Brass Salesman* pinpoints the date of one significant piece: "Frank M. Miller, New York representative of the H. Northwood Co., Wheeling, W. Va., has on display

Original Northwood paper label on the underside of a Grape and Cable hatpin holder; the date "Apr 3 1911" may be written near the lower right corner.

at his showrooms, 25 West Broadway, a rather unique novelty in iridescent glassware. This consists in a candlestick equipped with a shade in the same material, the latter being supported by a metal holder which attaches to the candle. This is shown in several styles [colors] and has proven a good seller since it has been on display" (see Fig. 650).

Some articles in Grape and Cable were made in Ivory glass later, after the enthusiasm for iridescent ware had died down. Several Ivory assortments appeared in Butler Brothers catalogs (see Chapter Six), but the selection was not nearly as varied as the Carnival glass line. Grape and Cable may also be found in several other colors. Some cobalt blue pieces (see Figs. 807-808 and 811-812) are not iridized, and the unusual yellow painted articles (see Figs. 801, 803-804 and 809-810) are quite scarce. Heacock pictured a handled nappie or bon-bon in canary opalescent (*CG1*, p. 23/photo 103); although this piece lacks the N-in-a-circle, it does have the distinctive Northwood Basketweave exterior. A canary opalescent bowl is shown in this book (Fig. 247).

Northwood's Grape and Cable pattern was the subject of some imitation in its own time (the Dugan firm has been mentioned above). The Fenton Art Glass Company made its #1746 footed and crimped novelty about 1915 in Carnival glass, but Fenton's #920 orange bowl may date from about 1911 (see the index to Heacock's *Fenton Glass: The First Twenty-Five Years* as well as p. 59). When a Grape and Cable piece is marked with the distinctive N-in-a-circle, of course, attribution is

easy—it's Northwood! But the manufacturer of unmarked pieces may be difficult to determine. One of the Grape and Cable centerpiece bowls shown in the color section (Fig. 646) has been attributed to Fenton on the basis of some detail differences. Color is not generally a reliable guide, for manufacturers often imitated one another's colors as well as designs. The Grape and Cable centerpiece bowl shown in Fig. 647, for example, was thought to be Northwood's Chinese Coral, c. 1924 (quite a while after the heyday of Carnival glass); but the bowl is indeed Fenton's Venetian Red, a hue being made about the same time. *Grape and Gothic Arches.* Most of the articles in this popular pattern are not marked with the familiar N-in-a-circle, but Heacock reported some marked items (*GC3*, p. 9), including the pitcher, which is a pressed glass piece. The only iridescent example of this pattern shown by the Butler Brothers is a tumbler described as "embossed grapes and trellis design" in the spring, 1915, catalog. The iridescence is not described, but the tumbler appears rather light compared to the Singing Birds mug next to it. Furthermore, Grape and Gothic Arches pieces are shown in later catalog assortments of Northwood's Ivory ware (see the G. Sommers & Co. ads in Chapter Six) with Grape and Cable pieces, so there can be no doubt that these are Northwood products.

Both water sets and table sets are known in these Carnival colors—blue, green, marigold and

Butler Brothers catalog (Spring, 1915).

purple—and the water set also occurs in amethyst (see Figs. 494-495, 597-600, and 612-613). The water set and berry set are known in Ivory glass, but these date from late 1914. The water set and table set were also made in Northwood's emerald green (not iridescent, see Figs. 280-283); this color was being made as late as 1912.

Greek Key. This attractive water set (see Figs. 288, 312 and 571-572) is known in amethyst, green and marigold. Three pitchers (perhaps in these very colors!) are in the photo of Northwood products in the August 17, 1911, issue of *Crockery and Glass Journal.* The general style of the pitcher is similar to one of Northwood's decorated lemonade sets (see Fig. 287).

The Greek Key motif is found on other Northwood-made articles, such as Greek Key and Scales (known in marigold, green and ice blue; see Fig. 394) and Greek Key and Ribs, both of which are also known in opalescent glass (not iridized); the pattern is on the exterior (see *CG6,* pp. 52-53). Carnival plates in Greek Key have the pattern on the interior, and the N-in-a-circle appears prominently in the center on a small button. Bowls have the N-in-a-circle on the outside of the marie. The exterior pattern may be Basketweave, Thin Ribs or Northwood's Vintage. Such Carnival glass bowls are known in marigold and, rarely, blue.

A lone Greek Key tumbler which is nearly covered with ruby-stain resided in Rose Preznick's museum for a number of years. The Northwood firm is known to have used ruby-stain for decorating its pattern No. 12 in 1906 (see the previous chapter), but whether or not the company decorated this tumbler cannot be ascertained. The scarcity of this tumbler, of course, does make it unlikely that another firm bought a large quantity from Northwood with the intent of ruby-staining them. This ruby-stained tumbler must not be confused with so-called red Carnival glass, which seems to have been absent from the Northwood's lines.

Hearts and Flowers. This pattern is much like Embroidered Mums. Flat plates (see Fig. 375) and ruffled bowls (see Figs. 544 and 563) are well-known. These are usually plain or have a ribbed exterior, but HOACGA's *Educational Series I* reported a Hearts and Flowers bowl with the Basketweave back. A graceful stemmed compote in Hearts and Flowers (both inside the bowl and on the stem) was made in many different Carnival treatments, including iridized Ivory glass (see Figs. 466-477, 516, 537, 564 and 679 for accurate color of more than a dozen different hues). The

iridized Ivory (custard) glass and milk glass examples are particularly interesting. A ruffled bowl and a compote appear in a Butler Brothers iridescent assortment for Mid-spring, 1912.

The Hearts and Flowers compote base mould was apparently also used, albeit infrequently, for a similar compote with the Peacocks at the Fountain interior (see Figs. 500, 517 and 536), which was imparted by the plunger during pressing. These have the Hearts and Flowers design on the stem, and they may be either plain or ribbed on the outside of the compote's bowl.

Memphis. Originally made in 1908 as the No. 19 line in gold-decorated crystal or emerald green, this pattern seems to have had only limited production in Carnival, primarily in large two-piece fruit or punch bowls. Memphis punch sets (see Fig. 542) are well known in a wide variety of Carnival glass colors: green, marigold, purple, ice blue, ice green and white. The punch bowl comes in several shapes, including one called a two-piece fruit bowl by Don Moore (*Shape of Things to Come in Carnival Glass,* pp. 63-64). Several of these can be seen in the photo which appeared in the August 17, 1911, issue of *Crockery and Glass Journal.* The Memphis berry set occurs in marigold (see Figs. 605-606). Like Northwood's No. 12 (Near-Cut) line, however, No. 19 (Memphis) contained a wide variety of articles, so other Carnival glass items may turn up. A Memphis sugar bowl has recently been reported in purple Carnival glass.

Oriental Poppy. Several iridescent tankard pitchers in this motif are visible in the photo of Northwood wares in the August 17, 1911, issue of *Crockery and Glass Journal.* The water set is shown by Butler Brothers in "golden [marigold], green and dark metallic" [probably purple] in their Mid-winter, 1912 catalog along with Dandelion. The Oriental Poppy water set is also known in these carnival colors—blue (rarely), ice

Northwood's Peacock at the Fountain sets, from a Butler Brothers catalog (August, 1914).

blue, ice green and white—as well as in two transparent colors—blue and green—both of which are decorated with bright gold. The tumblers typically bear the N-in-a-circle, but the blown pitchers, of course, do not. See Figs. 489-490, 512, 540-541, and 566.

Peach. A relatively full line in Carnival, Northwood's Peach includes the berry set, table set and water set (Figs. 425-426 and 601). The most abundant Carnival color would seem to be white, which Northwood originally called Pearl, and the lustrous gold-decorated peach is shown to good advantage on this color (see Figs. 527-534). The water set is known in blue, and marigold tumblers and spooners have been reported. This pattern was made (but not iridized) in decorated crystal (Figs. 359 and 365-366) and emerald green (Figs. 341-342, 349-352), probably prior to Carnival production. The N-in-a-circle is ever-present. The shapes of most articles correspond closely to their counterparts in Peacock at the Fountain.

Peacocks on the Fence. Sometimes these plates or bowls are called simply Northwood's Peacocks, but the full name, as suggested by Presznick and adopted by Heacock, is much more descriptive. Peacocks on the Fence plates may be flat, ruffled or crimped in the "piecrust" fashion, and they come in a wide range of Carnival glass colors—marigold, blue, teal blue, purple, green, white, ice blue and ice green—as well as the rare aqua opalescent. Some plates or bowls may exhibit internal stippling, too. An unusual marigold iridescence on blue marble glass is shown on this book's cover (see Fig. 719 for the Thin Rib pattern on the reverse). A flat plate is among the items in a Butler Brothers iridescent assortment from Mid-spring, 1912. In addition to the front cover, see Figs. 385, 514-515, 560, 591 and 678. For a blue opalescent (not iridized) example, see Fig. 251.

Peacock at the Fountain. There is some evidence available to date this pattern. The berry set (the peacock is not present on the small dishes), table set and water set were offered by Butler Brothers in "golden and florentine iridescent" in their Mid-spring, 1912 catalog (Northwood introduced Florentine in January, 1912). Carnival glass articles may be found in marigold, blue and purple as well as white, ice green and ice blue and a few pieces in aqua opalescent (see the front and back covers as well as Figs. 406-407, 498-504, 520, 524-526, 569, 589, 614-615, and 681).

Heacock (*GC6*, p. 44) reported the existence of a gold-decorated, emerald green water set (not iridized), and there are mentions of this sort of

glassware from the Northwood firm in 1912, but no patterns were described. Other items in the Peacock at the Fountain line include the two-piece punch bowl with matching cups (see Figs. 509-510, 525-526, and 698) as well as a related piece—a small compote which has the Hearts and Flowers stem and the Peacock at the Fountain motif inside the bowl (see Figs. 500, 517 and 536).

Harry Northwood submitted this design to the United States Patent Office on February 7, 1914, and a design patent was granted on July 7, 1914 (#46,059). Northwood's design patent protected his Peacock at the Fountain pattern, but it did not preclude other manufacturers from producing Peacock articles. Indeed, Northwood's Peacock and Urn was being imitated (or perhaps he was imitating others!), so the design patent for Peacock at the Fountain may have reflected his desire to deter or halt copying. In his landmark article in the *Antique Trader* (February 25, 1981), Heacock reported Carnival glass fragments in

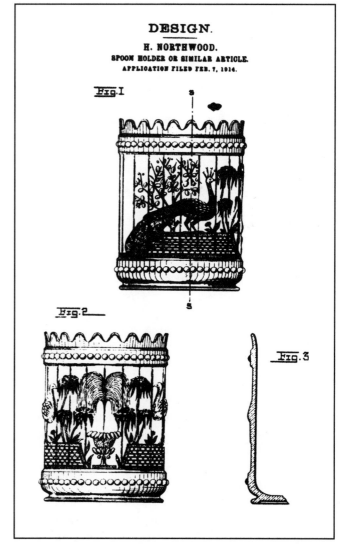

Northwood's drawings of the Peacock at the Fountain pattern, taken from his design patent specifications.

Peacock at the Fountain from the site of Northwood's Indiana, Pennsylvania, plant, which had become the Dugan Glass Company in 1904, so this firm may have been Northwood's target. There is no evidence to suggest that Northwood and Dugan sold, traded or leased moulds to each other. On the contrary, they were erstwhile competitors.

Edwards reported a "copy cat" water set by Dugan in his *Encyclopedia* (1989), and John and Lucile Britt made a close comparison of Peacock at the Fountain tumblers in the HOACGA newsletter, and they reported Northwood examples in these unusual colors—smoke, lavender and amber. Most Northwood-made tumblers have the N-in-a-circle on the inside bottom, but the Dugan versions have the pattern in lower relief and are generally less distinct (see also Owens' *Carnival Glass Tumblers,* pp. 94-95).

Peacock and Urn. Three different factories—Fenton, Millersburg, and Northwood—made separate versions of this motif (see Heacock's *Fenton Glass: The First Twenty-five Years,* p. 60), but, unfortunately, chronological priority for one plant over the others cannot be determined. Those made by Northwood often bear the N-in-a-circle, and they are found in his typical carnival colors—marigold, blue, green, purple, white, ice green, and ice blue. The extraordinarily scarce large plate is about 11" d., and the bowls are about 10" d. Small plates (or ice cream bowls about 5 1/2 to 6" d.) are reported in marigold and amethyst as well as aqua opalescent, but these are all quite scarce. See Figs. 386-387, 507-508, 699-700.

Hartung (7, pp. 134-7) made a detailed, convincing study of all versions of this pattern, concluding that Northwood's invariably displays three rows of beads on the urn, enabling collectors to distinguish the Northwood product even if it does not have the N-in-a-circle. Fenton's version uses the Bearded Berry pattern on the exterior, and the Millersburg examples have a rayed star on the outside of the marie in addition to other minor detail differences.

Raspberry. This pattern, which is similar to Northwood's Springtime, can be dated using Butler Brothers catalogs, for a water set appeared there as a sales special in April, 1911, along with baseball gloves, buckets and baskets! Charles Broadway Rouss offered the same sets at the same price in his February, 1912, catalog. Both the Butler Brothers and the Rouss firm described the fruit as blackberries, however. Three iridescent colors are mentioned in these catalogs— golden (obviously marigold), green and amethyst. Collectors also report the water set in blue, white, ice blue and ice green. The Raspberry pitcher comes in two different sizes, and the smaller one is often called a milk pitcher (see Figs. 493, 511, 546, 561-562, 603-604, and 607-609). An oddly-shaped creamer (or "sauce boat") rests on four feet (Fig. 377).

Singing Birds. This is one of the few Northwood patterns to feature animals—a pair of songbirds. Water sets and table sets are known in amethyst, green and marigold, and tumblers are reported in olive green and amber. Many articles—table sets, water sets and berry bowls—are visible in the photo of Northwood products which appeared in the August 17, 1911, issue of *Crockery and Glass Journal.* The earliest appearance in Butler Brothers is a January, 1912, catalog in which water sets and table sets were combined with berry sets in Grape and Cable. The berry set is well-known in marigold, green and purple, and John Britt reports a few small sauce dishes in blue. Footed sauce dishes (also called sherbets) have also been found in marigold; these are very scarce. See Figs. 496-497.

Singing Birds and Grape and Cable items from the February, 1912, Butler Brothers catalog.

The Singing Birds handled mug (see Fig. 691) must have been a popular article in Carnival glass, for it is known in more than a dozen different colors: amber, amethyst, aqua opalescent, blue opalescent, cobalt blue, electric blue, marigold pastel, lavender, marigold, green, ice blue, purple, smoke, and teal blue as well as iridized Ivory or custard (called "pearl" by some Carnival glass collectors).

Shops making such high-production items as small mugs and tumblers generally used two moulds, and Carnival glass collectors have spotted some variations in Singing Birds mugs which tend to confirm this. A major difference is the stippled background Singing Birds mug, which is known in five colors: amethyst, blue,

Butler Brothers catalog (April, 1911).

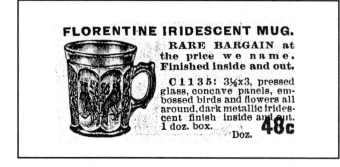

marigold pastel, marigold and green. Some of these have had the name of a city stencilled near the top rim.

A number of pieces in Singing Birds are found in clear glass (with the birds decorated in blue), and the footed sauce (or sherbet) and handled mug are known in Ivory glass (see Fig. 789). These date from about 1914-15. Production in blue opalescent glass (Fig. 194) was probably contemporary with Carnival, for these were the base glass for aqua opalescent Carnival glass.

The general shape of the Singing Birds table set is reminiscent of an undated Northwood "Colonial" pattern called No. 21 (Flute) in both general proportions and in the shapes of the handles. The Imperial Glass Co. made a similar article (called the Robin mug) which has three individual birds evenly-spaced around the mug.

Springtime. Another full line in Carnival glass, Springtime is reminiscent of both Northwood's Raspberry in Carnival glass and the Gold Rose line in colored glass. The flowers and butterflies are well-detailed and realistic. Production in Carnival glass is generally limited to three major colors, and the berry set, table set and water set are known in purple, green and marigold (see Figs. 420-421 and 602). The N-in-a-circle is usually present.

Three Fruits. Like the Fruits and Flowers pattern described above, the bowls and plates in this design depict three of Northwood's favorite fruits—apples, cherries, and pears (see Figs. 422, 432-436, 688, 705 and 716-717 for a look at variations). Some pieces are known in opalescent glass (Fig. 249) as well as Ivory (custard) glass (Fig. 785). A similar pattern, called Three Fruits Medallion (or Three Fruits Variant in Edwards' *Encyclopedia*) has the Meander exterior (see Figs. 432 and 436). See also Fruits and Flowers.

Waterlily and Cattails. Known only in the water set, this pattern was likely a short-lived imitation of Fenton's extensive line called No. 8. The Northwood pitcher is a tankard style, and it has the N-in-a-circle mark, as do the tumblers (for color, see Heacock's *Fenton Glass: The First*

Twenty-five Years, p. 30). Northwood's marigold pitchers display iridescence only on the top one-third or so; John Britt reports a blue Carnival glass pitcher with excellent all-over iridescence, and this piece was pictured in the International Carnival Glass Association's *Carnival Pump* (September, 1985). Unlike Fenton's, the Northwood tumbler has no basketweave near the base, and the water surface is represented by tiny dashes (see John and Lucile Britt's article in the December, 1988, HOACGA newsletter and Owens' *Carnival Glass Tumblers,* plate 18 and pp. 106-107).

Wishbone. This pattern, called Melinda by Presznick, is a short line of tableware consisting of the water set, bowls, plates and an attractive epergne (see Figs. 353, 380, 393, 401, 565, 588 and 592). The orchid-like flowers are nicely executed, but the pattern derives its name from the wishbone-shaped figures. The blown pitchers lack the N-in-a-circle, of course, but it is usually present on tumblers.

Wishbone bowls and plates, along with the base to the epergne, may have the Northwood Basketweave as an exterior pattern; footed bowls and plates have the Ruffles and Rings pattern on the exterior. Three Wishbone pitchers are prominent in the photo of Northwood products in

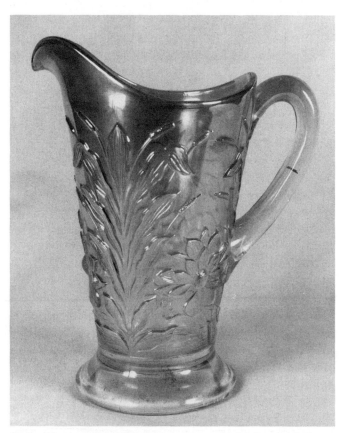

Waterlily and Cattails pitcher in marigold Carnival glass. Courtesy of the Fenton Museum.

the August 17, 1911, issue of *Crockery and Glass Journal*. The Carnival colors available—marigold, blue, green, purple, white, ice blue and ice green (plus the occasional aqua opalescent)— suggest a production time of 1911-12.

Wisteria. This extraordinarily scarce, attractive water set comes in white, ice blue (Fig. 702-703) and ice green, the iridescent colors introduced by Northwood as Pearl, Azure and Emerald, respectively, in 1912. Wisteria may have been designed especially for the introduction of these three new iridescent colors, although many other Northwood patterns and articles were also made in these hues. One enterprising Northwood glassworker fashioned a Wisteria tumbler into a bank with coin slot, creating a rare and most delightful "whimsey" (see the June, 1983, *Carnival Pump*, p. 10).

Carnival Glass Novelties and Other Items

Advertising pieces. Fortunately for Carnival glass collectors, there is a superb reference book available on these special items, John D. Resnik's *Encyclopedia of Carnival Glass Lettered Pieces*. Several major Carnival glass firms—including Millersburg, Fenton and Northwood—made such pieces, and Resnik has done a remarkable job of ferreting out the historical details behind many advertising and commemorative articles.

The Northwood-made plates are amethyst glass, about 6" in diameter, have 64 tiny scallops on the rim and display the Basketweave pattern on the back side. They may be ruffled to create a six-sided bowl, or they may be found with a portion of the edge gently rolled up, creating what Carnival glass collectors call a "hand grip" plate. Some have two opposite edges rolled up, creating a double hand grip. Northwood's are usually found with the N-in-a-circle. Most of the Northwood plates are plain except for the lettering, of course, but some have a floral motif similar to Fenton's Garden Mums.

Some advertising plates are pictured together (see Figs. 581-586) elsewhere in this book—Eagle Furniture; E. A. Hudson Furniture; Fern Brand Chocolates; Davidson's Society Chocolates; and Jockey Club—and the Dreibus Parfait Sweets is also shown (Fig. 595). Resnik records two other similar Northwood-made plates—Broeker's Flour and Ballard's of Merced, California. In the December, 1986, issue of the International Carnival Glass Association's *Carnival Pump*, Ray and Verda Asbury provided some interesting history of the Fern Brand plate. They report that these were given to merchants (not the general public) as tokens "of appreciation for promoting their chocolates." The Carnival glass plates were packed within large wooden crates of bulk chocolates, one plate to a crate!

Amaryllis. Just one article is known in this design, a small compote which has a short stem (Fig. 596). These have been found in marigold, blue and purple. The pattern on the exterior is a poppy motif which is reminiscent of Oriental Poppy as well as the Poppy and Scroll pieces in the Intaglio line and some "goofus" articles.

Basketweave. This pattern is typically found on the exterior (or "back") of plates, bowls, comports or two-handled bon-bons, but it is worthy of discussion here, for the distinctive design is a Northwood hallmark (see Fig. 586). A Butler Brothers fall, 1910, catalog clearly shows Basketweave on the back of Grape and Cable items.

Beaded Cable. There are two articles in this motif, a crimped rose bowl and a "candy dish." The latter was probably called a card receiver in its own time (Fig. 201 in opalescent glass). The crimping sometimes results in a nearly vertical pie crust look (see Fig. 30 in Mosaic glass), but the rose bowls in Carnival glass typically underwent additional cupping.

Both the rose bowls and the candy dishes were made from the same pressed article, and they occur in virtually all of the Carnival glass colors, including one in "peach opalescent" (flint opalescent with marigold treatment), an extraordinarily rare Northwood color. The rose bowl may be plain inside or it may be ribbed (see Figs. 459-463, 689 and 793). Beaded Cable articles are shown in opalescent glass in Northwood's fall, 1906, catalog, which predates carnival production, and the Jefferson firm may have been making similar items at this time. The rose bowl is shown in a Butler Brothers iridescent assortment of Northwood items in a Mid-spring, 1912, catalog.

Heacock (*CG3*, p. 16) noted that the outside base may display either two rings or three rings, and he thought this might shed light on the relationship between Jefferson and Northwood. Unfortunately, it cannot be determined whether Northwood purchased any of these particular moulds from Jefferson, so these similar items may be a case of one firm imitating another's designs. Many Beaded Cable pieces carry the N-in-a-circle, so their manufacture is certain. Carnival production, of course, is all Northwood, and these items also occur in the Antique Ivory line, c. 1914 (see Fig. 793).

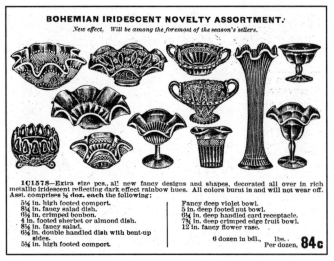

Beads. Heacock called this motif Posies and Pods, and he documented its production in emerald green (see Figs. 265-271), including a berry bowl with the N-in-a-circle. An iridescent berry bowl is shown as part of an assortment in the spring, 1909 Butler Brothers catalog. These are best known in green Carnival, but other Carnival colors may turn up someday.

Blackberry. Both a bowl and a compote are known, the latter having Daisy and Plume on the exterior. A similar compote, called Northwood's Small Blackberry (Hartung 8, p. 76) has the Basketweave exterior.

Blossomtime. Like Amaryllis, this design is known only in a compote. The stem has a distinctive spiral effect (see Fig. 587), and a design called Wild Flower is on the exterior. Two such compotes appear in a fall, 1908, Butler Brothers assortment of Northwood iridescent ware which also includes a Sunflower bowl. These occur in marigold, purple and green.

Bull's Eye and Leaves. Apparently, the only items in this design are Carnival glass bowls in either marigold or green (see Fig. 412).

Bushel Basket (sometimes called *Basket*). This interesting novelty item comes in a wide variety of hues, ranging from blue, canary, Ivory (custard), and black amethyst (which are not iridescent) to these Carnival glass colors: marigold, blue, green, purple, white, ice blue, and ice green as well as aqua opalescent, lime green opalescent and other hues described as "clambroth," "vaseline" (canary) and "smoke" (see Figs. 478-484, 513, 548-549, 687, 718 and 791).

There are several design variations; most Bushel Baskets are round, but some are eight-sided. Most Bushel Baskets have handles with an all-over ribbed motif, but some are smooth where the handle joins the body. The eight-sided version is shown in a Butler Brothers iridescent assortment in a Mid-spring, 1912, catalog. The Bushel Basket almost always displays the N-in-a-circle.

Butterfly bon-bon. This attractive two-handled piece occurs in many Carnival glass colors (including a rare example in ice blue), and the exterior may be plain or threaded. The butterfly is at the center of the bowl, and the rays which emanate therefrom alternate in plain and stippled (see Fig. 590). The N-in-a-circle mark is on the outside of the marie. A Butterfly bon-bon appears in the "Pompeiian" assortment in a June, 1910, Butler Brothers catalog.

Cherry and Cable. This pattern dates from about 1908 in clear glass, and the Carnival items seem to be marigold only, so this is likely one of Northwood's earliest efforts in the iridescent glass field. The marigold iridescence typically covers the top half of pitchers, although it is usually more extensive on other pieces. The berry set, table set and water set are known, although all are rather scarce. This pattern should not be confused with the Cherries motif in Northwood's Intaglio line, which also occurs in Carnival glass (see Fig. 429).

Christmas compote. The marigold and purple examples of this compote often recall Northwood's typical iridescence, and the carefully-crafted holly design is similar to both his Panelled Holly and a motif found with "goofus" decoration. However, the Christmas compote (Fig. 574) is not marked with the N-in-a-circle and it has yet to turn up in any Butler Brothers groupings, so it cannot be definitely established as a Northwood-made piece.

Coin Dot. The only articles listed in this motif are tumblers, which occur in marigold. Hartung (7, p. 102) reports a pitcher in marigold and a tumbler in amethyst. John Britt notes that the tumblers, which display the N-in-a-circle, have six rows of dots while a similar Fenton product has just five rows.

Corn vase. This article is among the iridescent items in a Butler Brothers assortment in their Mid-spring, 1912, catalog. There are two versions, the standard shape (see Fig. 354, 732 and 736), which is 6 3/8" tall, and a slightly taller one which has several husks curling out from the surface in a realistic fashion (see back cover and Fig. 578). The latter, which is sometimes called the Corn Husk vase, occurs in purple and green, while the standard version is known in these colors plus marigold, blue, teal blue, white, ice green, ice blue and aqua opalescent. The smaller versions may be plain on the underside of the base or there may be a motif consisting of finely-detailed corn husk leaves. All were made by Northwood, and they are typically marked with the N-in-a-circle on the inside bottom.

Daisy and Drape. The lone item in this motif is a vase about 6 1/4" tall, and it can be found in many Carnival glass colors—marigold, blue, purple, white, ice green, ice blue—plus the desirable aqua opalescent and a rare green. These usually display the N-in-a-circle, although the circle may be hard to see. The top rim may be slightly flared or slightly cupped (see Figs. 551, 680 and 738). An example is shown in a Butler Brothers iridescent assortment in a Mid-spring, 1912, catalog.

Daisy and Plume. Four articles are known with this motif—a stemmed, crimped item which resembles a goblet (Figs. 456-458 and 620) or is flared into a small compote (Fig. 409) and a three-footed, crimped rose bowl (Fig. 465 and 704), which may be flared into a card receiver or candy dish. A plain Fern motif or Blackberry may appear on the inside.

Attribution of some Daisy and Plume pieces is a bit of a puzzle, for both Northwood and the Dugan Glass Company of Indiana, Pennsylvania, had their versions of this pattern. Collectors should note that the N-in-a-circle is often hard to see or to distinguish clearly, probably because of distortions in pressing and subsequent shaping of the piece as well as in the iridizing process itself.

In the first volume of his *Collecting Glass*, Heacock made a close study of the three-footed rose bowls, concluding that Northwood's have a thin rib which runs parallel to the center of each foot. He also found that Northwood's have 74 to 76 beads around each flower, while the Dugan

versions have at least 80 per flower. Most of these Northwood Daisy and Plume pieces have the N-in-a-circle, but the stemmed piece lacks this mark.

Diamond Point vases. Initially were made in opalescent glass about 1906, these occur in many Carnival glass colors. Most have the N-in-a-circle (see Figs. 701 and 737).

Double Loop. Just two pieces occur in this pattern, the creamer and its companion open sugar which has a stem foot (see Figs. 424, 619 and 690). The aqua opalescent pieces are of great interest to Carnival glass collectors, of course, but Double Loop is also known in marigold, green and purple; the N-in-a-circle is usually present. Both pieces may also be found in Northwood's Ivory glass, which was first made in 1903 and was re-introduced in 1914 (see Figs. 780-781). The Mansion Museum at Oglebay Institute in Wheeling has a small creamer in dark cobalt blue (not iridescent).

Drapery. This was, of course, an earlier Northwood pattern line, but just a few articles were made in Carnival glass, primarily vases (Fig. 553) or various smaller pieces, such as rose bowls or candy dishes which may have been made from the spooner mould (Figs. 464 and 567). Drapery items occur in a wide variety of iridescent hues: marigold, purple, amethyst, blue, green, white, ice blue, and ice green. John Britt notes that the Drapery rose bowl, which has six panels of drapes, is not uncommon in aqua opalescent, a hue which is otherwise rather hard to find. Most Drapery articles have the N-in-a-circle on the inside of the bottom. A small vase appears in a Butler Brothers iridescent assortment for Mid-spring, 1912.

Embroidered Mums. This highly-detailed pattern, which is similar to Northwood's Hearts and Flowers, occurs in a variety of bowls as well as a flat plate and a two-handled bon-bon, which is quite scarce (HOACGA's *Educational Series I* reports it in white Carnival only). The bowls may be ruffled or crimped in several different ways, and they may be found in a wide variety of Carnival glass colors (see Figs. 557 and 617).

Feathers. Swung vases are the only articles known in this pattern, but they occur in a variety of sizes and have been found in marigold, purple, green and ice blue (see Fig. 734).

Fern. This rather plain motif occurs inside some Daisy and Plume stemmed compotes (Fig. 409). One of these is clearly shown in a Butler Brothers assortment of Northwood iridescent items in a Mid-spring, 1912, catalog.

Fine Cut and Roses. Like its counterpart in Beaded Cable, this three-footed rose bowl is usually found

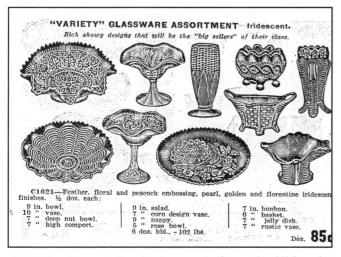

This Northwood Carnival ware is from the Mid-spring, 1912, catalog issued by the Butler Brothers.

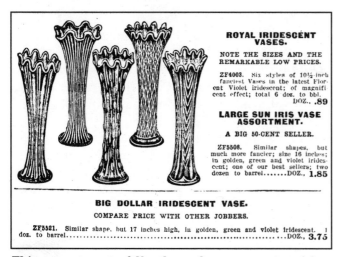

This assortment of Northwood vases appeared in a February, 1912, catalog issued by Charles Broadway Rouss. Note the references to vases as tall as 16 and 17 inches.

tightly crimped (see Figs. 450-455, 559 and 685), although some were flared out to make a card receiver (Fig. 558). The interior may be smooth (these have the N-in-a-circle) or it may bear the pattern called "Fancy" (Hartung 6, p. 38). These rose bowls and flared dishes are available in a great variety of carnival colors. HOACGA's *Educational Series I* (p. 97) shows one rose bowl which was not crimped.

Fine Rib vases. These are likely contemporaries of the Diamond Point vases, for both come in a wide variety of iridescent and non-iridescent colors and range from 7" to about 12" tall (see Figs. 543, 722-724, 726 and 731). John Britt reports examples in teal blue, sapphire blue, canary, ice blue, ice green and white. Most display the N-in-a-circle. A vase described as "12 in. fancy flower vase" appears with other Northwood articles in the April, 1909, Butler Brothers catalog. Collectors should be aware of Fenton's similar pattern, also called Fine Rib.

Flute vase. A likely contemporary of the Diamond Point, Feathers, and Fine Rib motifs, these swung vases occur in marigold and in green glass with marigold iridescence (see Fig. 735).

Flute. A plain pattern of the type generally known as "Colonial" among glass manufacturers, this line, originally called No. 21, includes the water set (see Figs. 370-371) and the table set, both of which are known in marigold and green. A small sherbet occurs in virtually every known Carnival color and in several "stretch" colors, such as opaque blue and russet, which were not made until about 1921. The mark inside the sherbets, nut cups and individual salts often appears to be an underlined N, but the full N-in-a-circle is

sometimes apparent under strong magnification. Initial Carnival production of the Flute pattern in marigold probably dates from 1908-09, for a sherbet appears in the spring, 1909 Butler Brothers catalog, and a sauce dish is also known (Fig. 378).

Four Pillar. The swung vases in this design occur in a variety of transparent colors and opalescent hues as well as Carnival glass. Sometimes the iridescence is rather light (see Figs. 727 and 730), but some aqua opalescent specimens with a pronounced "butterscotch" effect are known (see Figs. 682-683).

Fruits and Flowers. The berry set occurs in this design as does a variety of plates and bowls as well as a two-handled bon-bon. The master bowl for the berry set is quite large, measuring about 10" in diameter. Northwood's Basketweave is the exterior pattern on most pieces, and all can be found in marigold, blue, green, purple, and ice green.

The Fruits and Flowers bon-bon, which may have either a smooth or a slightly stippled background, is also known in white, ice blue and aqua opalescent (see Fig. 694), and it often bears the Basketweave exterior. John Britt reports rare examples in teal blue and sapphire blue. The centers of the plates and bowls may be either plain or a group of three leaves, and Carnival glass collectors are still sorting out the many variations of this pattern and its close relative, Three Fruits.

Graceful. The sole item in this design, a relatively small vase, reminds one of Northwood's Spool, which dates from 1903. Perhaps the vase (Fig. 411) represents a rebirth of the design. Graceful

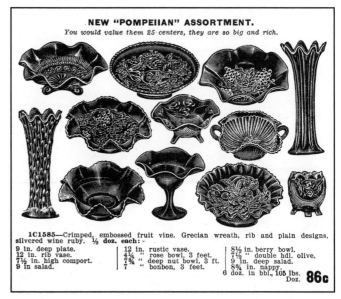

Many Northwood motifs appeared in the "New Pompeiian" assortment in a Butler Brothers catalog.

(Continued on page 150)

Introduced in 1904, the decorated Ivory (custard) glass Carnelian line is called Everglades by collectors today. It is similar in both design and decoration to Northwood's Intaglio (Fig. 1), which was introduced at Indiana, Pa., in 1899.

2-4. Carnelian (Everglades) tumbler, pitcher and jelly compote.

5-8. Carnelian (Everglades) table set.

9-12. Carnelian (Everglades) sauce dish, berry bowl, salt/pepper shakers and cruet.

13-14. Carnelian (Everglades) pitcher and tumbler in canary opalescent. 15-19. Carnelian (Everglades) jelly compote, salt/pepper shakers, cruet, tumbler and pitcher in blue opalescent.

20-23. Carnelian (Everglades) table set in canary opalescent.

24-28. Canary opalescent Carnelian (Everglades) sauce, berry bowl, s/p shakers, cruet and jelly compote.

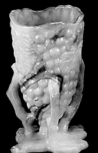

An assortment of Northwood's Mosaic glass, c. 1903 (note the range of colors). 29. Floralore crimped bowl. 30. Beaded Cable rose bowl with crimped edge. 31. Spool compote with crimped edge. 32-33. Northwood's Hobnail spooner and bowl with ruffled edge. 34. Rose bowl with vertical panels. 35-38. Scroll with Acanthus spooner, tumbler, creamer and jelly compote (see Fig. 63). 39. Carnelian (Everglades) creamer.

40. Grapevine Cluster vase. 41. Spool of Threads compote. 42. Jack-in-the-pulpit vase. 43. Ocean Shell vase. 44. Maple Leaf Chalice vase. 45. Beads and Bark vases.

46-49. *Oriental Poppy pitchers and tumblers in green and blue.* 50-52. *Poinsettia pitcher and tumbler in blue opalescent; pitcher in pink opalescent (cranberry).*

53, 58-59. *Teardrop Flower cruet, creamer and spooner in amethyst.* 54-57. *Poinsettia sugar shakers in green opalescent and blue opalescent, pitcher in pink opalescent (cranberry) and syrup jug in blue opalescent.*

60-67. *Scroll with Acanthus salt/pepper shaker in light green, toothpick holder in blue (note gold decoration) and butterdish in Mosaic glass (see Figs. 29-45); the covered sugar, spooner, creamer, tumbler and pitcher are blue opalescent, although the spooner is rather light in color.*

68   69   68   70   71

72   73   74   75

68-69. Panelled Holly tumblers and pitcher in green with gold decoration. 70-71. Regent (Leaf Medallion) cruet (stopper not original; see Figs. 79, 94 and 97 as well as the ad below) and pitcher in green with gold decoration. 72-75. Regent (Leaf Medallion) table set in green with gold decoration.

This advertisement, depicting all the known Regent pieces including the rare tray, appeared in early 1904.

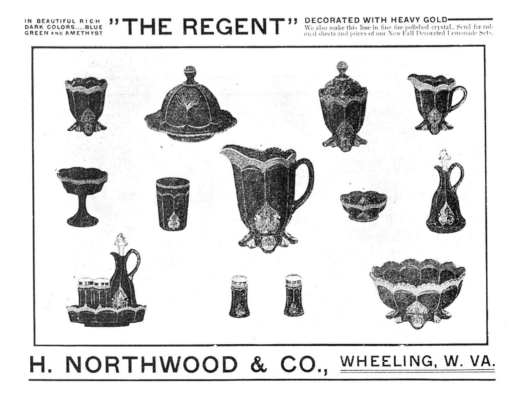

IN BEAUTIFUL RICH DARK COLORS....BLUE GREEN AND AMETHYST "THE REGENT" DECORATED WITH HEAVY GOLD——— We also make this line in fine fire polished crystal. Send for colored sheets and prices of our New Fall Decorated Lemonade Sets.

H. NORTHWOOD & CO., WHEELING, W. VA.

76   77   76   78   80   78   81   82   81

83   84   85   86   87   88   89   90

91   92   93   94   95   96   97   96   99   98

76-77. *Regent (Leaf Medallion) tumblers and pitcher in amethyst. 78-81. Regent (Leaf Medallion) salt/pepper shakers, cruet (note original stopper), tray, tumblers and pitcher in blue.*

83-86. *Regent (Leaf Medallion) table set in amethyst. 87-90. Regent (Leaf Medallion) table set in blue.*

91-95. *Regent (Leaf Medallion) berry bowl, sauce, salt/pepper shakers, cruet and jelly compote in amethyst. 96-97. Regent (Leaf Medallion) salt/pepper shakers and cruet in green. 98-99. Regent (Leaf Medallion) sauce and berry bowl in blue.*

100   101   102   103   104   105

106   107   108   109   110   111   112   113

115   117

114   116   118   119

100-101. *Dandelion pitcher and tumbler in green.* 102-103. *Gold Rose pitcher and tumbler in green (note decoration).* 104-105. *Dandelion pitcher and tumbler in blue.*

106-109. *Frosted Leaf and Basketweave table set in canary opalescent.* 110-113. *Frosted Leaf and Basketweave table set in blue opalescent.*

114-119. *Mikado (Flower and Bud) cruet, table set and tumbler; note the characteristic multi-color decoration on the indivdual flowers.*

120-123. Encore (Jewel and Flower) pitcher, tumbler, cruet and salt/pepper shaker in canary opalescent. 124. Encore (Jewel and Flower) cruet in flint opalescent. 125-128. Encore (Jewel and Flower) salt/pepper shakers, cruet, tumbler and pitcher in blue opalescent.

129-132. Encore (Jewel and Flower) table set in flint opalescent; note the similarity of the red decor to Mikado on the previous page. 133-136. Encore (Jewel and Flower) table set in blue opalescent.

137-144. Lustre Flute table set, pitcher, tumbler, berry bowl and sauce in blue opalescent.

145   146   147   148   149   150

151   152   153   154   155

151-155. Encore (Jewel and Flower) pitcher in blue opalescent and table set—spooner, butterdish, covered sugar and creamer—in canary opalescent.

156   157   158   159   160

161   162   161   163

156-160. Drapery table set and pitcher (note worn gold decoration). in blue opalescent.

161-163. Drapery sauce dishes, berry bowl and tumbler in blue opalescent (note gold).

164-168. *Diadem (Sunburst on Shield) cruet in flint opalescent, tumbler and pitcher in canary opalescent, and tumbler and cruet in blue opalescent.*

169-171. *Diadem (Sunburst on Shield) covered sugar, covered butterdish, and spooner in canary opalescent.*
172-175. *Diadem (Sunburst on Shield) table set in flint opalescent.*

176-180. *Diadem (Sunburst on Shield) berry bowl in flint opalescent, sauce and berry bowl in canary opalescent, spooner in blue opalescent, and celery tray in bluish-green opalescent.*

181-182. Teardrop Flower tumblers and pitcher in amethyst.

183-186. Teardrop Flower table set—covered sugar, creamer, butterdish and spooner—in pale emerald green. Note the gold decoration.

187-190. Northwood's #31 (Belladonna) table set—butterdish, covered sugar, spooner and creamer—in blue with enameled decoration in daisy motif; the floral decoration shown in Northwood's 1906 catalog differs from this.

191   192   193   194   195   196   197

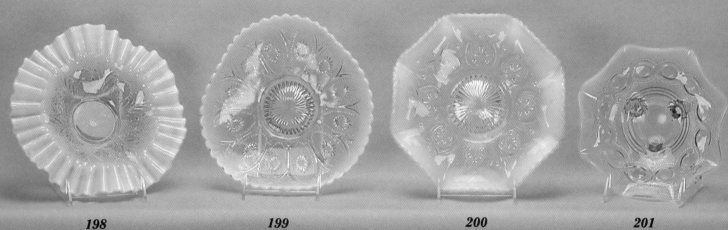

198   199   200   201

202   203   204   205   206

191-192. Decorated green tumbler and pitcher. 193. Rose Show ruffled bowl in blue opalescent. 194. Singing Birds mug in blue opalescent. 195-197. Oriental Poppy pitcher and tumblers in blue and green.

198-199, 201. Blue opalescent Netted Roses crimped bowl, Spokes and Wheels plate and Beaded Cable candy dish. 200. Cashews plate in green opalescent. Note the various crimping styles.

202-205. Northwood's No. 12 table set in emerald green with gold decoration. 206. This unidentified vase is probably not a Northwood product.

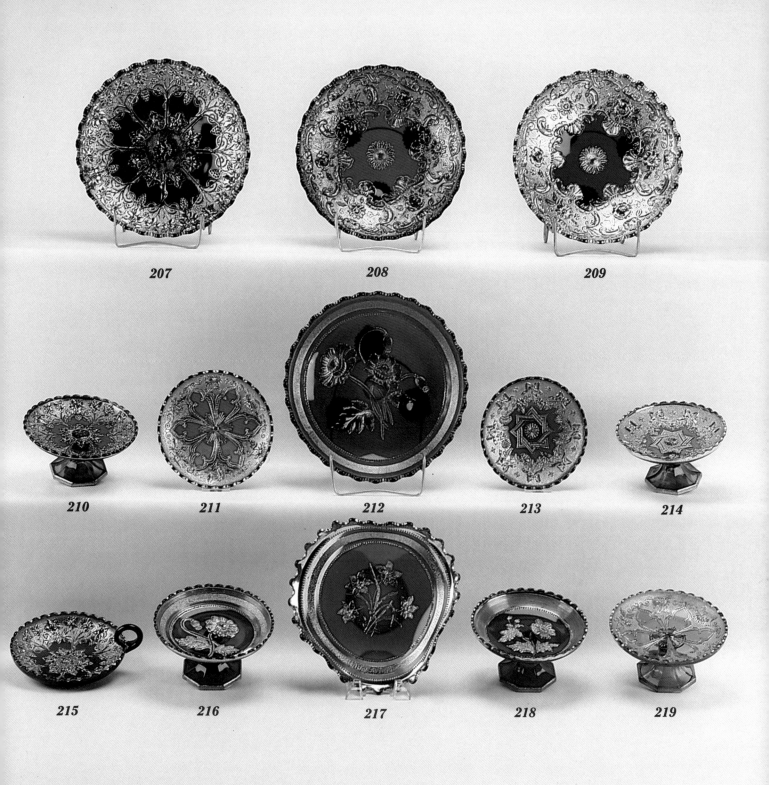

207   208   209

210   211   212   213   214

215   216   217   218   219

All of these items are from Northwood's Verre D'or line.

207. Blue Grape Frieze 10" fruit. 208-209. Southern Gardens 10" fruits in green and amethyst.

210. Green Grape Frieze comport. 211. Green Beaded Star and Mums 6" sweet. 212. Green 10" fruit in Iceland Poppy motif. 213-214. Ribbons and Overlapping Squares 6" sweet in blue and comport in green.

215. Grape Frieze handled bon bon in amethyst. 216. Blue Iceland Poppy comport. 217. Blue Violet Bouquet crimped 10" fruit. 218. Blue comport in Shasta Daisy. 219. Beaded Star and Mums comport in amethyst.

220-223. Decorated tumblers and pitchers. 224. Daffodil pitcher in flint opalescent. 225-226. Poinsettia tumbler and pitcher in flint opalescent.

227-228. Grapevine and Cherry Sprig tumbler and pitcher in crystal with satin-finished fruit. 229. Atlas pitcher in crystal. 230-231. Crystal Oriental Poppy tumbler and pitcher in a similar poppy motif. 232. Crystal Gold Rose pitcher with red/gold decoration.

233. Daffodil pitcher in canary opalescent. 234-235. Northwood's Hobnail tumbler and pitcher in canary opalescent. 236-237. Crystal Panelled Holly tumbler and pitcher with gold decoration. 238. Lustre Flute pitcher in flint opalescent.

239-240. **Poinsettia tumbler and pitcher in blue opalescent. 241-242. Decorated lemonade pitchers in blue. 243. Coinspot pitcher in blue opalescent.**

244. **Grapevine Cluster vase in canary opalescent. 245-246. Decorated tumbler and lemonade pitcher in amethyst. 247. Grape and Cable bowl in canary opalescent. 248. Regent (Leaf Medallion) pitcher in amethyst.**

249-251. **Blue opalescent bowls in Three Fruits with Ribbed exterior, Palm and Scroll, and Peacocks on the Fence (note the various edges and crimping styles).**

252-256. *Decorated pitchers in blue, green and ruby (cranberry); 252, 253 and 355 were made from the same shape mould as other Northwood pitchers—see Figs. 221, 223-224, 284-286.*

257-260 *Decorated crystal pitchers in Cherry Lattice, Cherry and Cable, Plums and Cherries (also called Two Fruits), and Strawberry and Cable.*

261. *Regent (Leaf Medallion) pitcher in green. 262. Regal pitcher in green opalescent. 263. Scroll with Acanthus pitcher in green with gold decoration. 264. Memphis pitcher in green with gold decoration.*

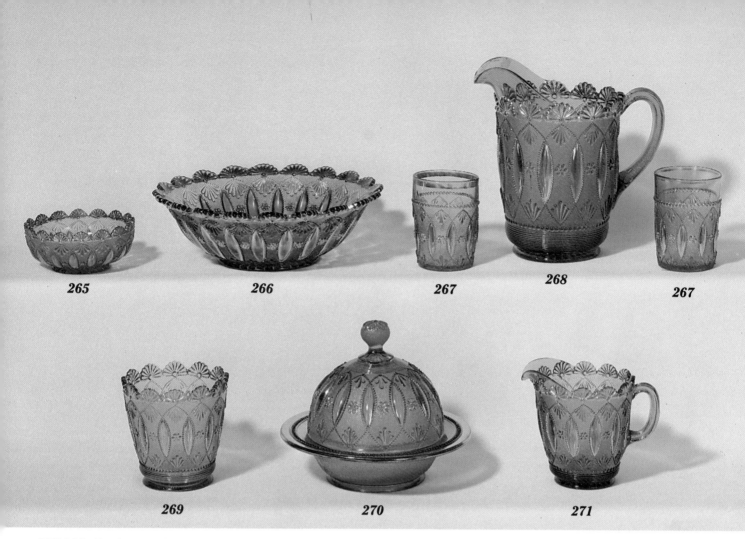

265-268. *Posies and Pods pieces in emerald green—sauce, berry bowl, tumblers and pitcher—with gold decoration.*

269-271. *Posies and Pods table set pieces—spooner, butterdish, and creamer—in emerald green with gold decoration.*

This pattern is also known in crystal with ruby stain and gold decoration (see Figs. 296-297), a decorating treatment which is similar to that used on Northwood's Encore (Jewel and Flower) line. Since Encore (Jewel and Flower) dates c. 1904, Posies and Pods may be from this same general time. Heacock reported that a berry bowl had been found with the N-in-a-circle mark.

272   273   274   275

276   277   278   279

280   281   282   283

272-275. Emerald green with gold Panelled Holly table set—covered sugar, butterdish, spooner and creamer.

276-279. Atlas covered sugar, butterdish, creamer and pitcher in crystal with gold decoration and "maiden's blush" treatment.

280-283. Emerald green with gold Grape and Gothic Arches table set—covered sugar, butterdish, spooner and creamer; compare the shapes of the creamer and covered sugar to Figs. 847-848.

284, 287. Daffodil pitchers in green opalescent and ruby opalescent (cranberry). 285, 287. Decorated pitchers in green and blue. 288. Greek Key pitcher in green Carnival (compare shape to 287).

289. Not Northwood. 290. Interior Swirl pitcher in marigold Carnival. 291-292. Green decorated tumbler and pitcher (290 and 292 were blown in the same shape mould). 293. Blue opalescent Coinspot blown pitcher. 294. Green opalescent Daffodil pitcher (293 and 294 were blown in the same shape mould).

295. Encore (Jewel and Flower) decorated pitcher in flint opalescent. 296-297. Posies and Pods tumbler and pitcher in crystal with ruby-stain and gold decoration. 298. Crystal Grape and Gothic Arches pitcher with ruby-stain and gold decoration. 299-300. Dark blue tumbler and pitcher (gold decorated) in the pattern Heacock named Barbella; these have an interior plain panel design (note the similarity in shape to Grape and Gothic Arches).

301-308. Decorated pitchers in blue, green and satin-finished crystal (note the variety of shapes and the different decorations). The pitcher shown as Fig. 301 appeared in a December, 1906 ad. Compare Fig. 308 to Figs. 290 and 292; Hartung called Fig. 308 Daisy and Drape.

309-310. Decorated Carnival glass; these are called "Cherries, Ground" in Whitley's book, and both the tumbler and pitcher have panels inside. 311. Green Pretty Panels tumbler decorated in Cara Nome style. 312. Decorated pitcher in green. 313-314. Decorated tumbler and pitcher in blue.

315   316   317   318   319   320   321   322   323

324   325   326   327   328   329   330   331

332   333   334   335   336   337   336   338   339

315-316, Regal pitcher and tumbler (note gold decoration) in blue opalescent. 317-320. Regal table set in green. 321. Regal cruet in green opalescent. 322-323. Panelled Holly tumbler and pitcher in blue opalescent with gold decoration.

324-327 Panelled Holly table set in blue opalescent with gold decoration. 328-331. Panelled Holly table set in flint opalescent with red and green decoration.

332-333. Panelled Holly sauce and berry bowl in blue opalescent with gold decoration. 334-336. Regal sauce dish and berry bowl in green with gold decoration and salt/pepper shakers and cruet in blue opalescent. 338-339. Panelled Holly sauce and berry bowl in flint opalescent with red and green decoration.

340. *Northwood's No. 21 (Flute) pitcher in green. 341-342. Northwood's Peach tumbler and pitcher in green with gold decoration. 343-344. No. 19 (Memphis) tumbler and pitcher in green with gold decoration.*

345-348. *Northwood's No. 19 (Memphis) table set in green with gold decoration.*

349-352. *Northwood's Peach table set in green with gold decoration. Compare the Peach creamer with the larger pitcher (Fig. 342); the creamer has two pieces of fruit visible, like the rest of the table set pieces, while the larger pitcher has three. The large berry bowl and smaller sauce dishes (Figs. 365-366), however, display two pieces of fruit.*

353-357. *Five pieces of Northwood's iridescent Pearl glass, which is called white Carnival today—Wishbone epergne, Corn vase (note stalk base), Wide Panel epergne and Grape Arbor tumbler and pitcher.*

358. *Plums and Cherries decorated tumbler (see Fig. 259 for the pitcher).* 359. *Northwood's Peach pitcher with ruby-stain.* 360-362. *Crystal Cherry and Cable butterdish, spooner and covered cracker jar with ruby-stained fruit and gold decoration.*

363-364. *Crystal Cherry and Cable covered sugar and creamer with ruby-stained fruit and gold decoration.* 365-366. *Northwood's Peach sauces and berry bowl with ruby-stained fruit and gold decoration.*

An impressive array of Northwood's Golden Iris (marigold Carnival). Note that the iridescence ranges from partial (Figs. 367, 369 and 371) to complete.

367. Swirl tumbler and pitcher, 12 1/4" tall. 368-369. Interior Swirl tumbler and pitcher (the pitcher is similar in shape to Northwood's Raspberry; see Figs 561-562). 370-371. No. 21 (Flute) tumbler and pitcher. 372. Greek Key pitcher.

373-374 Good Luck plates with Basketweave and plain backs. 375. Hearts and Flowers 9" plate. 376. Poppy Show ruffled bowl, 8 3/4" d.

377. Raspberry gravy boat made from creamer mould. 378. No. 21 (Flute) sauce. 379. Strawberry hand-grip type 7 1/4" plate with Basketweave exterior. 380. Wishbone tumbler. 381. Grape and Cable whimsey made from a tumbler. 382. Northwood's jack in the pulpit style vase, 6 1/2" tall (note exterior ribbing)..

383. Not Northwood; this is Dugan's Victorian pattern. 384. Nippon 8 1/2" ruffled bowl in purple Carnival. 385. Peacocks on the Fence 9" plate with sawtooth edge in blue Carnival. 386-387. Peacock and Urn 5 1/2" d. and 9 3/4" d. shallow bowls in blue Carnival (these are called the "ice cream set").

388-390. Tornado vases in green, marigold (note smaller size) and blue Carnival (390 has a ribbed background). 391-392. Wild Rose open edge bowls (note the different styles) in purple and green Carnival (391 has the Stippled Rays interior; 392 is plain). 393. Wishbone 9 1/2" bowl with pie crust edge in an unusual color for Northwood Carnival—"smoke."

394. Greek Key and Scales footed bowl with Stippled Rays interior in green Carnival. 395-397. Lustre Flute tumbler whimsey in marigold carnival; open sugar and creamer in green with marigold iridescence (the creamer is smaller than Fig. 140). 398. Rainbow 8 1/4" bowl with pie crust edge in green Carnival.

399-400. *Swirl pitcher and tumbler; note the marigold color at the top of the green pitcher.* 401. *Wishbone pitcher in purple Carnival.* 402. *Crystal with satin finish (not iridized) decorated pitcher (note similarity in shape to Wishbone).* 403-404. *Blue decorated tumbler and pitcher.*

405, 408. *Grape and Cable orange bowls in purple and blue Carnival; the interior of 408 is smooth, without any pattern.* 406-407. *Peacock at the Fountain tumbler and pitcher in ice blue Carnival.*

409. *Fern compote in green Carnival (note Daisy and Plume exterior).* 410. *Panelled Holly bon bon in green with marigold iridescence.* 411. *Graceful vase in green Carnival.* 412. *Bull's Eye and Leaves crimped bowl in green with marigold iridescence.* 413. *Grape and Cable 8 1/2" bowl, stippled interior except for the pie-crust edge, in aqua opalescent Carnival (note Ribbed exterior).*

414   415   416   417   418   419   420   421

422   423   424   425   426

430

427   428   429   431

414-415. *Grape Arbor tumbler and pitcher in ice blue Carnival. 416-419. Dandelion tumblers and pitchers in purple and ice blue Carnival. 420-421. Springtime tumbler and pitcher in purple Carnival.*

These are all blue Carnival. 422. Three Fruits 9 1/4" plate. 423. Grape and Cable 10 1/2" ice cream bowl. 424. Double Loop open sugar. 425-426. Northwood's Peach tumbler and pitcher.

427-428, 431. Grape and Cable banana bowl (ice blue), handled bon bon in purple Carnival (note Basketweave exterior) and covered cracker jar in ice green. 429-430. Cherries motif, Intaglio line, bowl and sauce dish in marigold Carnival.

432. *Three Fruits footed bowl with leaves in the center and Meander exterior in purple Carnival.* 433. *Three Fruits plate with cherries in center and Basketweave exterior in green Carnival.* 434. *Fruits and Flowers pastel marigold plate with plain center and Basketweave exterior.* 435. *Three Fruits Marigold bowl with cherries in center.* 436. *Three Fruits footed bowl with Meander exterior and leaves in the center (432 and 436 are sometimes called Three Fruits Medallion; 434 is sometimes called Fruits and Flowers).*

437-438. *Poppy Show ruffled bowl and 9 1/2" plate in blue Carnival.* 439-440. *Rose Show plates in green and purple Carnival.*

441. *Stippled Strawberries 9" plate in purple Carnival.* 442-443. *Strawberries 9" plates in purple and marigold Carnival (443 has the Basketweave exterior).*

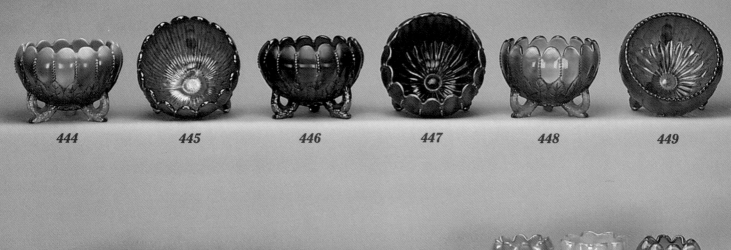

444-449. Leaf and Beads rose bowls in several Carnival colors—444-aqua opalescent; 445-green; 446-blue; 447-purple; 448-green; and 449-amethyst. Note the different interiors—444, 446 and 449 are plain; 445 is Stippled Rays; 447 and 449 have a 24-petalled flower.

450-455. Finecut and Roses rose bowls in a variety of Carnival colors—450-marigold; 451-green; 452-aqua opalescent; 453-amethyst 454-dark amber (not iridized on exterior); and 455-ice blue. **456-458.** Daisy and Plume stemmed rose bowls in marigold and green Carnival (note the slightly different crimps).

459-463. Beaded Cable rose bowls in marigold, ice green, aqua opalescent, purple and blue, respectively. **464.** Drapery rosebowl in aqua opalescent. **465.** Daisy and Plume 3-footed rose bowl with Blackberry interior in purple Carnival.

466 467 468 469 470 471

472 473 474 475 476 477

478 479 480 481 482 483 484

466-471. Hearts and Flowers 6" tall compotes in the following Carnival colors: 466-amethyst; 467-amethyst; 468-marigold; 469-unusual "clambroth"; 470-ice green; and 471-ice blue.

472-477. Hearts and Flowers compotes in the following Carnival colors: 472-blue; 473-ice blue opalescent; 474-aqua opalescent; 475-blue; 476-green; 477-marigold on Ivory (custard).

478-483. Bushel Baskets in various Carnival colors: 478-amethyst; 479-ice green; 480-black (not iridized); 481-purple; 482-aqua opalescent; and 483-marigold. 484. Bushel Basket, eight-sided, in purple Carnival.

485   486   487   488   489   490   491   492

493   494   495   496   497   498   499

500   501   502   503   504

This stunning display captures the original phrase "metallic sheen" used to describe Northwood's iridescent wares in 1910.

485-486. Acorn Burrs tumbler and pitcher in green Carnival. 487-492. Tumblers and pitchers in Grape Arbor, Oriental Poppy, and Dandelion—all in purple Carnival.

493. Raspberry milk pitcher in green Carnival. 494-499. Tumblers and pitchers in Grape and Gothic Arches, Singing Birds, and Peacock at the Fountain—all in purple carnival.

500. Peacock at the Fountain compote in purple Carnival (note the Hearts and Flowers pattern on the base). 501-504. Peacock at the Fountain table set in purple Carnival.

505   506   507   508   509   510

511   512   513   514   515

516   517   518   519   520

A nice array of carnival pieces in various shades of "ice green," dubbed "Emerald" by Northwood in 1910.

505-506. Acorn Burrs punch cup and punch bowl. 507-508. Peacock and Urn small and large ice cream set pieces. 509-510. Peacock at the Fountain punch bowl and punch cup.

511. Raspberry milk pitcher. 512. Oriental Poppy tumbler. 513. Bushel Basket. 514-515. Peacocks on the Fence 9" plates (514 has Ribbed back).

516. Hearts and Flowers compote. 517. Peacock at the Fountain compote (note Hearts and Flowers pattern on base). 518. Grape and Cable tumbler. 519. Poppy Show bowl. 520. Peacock at the Fountain berry bowl.

521 522 523 524 525 526

527 528 529 530 531 532

533 534 535 536 537

These articles are in "white" Carnival glass, which was originally called Pearl by Northwood.

521-522. Grape and Cable punch cup and punch bowl. 523. Not Northwood; this is Dugan's Grapevine Lattice. 524-526. Peacock at the Fountain pitcher, punch bowl and punch cup.

527-532. Northwood's Peach table set, tumbler and pitcher (note the gold decoration).

533-534. Northwood's Peach berry bowl and sauce dish (note the gold decoration). 535. Grape and Cable covered cracker jar. 536-537. Peacock at the Fountain compote and Hearts and Flowers compote (note that these have the same design on the bases).

538 539 540 541 542 543

544 545 546 547

548 549 550 551 552

These articles are in "white" Carnival glass, which was originally called Pearl by Northwood.

538-539. Acorn Burrs punch cup and two-piece punch bowl. 540-541. Oriental Poppy tumbler and pitcher. 542. Memphis 10 1/2" fruit bowl and base. 543. Fine Rib 10 1/2" vase.

544-545. Hearts and Flowers and Poppy Show crimped bowls. 546. Raspberry milk pitcher. 547. Rose Show plate, 9 1/2" diameter.

548-549. Bushel Baskets (548 is eight-sided). 550. Grape and Cable 9 1/4" bowl (this piece is generally called a "centerpiece" bowl; see Figs. 643-649). 551. Daisy and Drape 6 3/8" tall vase. 552. Grape Arbor whimsey made from tumbler.

553 554 555 556 557

558 559 560 561 562

563 564 565 566 567

553-554. *Aqua opalescent Drapery vase and Leaf and Beads candy dish with the type of marigold iridescence called "butterscotch." 555-557. Pastel aqua opalescent bowls—Good Luck, Poinsettia Lattice, and Embroidered Mums.*

558-559. *Fine Cut and Roses candy dish in aqua opalescent and rose bowl in ice blue. 560-562. Three ice blue pieces—Peacocks on the Fence 9 1/4" plate (Ribbed back), Raspberry milk pitcher and water pitcher.*

563-567. *All in ice blue—Hearts and Flowers bowl and compote, Wishbone footed bowl, Oriental Poppy tumbler and Drapery candy dish, 6 1/2" wide. Ice blue was originally called Azure by Northwood.*

Except for Figs. 568-569 and 573, these are all purple Carnival pieces.

568-569. Dandelion and Peacock at the Fountain pitchers in green Carnival. **570-572. Grape and Cable** pitcher, **Greek Key** tumbler and pitcher.

573. Blue Carnival Grape and Cable orange or fruit bowl with applied handle (the handle is not iridized). **574. Christmas compote,** probably not Northwood-made. **575. Grape and Cable** orange or fruit bowl made into an unusual whimsey piece.

576. Tree Trunk vase. **577. Grape and Cable** spittoon made from powder jar base. **578. Corn Husk** vase (note the pulled husk style; compare with Figs. 354, 732 and 736). **579. Wheat** sweetmeat and cover. **580. Goblet** in No. 12 pattern (known as Northwood's Near-Cut).

116

581   582   583

584   585   586

The Northwood firm produced some delightful advertising items in Carnival, almost always in amethyst glass and often with outstanding iridescence, as shown by these pieces. Furniture and candy merchants seem to have been most interested in utilizing the Northwood glass medium. All of these began as 6" plates, but several interesting variations are illustrated and noted.

581. Eagle Furniture "handgrip" style. 582. E. A. Hudson Furniture. 583. Fern Brand Chocolates (note plain back). 584. Davidson's Society Chocolates, "double handgrip style." 585. Jockey Club ruffled bowl. 586. The Basketweave back pattern on a "handgrip" plate.

Other Carnival glass manufacturers, notably Fenton (see Fig. 594) and Millersburg, made advertising items, too. Readers should consult John D. Resnik's excellent book, The Encyclopedia of Carnival Glass Lettered Pieces. Resnik pictures three other Northwood advertising plates— "Ballard [of] Merced, Cal.," "We Use Broeker's Flour," and "Dreibus Parfait Sweets" (see Fig. 595).

587. Blossomtime compote in amethyst Carnival. 588. Wishbone epergne in green Carnival (the base has Northwood's distinctive Basketweave exterior). 589. Peacock at the Fountain orange or fruit bowl in blue Carnival. 590. Butterfly bon bon with Stippled Rays interior in purple Carnival. 591. Peacocks on the Fence 8 3/4" crimped plate in unusual "electric blue" Carnival.

592. Wishbone footed plate, 8 1/4" d. in green carnival. 593. Leaf and Beads candy dish with Lovely interior in purple carnival. 594. Not Northwood; this is a Fenton advertising plate. 595. Northwood Dreibus Parfait Sweets "handgrip" plate in amethyst (note Basketweave back). 596. Amaryllis compote in purple Carnival.

597-600. Grape and Gothic Arches table set in blue carnival. 601. Northwood's Peach tumbler in blue carnival. 602. Springtime tumbler in amethyst Carnival.

118

603-604. Marigold Raspberry tumbler and pitcher. 605-606. Marigold No. 19 (Memphis) sauce and berry bowl. 607-609. Raspberry milk pitcher, tumbler and pitcher in purple Carnival.

610-611. Marigold Acorn Burrs sauce and berry bowl. 612-615. Blue Carnival sauces and berry bowls, Grape and Gothic Arches and Peacock at the Fountain.

616. Hearts and Flowers compote in purple Carnival. 617. Embroidered Mums 8 3/4" ruffled bowl in blue Carnival. 618. Marigold Panelled Holly spooner. 619. Double Loop open sugar in blue Carnival. 620. Daisy and Plume stemmed rose bowl in green Carnival. 621. Town Pump in purple Carnival.

This page and the three following display a wide variety of pieces in Northwood's Grape and Cable pattern.

622. *Covered compote in purple Carnival.* **622-623.** *Tumbler (typical size, 4" tall) and pitcher in purple Carnival.* **625-626.** *Tumbler (4 1/4" tall) and tankard pitcher in green Carnival.* **627-629.** *Hatpin holders in purple, green and marigold Carnival.*

630. *Banana bowl in purple Carnival.* **631-633.** *Marigold open compote, covered cracker jar and humidor.*

634-637. *Table set in green Carnival.* **638.** *Fernery bowl in purple Carnival.*

639   640   641   642

643   644   645   646

647   648   649

639, 642. Grape and Cable centerpiece bowls in purple and green Carnival, respectively (both have the N-in-a-circle) . 640-641. Punch cups and master punch bowl with base in purple carnival.

643-645. Centerpiece bowls in ice blue, ice green, and white Carnival (all have the N-in-a-circle). 646. Not Northwood; probably made by Fenton.

647. Not Northwood; probably Fenton's Venetian Red, c. 1924. 648-649. Centerpiece bowls in marigold Carnival (649 has the N-in-a-circle; 648 does not).

650   651   652   653   654   655   656

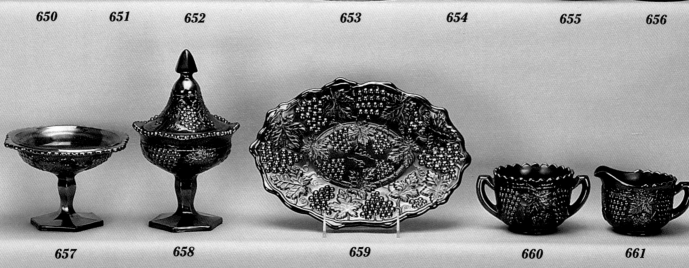

657   658   659   660   661

662   664   665

663

650. *Grape and Cable marigold Carnival candle lamp.* 651-652. *Shot glass and whiskey decanter in purple Carnival.* 653-654. *Marigold 10" d. punch bowl and punch cup.* 655-656. *Cologne bottle in amethyst and candlestick in purple Carnival.*

657. *Amethyst compote made from sweetmeat base.* 658. *Covered sweetmeat in blue carnival.* 659, *Large dresser tray in purple Carnival.* 660-661. *Breakfast set—open sugar and creamer—in purple Carnival.*

662, 664. *Banana bowls (note the slightly different shapes) in green and marigold Carnival.* 663. *Small pin tray in marigold.* 665. *Powder jar (originally called Puff Box) in amethyst Carnival.*

122

666. *Grape and Cable 10 1/4" ice cream bowl in marigold (Basketweave back).* 667. *Ruffled bowl in marigold (Basketweave back).* 668. *Crimped plate, 8 1/2" in marigold (Basketweave back).* 669. *Plate, 8 3/4" d. in blue Carnival (note stippled center area and Ribbed back).*

670. *Plate, 8 3/4" d. in green Carnival (Ribbed back).* 671. *Crimped plate, 9 3/4" in purple Carnival (Basketweave back).* 672. *Not Northwood; this is Fenton's Grape and Cable in red carnival.* 673. *Grape Leaves crimped bowl in green Carnival (stippled Shell and Wild Rose back).*

674. *Plate, 7 3/4" d. (Basketweave back) with "handgrip" in green Carnival.* 675-676. *Banana bowl and tumbler in ice green Carnival.* 677. *Plate, 7 1/2" d., with "handgrip" in purple carnival.*

678   679   680   681   682   683

684   685   686   687   688

689   690   691   692   693   694

A superb selection of Northwood pieces in aqua opalescent (unless indicated otherwise), considered a premier color in Carnival glass by collectors today. Note the range of colors from pastel to butterscotch.

678. Peacocks on the Fence 8 1/2" bowl (Ribbed back). 679. Hearts and Flowers compote. 680. Daisy and Drape 6 1/4" vase. 681. Peacock at the Fountain orange or fruit bowl. 682-683. Vases in Four Pillar. Note differences in color near foot of each.

684. Rose Show ruffled bowl in ice blue opalescent. 685. Fine Cut and Roses rose bowl. 686. Rose Show plate, 9 1/2" d., in lime green opalescent. 687. Bushel Basket. 688. Three Fruits 9" plate (Ribbed back).

689. Beaded Cable rose bowl. 690. Double Loop open sugar. 691. Singing Birds mug. 692. Dandelion mug (note stippled background). 693. Leaf and Beads rose bowl 694. Fruits and Flowers handled bon bon with Basketweave exterior.

695. *Wide Panel epergne in aqua opalescent.* **696-697.** *Grape and Cable punch cup and punch bowl with base in ice blue.* **698.** *Peacock at the Fountain punch bowl with base in aqua opalescent.*

699-701. *Aqua opalescent Peacock and Urn ice cream set pieces and Diamond Point vase.* **702-704.** *Wisteria pitcher and tumbler and Daisy and Plume three-footed rose bowl in ice blue (note the Blackberry interior; see Fig. 465).*

705-709. *Aqua opalescent—Three Fruits ruffled bowl, Poppy pickle dish, Tree Trunk vase, Grape and Cable two-handled bon bon (Basketweave exterior), and Grape and Cable bowl with pie-crust edge (note the stippled center area and the Ribbed exterior).*

710   711   712   713

714   715   716   717

718   719   720   721

710. Wide Panel epergnes in green opalescent and marigold Carnival (note differences where the trumpets fit into the holders). 712-713. Tree Trunk vases in Ivory with "nutmeg" stain and with marigold iridescence.

714. Unusual Ruffles and Rings flint opalescent bowl with marigold Carnival iridescence on the interior (note the floral motif on the opalescent edge). 715. Marigold iridescence on Ivory (custard) Rose Show plate. 716-717. Three Fruits bowls in Ivory (custard) with some iridescence. 718. Bushel Basket in canary opalescent. 719. Ribbed back of Peacocks on the Fence bowl in iridized blue marble glass, note lack of iridescence on the marie (see front cover). 720-721. Poinsettia Lattice plate in Ivory (custard) and ruffled bowl in canary opalescent.

126

An excellent assortment of Northwood's famous swung vases.

722-724, 726. Fine Rib vases in purple carnival, teal blue (iridized), vaseline or canary (iridized) and marigold "butterscotch" carnival (726 is 16 1/4" tall). **725.** Tree Trunk "funeral" vase in purple Carnival.

727, 730. Four Pillar vases in teal blue and green, both iridized (note gold decoration on 727). **728-729.** Tree Trunk vases in ice green and marigold (728 is 17 1/2" tall). **731.** Fine Rib vase in purple Carnival.

732, 736. Corn vases in ice green and green Carnival. **733.** Tree Trunk vase in purple Carnival. **734.** Feathers vase in marigold. **735.** Flute vase in green with marigold iridescence (12" tall). **737.** Diamond Point vase in blue Carnival. **738.** Daisy and Drape vase in ice blue. **739.** Leaf Columns vase in ice green.

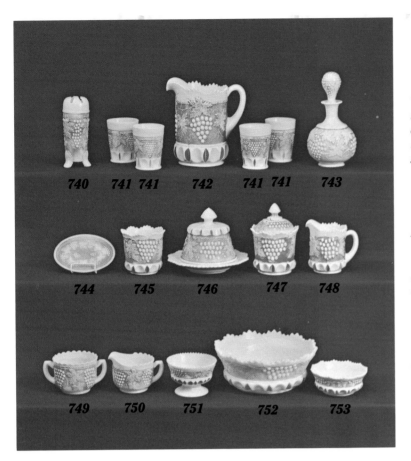

740   741 741   742   741 741   743

744   745   746   747   748

749   750   751   752   753

These Grape and Cable items, c. 1914, have the original decoration, a brown stain called "nutmeg" today. Other articles may be gold decorated or have pink or blue stain, as shown on the next several pages.

740. Grape and Cable hatpin holder. 741-742. Grape and Cable tumblers and pitcher. 743. Grape and Cable cologne bottle (see Fig. 801).

744. Grape and Cable pin tray (see Figs. 770 and 810-811 for larger size). 745-748. Grape and Cable four-piece table set--spooner, butterdish, covered sugar and creamer.

749-750. Grape and Cable "breakfast set" creamer and open sugar. 751-753. Grape and Cable pedestal sauce, berry bowl and flat sauce.

754-755. Grape and Cable punch cups and master punch bowl.

756. Grape and Cable fernery bowl (these originally were furnished with a thin white inner liner). 757. Grape and Cable humidor. 758. Grape and Cable centerpiece bowl, note crimping.

759-761. Grape and Cable two-handled bon bon (note Basketweave exterior), crimped 8" plate and flat 8" plate.

754   754   755   754   754

756   757   758

759   760   761

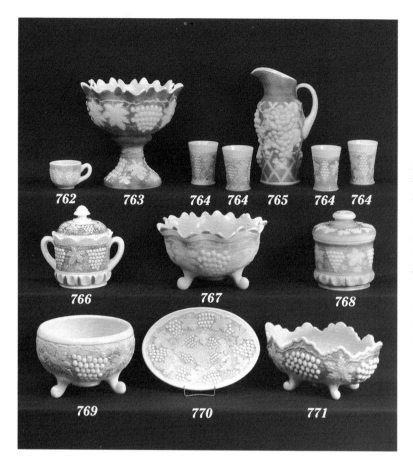

762-763. *Grape and Cable punch cup and punch bowl with blue stain.* 764-765. *Grape Arbor tumblers and pitcher with original pink stain.*

766. *Grape and Cable cracker jar with nutmeg stain.* 767-768. *Grape and Cable orange or fruit bowl and humidor with pink stain.*

769-771. *Grape and Cable bowl (contrast the edge with Fig. 767), large dresser tray (see Figs. 810-811), and banana bowl, all with nutmeg stain.*

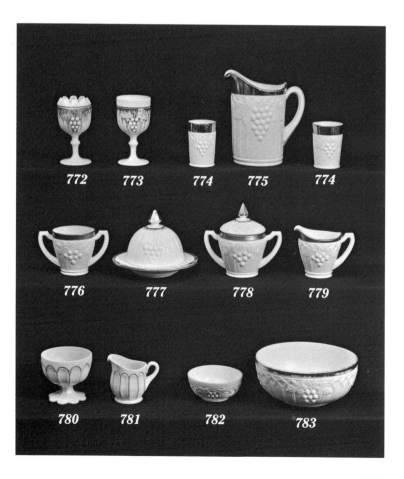

772-773. *Grape and Gothic Arches crimped goblet and regular goblet, both with nutmeg stain.* 774-775. *Grape and Gothic Arches tumblers and pitcher with gold decoration.*

776-779. *Grape and Gothic Arches table set with gold decoration.*

780-781. *Double Loop open sugar and creamer with nutmeg stain.* 782-783. *Grape and Gothic Arches sauce (nutmeg stain) and berry bowl with gold decoration.*

The original name for this impressive Northwood shade in their "Luna Ivory" glass was Louis XIV (Heacock called it Panelled Poppies).

These shades could be drilled for hanging from three cords (note the metal inserts), or they could be hung with special clamps instead of drilling holes in the glass.

784

785. Three Fruits plate. 786-787, 789. Good Luck crimped bowl, Drapery vase and Singing Birds sauce on pedestal with nutmeg stain. 788. Poinsettia Lattice crimped plate with blue stain.

790-794. Dandelion mug, Bushel Basket, Finecut and Roses rose bowl, Beaded Cable rose bowl, and Grape Arbor whimsey (made from tumbler)—all with nutmeg stain. 795. Probably not Northwood; could be Jefferson's "Spool."

796. Not Northwood. 797-799. These pieces all have nutmeg stain–Three Fruits bon bon (note Basketweave exterior), crimped plate and Poppy oval bowl with typical fluted edge. 800. Northwood's No. 21 (Flute) goblet with rolled edge.

801. Grape and Cable cologne bottles in white satin with yellow paint. 802. Electric shade in Luna Ivory.

803-804. Puff box and hatpin holder in white satin with yellow paint. 805-806. Haptpin holders with pink and blue stain. 807-808. Hatpin holder and puff box in dark transparent blue.

809-812. Small and large dresser trays in white satin with yellow point and dark transparent blue.

131

813. Luna No. 10 electric shade (this shade is marked in the fitter "10 Luna"). 814. Etruscan vase (for the same shape, see Fig. 886).

815-816. Brecciated Marble two-piece compote and vase.

817. Bear bookend or doorstop in Luna glass.

818   819   820   821   822   823   824

825   826   827   826   828

829   830   831   830   832   833

All of these except Fig. 818 are Northwood's "Blue Iridescent" (note the range of color intensity); items are described using original Northwood terms—covered almond, sweet pea vase, etc.

818-819. No. 725 candlestick (10 3/8" t.) and No. 727 tall twisted vase. 820, 822. No. 636 1-lb. candy jars (Fig. 822 is decorated with gold band by the Lotus Glass Co.; see the color plate following Fig. 919). 821. No. 691 covered almond or bon bon. 823-824. Tumbler and pitcher (pattern is called "Concave Diamond" by collectors today..

825. No. 698 sandwich tray. 826-827. Console set consisting of No. 660 bowl with black base and No. 657 candlesticks (note that these are slightly lighter than Northwood's typical Blue Iridescent). 828. Unusual open piece (perhaps a vase?) made from No. 605 footed bowl.

829. No. 699 cheese and cracker. 830-831. Console set consisting of No. 642 bowl with black base and No. 719 candlesticks. 832. No. 621 mayonnaise bowl with No. 674 plate. 833. No. 569 sweet pea vase (note ribbing).

834   835   836   837   836   838   838

841

839   840   842   843   844

845   846   847   848   849   850

All of these are Northwood's "Topaz Iridescent;" items are described using original Northwood terms.

834-835. No. 636 1-lb. and No. 659 1/2-lb. candy jars. 836-837. Console set consisting of No. 648 bowl (13" d.) with black base and No. 696 candlesticks (10 1/2" t.). 838. Pair of No. 708 candlesticks.

839-840. No. 637 tall comport, bell shape (note vertical panels) and a similar comport, undoubtably Northwood-made, in an unlisted shape. 841-842. No. 301 8" bowl and No. 631 11 1/2" cake plate (this is sometimes called a "salad set"). 843. Unlisted bowl with cupped edge and square foot. 844. Unlisted bowl with cupped edge and twelve-sided base.

845. No. 613 5 1/2" crimped vase (these may have a diamond pattern, too). 846. No. 301 6" cake plate. 847-848. Covered sugar and creamer in Barbella; compare shapes to Grape and Gothic Arches pieces in Figs. 282-283). 849. Unlisted shallow comport 6" d., octagonal base. 850. No. 707 bulb bowl, cupped.

851   852   853   854   853   855   856

857   858   859   860   861

862   863   864   863   865   866

Most of these pieces are Northwood's exclusive "Russet" color.

851. No. 989 swung vase, 11 3/4" tall. 852. No. 637 comport with rolled edge. 853-854. Console set consisting of No. 647 bowl with black base and No. 657 8 1/4" candlesticks. 855. Tumbler (Concave Diamond pattern). 856. No. 651 10 1/2" candlestick.

857. No. 657 candlestick, dark amethyst with iridescence. 858. No. 807 footed bowl (perhaps in Northwood's "Royal Purple"). 859. No. 807 bowl in "Pearl." 860-861. No. 617 and No. 669 bowls with black bases.

862. No. 654 footed nut bowl. 863-864. Console set consisting of No. 640 bowl with black base and No. 658 7" candlesticks. 865. No. 675 handled candlestick. 866. No. 645 footed bowl.

Rosita Amber was one of the last colors developed at the Northwood firm before its closure. The opaque blue was called "Jade Blue" when it was introduced.

867. No. 727 tall twisted vase. 868. No. 695 8 1/2" candlestick. 869. No. 636 1-lb. candy jar in crystal with unusual iridescence, perhaps a variation of Northwood's Russet. 870. No. 643 jelly or bon bon and cover. 871. No. 725 10 1/2" candlesticks.

These bowls and candlesticks could be mixed to form different console sets. 872. No. 657 8" candlesticks. 873. No. 617 bowl with black base. 874. No. 660 bowl with black base. 875. No. 658 candlesticks. 876. No. 669 bowl with black base.

877. No. 643 jelly or bon bon and cover. 878. No. 672 bulb bowl. 879. No. 666 footed comport. 880. No. 638 bowl, cupped, 6 1/2" d. 881. No. 656 footed comport.

136

882-883. *No. 1005 lamp vase and No. 1001 lamp vase in Blue and Chinese Coral, respectively, with black bases.* 884. *No. 616 bowl in iridized Ivory with black decoration and No. 712 black stand.* 885. *No. 659 1/2-lb. candy jar in iridized Ivory.* 886. *Vase, 10 1/4" tall, in unusual purple color (compare the shape to Fig. 814).*

887-888. *No. 640 bowl with black base and No. 643 jelly or bon bon and cover in iridized Ivory.* 889. *Crystal Poppy and Scroll 11" shallow bowl with the typical red and gold decoration of Northwood's Intaglio line (collectors call this "goofus").* 890. *No. 649 bowl with black base (this bowl may be a special "white" glass, for it is not like the ivory articles on this page).*

These four comports have similar octagonal bases on their stems; 891 and 893 are plain, but the others have a "tree of life" motif. 891. *Amethyst Beaded Star and Mums comport, Verre D'or line (see Figs. 207-219).* 892. *Topaz iridescent comport.* 893. *Crystal Poppy and Scroll comport with red and gold "goofus" decoration.* 894. *Cupped bowl comport in crystal with Russet-like iridescence (see Figs. 869, 900 and 902).*

137

895. Cake plate, 11 1/2" d., Topaz Iridescent in the pattern Heacock named Barbella. 896-897. No. 631 cake plates, 11 1/2" d., in Jade Blue and emerald green.

898-899. No. 685 sherbet and No. 723 ash tray in Blue Iridescent. 900, 902. No. 636 1-lb. candy jars and covers in crystal with Russet-like iridescence (see Figs. 869 and 894) and Blue Iridescent (gold decoration by Lotus). 901. No. 691 covered almond dish or bon bon (the lid is Topaz (not iridized); the base is Jade Green). 903. No. 655 Topaz Iridescent comport, decorated at the Lotus firm. (see the color plate following Fig. 919).

904-906. Jade Green articles: No. 713 10 1/4" footed bowl with Jade Green foot, No. 616 bowl with No. 712 black stand (a No. 595 Turtle Flower Block is inside) and No. 620 8" bowl with black base.

907   908   909   908   907

910   911   912   911   913

915

914   916   917   916   918   919

Northwood's Jade Green varies considerably in its depth of color.

907. *Pair of No. 725 10 1/2" candlesticks in Northwood's black.* 908-909. *Console set consisting of No. 724 oval bowl and No. 725 candlesticks.* 910. *No. 695 candlestick with gold decoration by the Lotus Glass Co.* 911-912. *Console set consisting of No. 694 bowl with white base and No. 657 candlesticks.* 913. *No. 727 short twisted vase, 7 1/2" tall.*

914-915. *No. 685 sherbet and No. 729 plate.* 916-917. *Console set consisting of No. 692 bowl (note interior twist pattern) with white base and twisted candlesticks.* 918-919. *Open sugar and creamer (Heacock believed these were Northwood products, but they were made by the Co-Operative Flint Glass Co.).*

139

The Lotus Glass Company of Barnesville, Ohio, began operations as the Lotus Cut Glass Company about 1912. The firm, which is still in business today, buys glass "blanks" from glassmaking firms and decorates the blanks with gold bands or etching and engraving in its own designs. Over the past three quarters of a century, the Lotus has seen many of its suppliers—the ranks of America's famed glass factories such as Heisey, Cambridge, Fostoria and Imperial—fall by the wayside.

This photo was made from an original "illustrated sheet," used by the Lotus firm's representatives to sell to the trade. The glass is Northwood's Jade Green with gold decoration, accented beautifully by white bases which have also been decorated. Courtesy of Francis Hanse and the Lotus Glass Company.

920 921 922 923 924 925

926 927 928 929

930 931 932 933 934

920-921. No. 698 sandwich tray and No. 695 candlestick in Chinese Coral. 922. Satin-finished Ivory "Dancing Ladies" covered urn with "nutmeg" stain. 923. No. 695 candlestick in Jade Green with gold decoration by Lotus. 924. No. 657 candlestick in a variation of Chinese Coral called "tan coral" by collectors. 925. Rosita Amber No. 725 candestick.

926, 928. Chinese Coral No. 1001 lamp vase with black base and No. 678 bowl with black foot. 927. Ivory No. 616 bowl with ususual black decoration and black base. 929. tumbler in Russet.

930. No. 636 in Ivory. 931, 934. No. 617 bowl and part of the No. 699 cheese and cracker set, both in Chinese coral (note orange color). 932-933. No. 727 tall twisted vase and No. 643 covered bon bon in Rosita Amber.

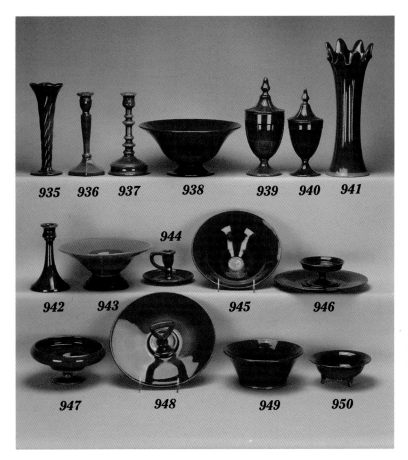

All the items here are Northwood's Chinese Coral.

935-941. No. 727 tall twisted vase, No. 695 candlestick, No. 708 candlestick, No. 678 footed bowl, 11 1/2" d., with black foot, Nos. 639 and 659 covered candy jars, and No. 930 swung vase (14 1/4" tall).

942-946. No 719 candlestick, No. 692 bowl with black base, No. 675 handled candlestick, No. 692 bowl, and No. 699 cheese and cracker set. The bowl shown in Fig. 945 bears the legend "CITIZEN'S MUTUAL TRUST CO. WHEELING W. VA." and the date "1924."

947-950. No. 656 footed comport, No. 698 handled sandwich tray, No. 669 bowl, and No. 707 nut bowl, flared.

951-952. Console set consisting of No. 708 candlesticks and No. 678 11 1/2" footed bowl with black foot. 953-954. Console set consisting of No. 657 candlesticks and No. 692 bowl with black base.

955-959. No. 643 jelly or bon bon with cover, twisted candlesticks, No. 698 handled sandwich tray (note gold band), No. 719 candlesticks and No. 636 1-lb. candy jar.

960-964. No. 722 plate and cup, No 707 bulb bowl with ribbed exterior (this bowl was available either with a matching cover or with the No. 706 ash tray), No. 618 vase, No. 676 candlestick, and No. 699 cheese and cracker set (note gold band).

Shortly after completing the eight grade at Ritchie School in Wheeling, Miss Bessie O. Kirsten became a decorator at H. Northwood and Company, which was just a few steps from her home on Wetzel Street. She marched with co-workers in a Liberty Loan parade in 1918, and she was an employee when the plant closed in 1925. On her last day, she was given the decorated compote below (Fig. 966) by the decorating room foreman, Charles Facer. The compote, not listed in any Northwood catalog, is similar to the nearby Central Glass Company's "High Footed Bon Bon." Perhaps a Central blank was decorated at the Northwood plant. The unusual decorated candlesticks in Fig. 965, Northwood's No. 708, were among her possessions until she presented them to friends recently.

965   966   965

Courtesy of Otto, Marion and Kurt Zwicker.

This page and the five following are from an original Northwood catalog, **The Rainbow Glassware**, *c. 1924.*

"NORTHWOOD"

THE universal recognition accorded the Northwood name wherever quality glassware is known has come only with the knowledge gained through many years close association with the glass working industry. Established as one of the pioneer glass factories on the American continent, Northwood leadership in design and manufacture has been consistently maintained.

Northwood designs are created by artists of traditional talent and long experience and are carried out by workers who spring from generations of skilled artisans in the glass working craft.

Thus it is that a piece of glassware, known to be of Northwood origin, carries with it the fullest assurance of originality, novelty and inherent quality.

"RAINBOW"

The very name is suggestive. The radiance and colorings of this ware are among the most beautiful ever achieved by skilled artists in the decorative glassworker's craft.

Rainbow ware is subject to imitation from many sources, yet its beauty of shape and design, and its originality of colors, remain unequaled. Its appeal is instant and universal to those who appreciate beautiful glassware, and wish to use it in decorating and beautifying the home.

The RAINBOW LINE

IS offered in a variety of unusually beautiful colors. Two of these, Blue and Topaz, are transparent and irridescent, reflecting from their specially treated surfaces all the values of light in the vari-colored hues of the rainbow.

The third, Rosita Amber, is a transparent glass with a deep golden effect. This color is not made in irridescent.

The other two colors are opaque and include the popular Jade Green, and new shade known as Chinese Coral. This new color is a distinctly novel introduction in colored glass, but its vividness of coloring has led to wide acceptance where a bizarre decorative note is desirable.

The entire Rainbow Line is obtainable either in plain colors or decorated with a band of coin gold. This produces a striking effect, adding appreciably to the beauty of any of the colors with which it may be used.

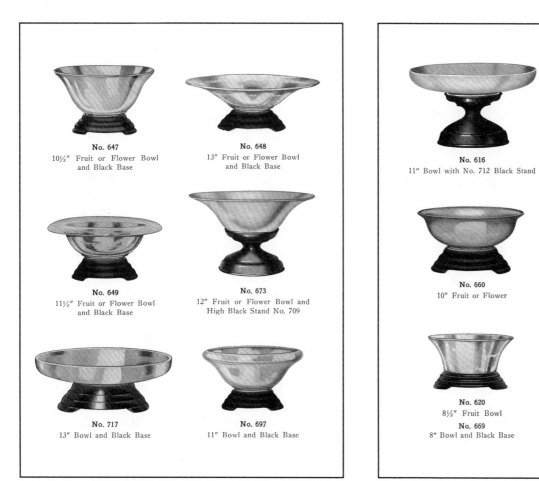

No. 647
10½" Fruit or Flower Bowl and Black Base

No. 648
13" Fruit or Flower Bowl and Black Base

No. 649
11½" Fruit or Flower Bowl and Black Base

No. 673
12" Fruit or Flower Bowl and High Black Stand No. 709

No. 717
13" Bowl and Black Base

No. 697
11" Bowl and Black Base

No. 616
11" Bowl with No. 712 Black Stand

No. 617
8½" Fruit or Flower Bowl and Black Base

No. 660
10" Fruit or Flower

No. 718
10" Rolled Edge Bowl and Black Base

No. 620
8½" Fruit Bowl
No. 669
8" Bowl and Black Base

No. 638
7½" Fruit or Flower Bowl and Black Base

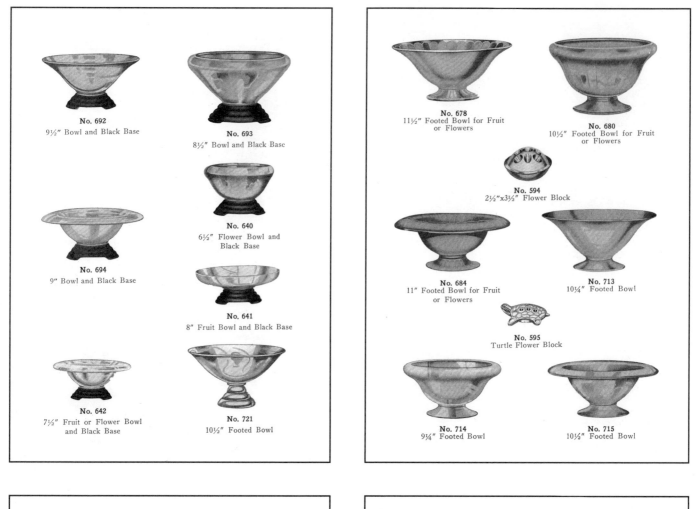

No. 692
9½″ Bowl and Black Base

No. 693
8½″ Bowl and Black Base

No. 694
9″ Bowl and Black Base

No. 640
6½″ Flower Bowl and
Black Base

No. 641
8″ Fruit Bowl and Black Base

No. 642
7½″ Fruit or Flower Bowl
and Black Base

No. 721
10½″ Footed Bowl

No. 678
11½″ Footed Bowl for Fruit
or Flowers

No. 680
10½″ Footed Bowl for Fruit
or Flowers

No. 594
2½″x3½″ Flower Block

No. 684
11″ Footed Bowl for Fruit
or Flowers

No. 713
10¼″ Footed Bowl

No. 595
Turtle Flower Block

No. 714
9¼″ Footed Bowl

No. 715
10½″ Footed Bowl

No. 724-725 Console Set
16″ Oval Bowl and 10½″ Candle Sticks

Console Set
Consisting of Bowl No. 692 with Black Base,
and 8½″ Candle Sticks No. 695

Console Set
Consisting of Bowl No. 694 with Black Stand No. 711,
and 8½″ Candle Sticks No. 708

Console Set
Consisting of Bowl No. 717 with No. 709 Black Stand
and 10½″ Candle Sticks No. 696

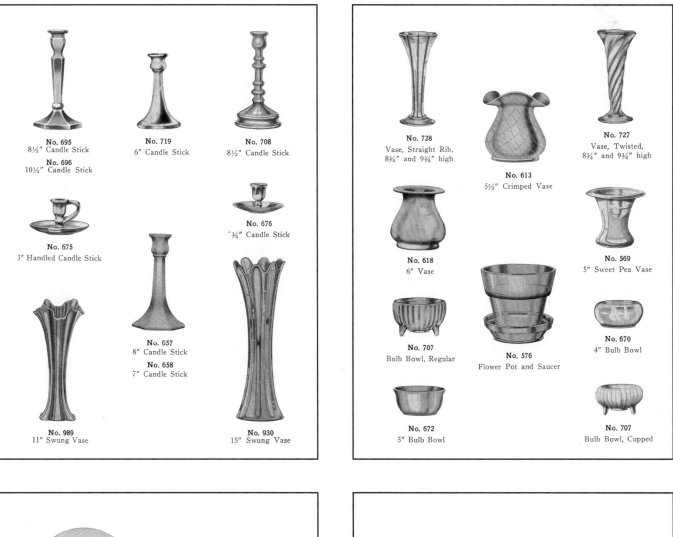

No. 695
8½" Candle Stick

No. 696
10½" Candle Stick

No. 719
6" Candle Stick

No. 708
8½" Candle Stick

No. 675
3" Handled Candle Stick

No. 676
7¾" Candle Stick

No. 657
8" Candle Stick

No. 658
7" Candle Stick

No. 989
11" Swung Vase

No. 930
15" Swung Vase

No. 728
Vase, Straight Rib,
8¾" and 9¾" high

No. 613
5½" Crimped Vase

No. 727
Vase, Twisted,
8¾" and 9¾" high

No. 618
6" Vase

No. 569
5" Sweet Pea Vase

No. 707
Bulb Bowl, Regular

No. 576
Flower Pot and Saucer

No. 670
4" Bulb Bowl

No. 672
5" Bulb Bowl

No. 707
Bulb Bowl, Cupped

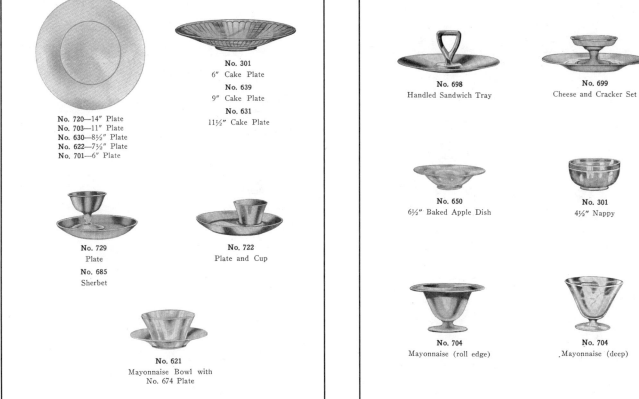

No. 720—14" Plate
No. 703—11" Plate
No. 630—8½" Plate
No. 622—7½" Plate
No. 701—6" Plate

No. 301
6" Cake Plate
No. 639
9" Cake Plate
No. 631
11½" Cake Plate

No. 729
Plate
No. 685
Sherbet

No. 722
Plate and Cup

No. 621
Mayonnaise Bowl with
No. 674 Plate

No. 698
Handled Sandwich Tray

No. 699
Cheese and Cracker Set

No. 650
6½" Baked Apple Dish

No. 301
4½" Nappy

No. 704
Mayonnaise (roll edge)

No. 704
Mayonnaise (deep)

147

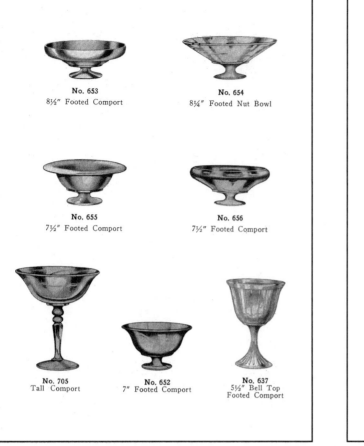

No. 653
8½" Footed Comport

No. 654
8¼" Footed Nut Bowl

No. 655
7½" Footed Comport

No. 656
7½" Footed Comport

No. 705
Tall Comport

No. 652
7" Footed Comport

No. 637
5½" Bell Top
Footed Comport

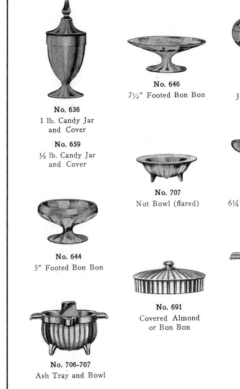

No. 636
1 lb. Candy Jar
and Cover

No. 659
½ lb. Candy Jar
and Cover

No. 646
7½" Footed Bon Bon

No. 643
Jelly or Bon Bon
and Cover

No. 707
Nut Bowl (flared)

No. 645
6¼" Footed Bon Bon

No. 644
5" Footed Bon Bon

No. 691
Covered Almond
or Bon Bon

No. 706
Ash Tray

No. 706-707
Ash Tray and Bowl

No. 723
Ash Tray

No. 688
Ice Tea Set (8 pieces)

3⅜" Coaster (No. 5)

No. 559
Bedroom Jug and Tumbler

No. 700
Water Set (7 pieces)

THE NEW NORTHWOOD AQUARIUM

THE New Northwood Aquarium, through its sheer novelty, is introducing a new note into the vogue of colored glass. A thoroughly radical departure from the common round "Fish Globe", its appealing difference in design, combined with the effect of its delicate colorings, is winning wide popularity wherever it is being shown.

The addition of a specially designed glass stand completes the Aquarium and presents it as an attractive unit. These stands are supplied in colors to match the bowls. By far the most pleasing effect, however, is obtained by the use of a stand of black glass which sets off the color of the bowl to better advantage and adds immeasurably to the appearance of the Aquarium when in use.

Colors—Blue, Amber, Canary and Crystal.

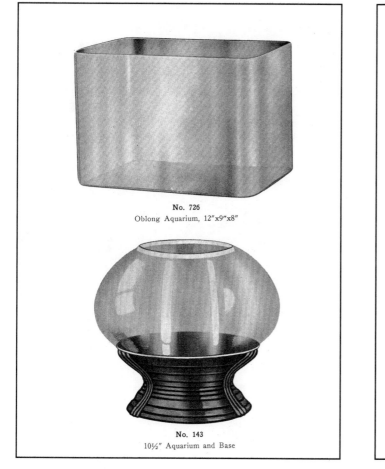

No. 726
Oblong Aquarium, 12"x9"x8"

No. 143
10½" Aquarium and Base

No. 134
9", 12" and 14" Aquarium and Base

No. 132
9", 12", 14" and 16" Aquarium and Base

NORTHWOOD LAMP VASES

The graceful shapes and brilliant colors of these lamp vases lend the necessary note of decoration in the lighting of the modern home. They are made in Blue, Canary, Jade Green, Chinese Coral and Black. Black bases are used with all colors.

No. 1003
12" Lamp Vase and
Black Base

No. 1001
10" Lamp Vase and
Black Base

No. 1006
7" Lamp Vase and
Black Base

No. 1005
11" Lamp Vase and
Black Base

No. 1004
15" Lamp Vase and
Black Base

No. 1002
12" Lamp Vase and
Black Base

(Continued from page 80)

vases are known in marigold, green and purple, all of which have good iridescence. Heacock (H2, p. 80) showed an opalescent vase in this pattern, which he then called Simple Simon.

Grape Leaves. The only articles in this design are crimped bowls which may have a Wild Rose exterior with stippled background. The grapes and leaves are pressed in rather low relief, but the iridescence on these bowls, particularly the blue Carnival, can be very striking indeed, often showing beautiful silver and gold highlights. These are also known in ice blue and green. The N-in-a-circle is generally present, but collectors should be aware of a similar pattern attributed to Millersburg which is not, of course, marked in any way. A Grape Leaves bowl appears in the "Pompeiian" assortment in a June, 1910, Butler Brothers catalog.

Good Luck. These Northwood plates and bowls have been popular Carnival collectibles for a number of years, and they can be found in many iridescent treatments, ranging from marigold, blue, and purple to white and aqua opalescent. The exterior may be plain, but either the Thin Ribs or the Basketweave design is usually present (see Figs. 373-374 and 555). John Britt reports a few Good Luck bowls with Thin Rib backs in ice blue, ice green and white.

Good Luck plates are about 9" in diameter, and bowls vary from 7" to 9" depending upon the ruffling and/or crimping. A Good Luck bowl was also made by Fenton; these are quite scarce, but the Fenton Heart and Vine pattern makes them easy to distinguish from the Northwood article.

Holiday. The lone item here is a large circular tray. It is known in crystal as well as marigold Carnival, and the N-in-a-circle is present. The design

Holiday pattern tray.

reminds one of Northwood's fondness for the Greek Key motif.

Leaf and Beads. There is great variety to be found here. The only item in this design is a modest-sized bowl which comes in many Carnival colors, but it may have either a heavy base or three twig-like feet. The edge may have 30 points, 15 rounded scallops (most often seen), or just eight gentle scallops. The interior may be plain, or it may have Stippled Rays, Fine Ribs, or a 24-petalled flower called the Floral Ribs motif (see Figs. 444-449, 554 and 693). Yet another interesting variation occurs when the bowl is flared into a candy dish and has the Lovely interior (Fig. 593).

When the bowl is left open, it is usually called a nut bowl or candy dish; when cupped in, it becomes a rose bowl. A footed Leaf and Beads bowl with the 30 point rim in dark purple is known with the Lovely pattern on the interior (*HOACGA Educational Series I*, p. 26). Most Leaf and Beads pieces have the N-in-a-circle.

Leaf Columns. Yet another motif in Northwood's extensive line of swung vases, these vases occur in ice blue and ice green (see Fig. 739) as well as

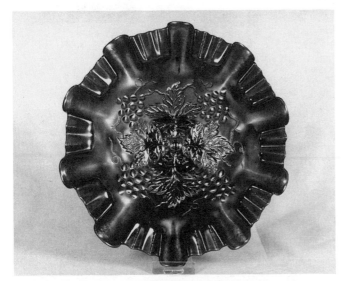
Grape Leaves bowl in blue Carnival glass (note the interesting pie-crust edge). **Courtesy of the Fenton Museum.**

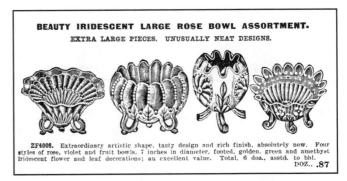

BEAUTY IRIDESCENT LARGE ROSE BOWL ASSORTMENT.
EXTRA LARGE PIECES. UNUSUALLY NEAT DESIGNS.

ZF4008. Extraordinary artistic shape, tasty design and rich finish, absolutely new. Four styles of rose, violet and fruit bowls, 7 inches in diameter, footed, golden, green and amethyst iridescent flower and leaf decorations; an excellent value. Total, 6 doz., asstd. to bbl.
DOZ., .87

Northwood rose bowls and candy dishes from a catalog issued by Charles Broadway Rouss (February, 1912). Note that they are called "rose, violet and fruit bowls."

an aqua shade which lacks the soft pastel usually associated with Northwood's aqua opalescent.

Lightning Flower. Presznick lists two pieces in this pattern, a 6" compote and a 9" plate, and she indicates that both had been found in several Carnival glass colors. John Britt recalls a small nappy with Lightning Flower on the exterior and a Pansy motif inside; this piece displayed the N-in-a-circle. Lightning Flower is well-known in the heavily gold-painted "goofus" glass (McKinley, p. 96, calls it Poppy) as well as emerald green; the N-in-a-circle is present on these. The flowers and rather stilted stems recall an earlier Northwood pattern, Mikado (Flower and Bud).

Lovely (also known as Northwood's Lovely). This pattern occurs as an interior motif on Leaf and Beads candy dishes (see Fig. 593). The one shown has 30 points and is a good purple iridescence. These are also known in green, but either color is hard to find.

Lustre Flute. Made in opalescent glass about 1908, the items known in Carnival are obviously a rebirth of the pattern. Three iridescent Lustre Flute items (two-handled bon-bon, small crimped nappie, and crimped tumbler) are shown in the spring, 1909 Butler Brothers catalog. A tumbler crimped somewhat differently is the lone Lustre Flute item in a later Butler Brothers assortment (October, 1909). Five Lustre Flute items—including the creamer, spooner and punch cup—

appear in a 1909 catalog issued by G. Sommers & Co., a St. Paul, Minnesota, wholesale firm which was most active in the Great Plains. The color is described as "a beautiful shade of green in semi-transparent iridescent effect." This is probably Northwood's marigold iridescence applied to emerald green glass (see Figs. 395-397). The punch cup is also known in green and purple Carnival glass.

Near-Cut. This is Northwood's No. 12 line from mid-1906 reborn, usually in marigold Carnival. Just a few pieces are recorded—pitcher, tumbler and goblet—so it would seem that a water set was the extent of its rebirth. The tumbler and goblet (see Fig. 580) are also known in purple Carnival, and Hartung mentioned a purple compote. Many different items are known in crystal, so more Carnival articles could turn up. Look for the N-in-a-circle.

Nippon. This pattern, which is found only on the interior of large bowls and plates (the exterior is Thin Ribs or, rarely, Basketweave), is often confused with a Fenton pattern called Peacock Tail. A flat plate is among the Northwood items in a Butler Brothers iridescent assortment for Mid-spring, 1912. Sizes range from about 8" to 9" in diameter, and items are known in marigold, purple, green, white, ice green and ice blue (Fig. 384). John Britt reports a few pie-crust edge bowls in lime green opalescent.

Octet. A footed berry bowl with eight large scallops on its rim and Northwood's Vintage on the exterior is the sole article in this design. The interior is an eight-petalled stylized flower with dots radiating from the ends of the petals. These are known in marigold, green, purple, white and ice green.

Panelled Holly (also called Holly Star). This is another resurrection of a pattern line introduced earlier (in 1908), but Northwood seems to have made only a few articles in Carnival glass. A 1909 catalog issued by G. Sommers & Co. shows a Panelled Holly two-handled bon-bon, which was likely made from the spooner mould. A purple pitcher and a marigold spooner (Fig. 410) are known, and perhaps other articles will turn up. This pattern bears some similarities to the holly motif on the mysterious Christmas compote.

Petals (Hartung 4, 58). The only articles in this seldom seen motif are low compotes and 7" plates. John Britt reports the compote in marigold, purple and green as well as a rare example in ice blue; these have the N-in-a-circle. The pattern is on the interior.

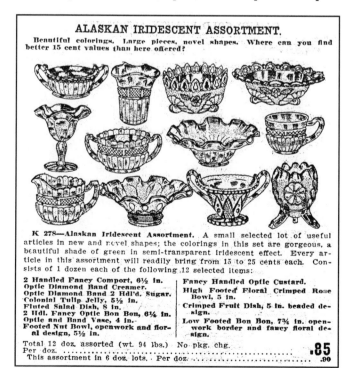

From a 1909 G. Sommers & Co. catalog. Note the five items in Lustre Flute and the two pieces in Wild Rose as well as the Panelled Holly bon bon and the Daisy and Plume rose bowl.

Plums and Cherries. Heacock's pattern name for the scarce Northwood line in decorated crystal discussed in the previous chapter ought to be retained for the few known Carnival glass items. A good-sized spooner in purple Carnival glass with excellent iridescence is on the outside back cover of this book, and John and Lucile Britt recently featured a tumbler which bears the N-in-a-circle (HOACGA *Bulletin,* June, 1990). The Britts note that the eight-paneled tumbler is shaped much like tumblers in well-known Northwood patterns—Dandelion, Greek Key, Oriental Poppy, Singing Birds, Springtime, and Wishbone—all of which were in production around 1912 (see Fig. 358 for a crystal tumbler). Edwards called this pattern "Two Fruits" in his *Encyclopedia* (1989), and he also reports a lidless sugar bowl. Since Fenton also made a well-known Two Fruits pattern, the name Plums and Cherries is preferable.

Poinsettia Lattice. Although these bowls are sometimes called simply Poinsettia, the full name is more descriptive (see Fig. 556). Known Carnival colors are marigold, blue, purple, ice blue and white as well as aqua opalescent. Heacock documented bowls in several opalescent hues—flint, blue and canary (see Fig. 721)—as well as Ivory (custard) glass which often bears characteristic Northwood decoration (see Figs. 720 and 788).

Poppy. Just a single article, an oval pickle dish, usually with crimped sides, occurs in this well-executed floral design (see Fig. 706). This item does, however, exist in a number of Carnival colors: marigold, light amethyst, blue, green, purple, white, ice blue and aqua opalescent. Like some other Carnival pieces, it was also made in Ivory (custard) in late 1914 (see Fig. 799). At least one of these is known with the N-in-a-circle.

Poppy Show. Like Rose Show, these bowls and plates are attributed to Northwood on the basis of known Carnival glass colors—marigold, blue, purple, white, ice blue, ice green and aqua opalescent (see Figs. 376, 437-438, 519 and 545). None is marked with the N-in-a-circle. Within recent years, this pattern has been very popular with Carnival glass collectors, especially when the iridescence is very good or the color a rare one.

Rainbow. These are perfectly plain pieces, but the name is derived from the iridescence. A compote and a crimped bowl appear in a Butler Brothers catalog for April, 1909, along with other Northwood items such as Lustre Flute, Panelled Holly and Wild Rose. These same two pieces appear in the "Pompeiian" assortment in a June,

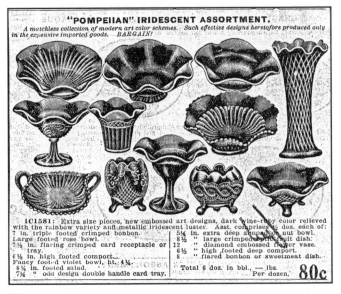

The Pompeiian assortment of Northwood's iridescent glass appeared in Butler Brothers catalogs throughout August-December, 1909.

1910, Butler Brothers catalog. A pie crust edge bowl is shown in this book (see Fig. 398). The small compote has been found in marigold Carnival with souvenir lettering and a 1909 date.

Rose Show and *Rose Show Variant.* Like Poppy Show, these plates and bowls are credited to Northwood because of the design, which Heacock noted is similar to Frosted Leaf and Basketweave, and by virtue of the confirmed Carnival glass colors—marigold, blue, green, purple, white, ice blue, ice green and aqua opalescent-as well as extraordinary examples in aqua (no opalescence), marigold over Ivory (custard) and lime green opalescent. Within recent years, unusual examples of Rose Show have been quite popular among Carnival glass fanciers, setting several price records at auctions.

Rose Show pieces typically have a gently scalloped rim (see Figs. 439-440, 547, 684, 686, and 715), while the Rose Show Variant has a sawtooth-type edge with 66 scallops as well as differences among the flowers on the interior (John Britt reports only two colors in Rose Show Variant, marigold and blue). No specimens with the N-in-a-circle have yet come to light, and further research continues on this design. For a blue opalescent (not iridized) example of Rose Show, see Fig. 193.

Rosette. The interior of these bowls resembles Stippled Rays, but some rosettes and prism-shaped ribs have been added. The N-in-a-circle is prominently displayed on a button in the center. The bowls typically have eight gentle scallops and have been found in marigold, green and purple. One of these bowls appears in the "Pompeiian" assortment in a June, 1910, Butler Brothers catalog.

Ruffles and Rings. This is a well-known pattern in opalescent glass from about 1906, and it may have been made by both the Northwood and Jefferson firms, unless, of course, Northwood acquired the moulds from Jefferson. A flint opalescent bowl was the basis for an interesting and unusual piece of Northwood Carnival glass with marigold iridescence in the interior (see Fig. 714).

Star of David and Bows. This motif resembles the Ribbons and Overlapping Squares motif in Northwood's Verre D'or line from 1906 (see Figs. 213-214), but the center is indeed a six-pointed Star of David made by overlapping triangles. The footed bowl, which is known in marigold, amethyst and green, typically has the Vintage back pattern.

Stippled Rays. An otherwise plain compote with Stippled Rays interior is depicted in the April, 1909, Butler Brothers catalog among other Northwood items.

Strawberry. These plates and bowls vary in diameter from 5" to 10," so a berry set can be assembled. Articles may be plain on the exterior, or they may have either the Thin Ribs exterior or the Basketweave exterior (see Figs. 442-443). A wide variety of Carnival colors can be found—marigold, blue, purple, green, ice green and, rarely, aqua opalescent; the edge may be curled to make a "hand grip plate (Fig. 379). John Britt recalls two examples in a "true smoke" color. The bowls or plates which exhibit heavy stippling in the center area (Fig. 441) are called Stippled Strawberries by many Carnival glass collectors. Those items with stippling also have three thin rings circumscribing the Strawberry pattern and usually exhibit the Thin Ribs exterior. This pattern is similar to Wild Strawberry.

Strawberry (Intaglio Line). These thick, heavy sauces and large, low bowls were part of the Intaglio line in 1906, as were the Cherries (see Fig. 429) and the Apples and Pears motifs. The lone Carnival color is marigold.

Swirl and *Interior Swirl and Panel.* Like Northwood's Pretty Panels, the tumblers in this design have the pattern on the inside surface. In his *Carnival Glass Tumblers,* Owens describes the "twenty-one swirls which move in a northeasterly direction when viewed through the glass," and he notes that the N-in-a-circle is almost always present. The pitchers are not so marked. A wholesale catalog from 1909 shows three Swirl pitchers in "Golden Iridescent," the Butler Brothers' euphemism for Northwood's Golden Iris (marigold).

Three Northwood swirl motif pitchers from a Spring, 1909, Butler Brothers catalog. "Golden Iridescent" means marigold Carnival glass.

The tall tankard is known in marigold (Fig. 367) as are a tall pitcher (Fig. 290) and a smaller, colonial style pitcher (Fig. 369), which is known as Interior Swirl and Panel; this latter piece has the N-in-a-circle. A green tankard in Swirl (Fig. 400) has marigold iridescence which is quite pronounced near its top. Edwards reports an unmarked mug in his *Encyclopedia* (1989, pp. 198-9), but there is some doubt concerning whether or not this pattern matches the known Northwood Swirl motifs.

Sunflower. This is yet another Carnival glass rebirth of a novelty made earlier, since a Sunflower plate in "goofus" is shown in Butler Brothers fall, 1908 catalog. Bowls and plates in Carnival are known in marigold, blue, purple and green, and John Britt reports a few in ice blue. Typically, the exterior pattern on the footed bowls is Meander.

Three Fruits. The bowls and plates in this design depict three of Northwood's favorite fruits—cherries, pears and peaches (see Figs. 422, 432-436, 688, 705, and 716-717 for a look at variations). Some pieces are known in opalescent glass (Fig. 249) as well as Ivory (custard) glass (Fig. 785), the latter having been made about 1914-15. A ruffled Carnival bowl appears in the "Pompeiian" assortment in a June, 1910, Butler Brothers catalog.

A similar pattern, called Three Fruits Medallion (or Three Fruits Variant in Edwards' *Encyclopedia*) has the Meander exterior (see Figs. 432 and 436). This pattern has a close cousin, Fruits and Flowers.

Thin Rib. This exterior or back pattern appears on such bowls as Northwood's Poppy, Strawberry, and Good Luck as well as the unusual Peacocks on the Fence bowl in iridized blue marble glass which is shown on this book's cover (see Fig. 719).

Tornado. These small vases, which range from about 5 1/4" to 6 1/2" tall, could easily be mistaken for Tiffany or Carder creations, for the iridescence is excellent, and the shape and design are quite atypical of Northwood in light of his fondness for realistic fruit and floral motifs. All seem to have the N-in-a-circle, however, and Carnival glass collectors report them in marigold, green, purple, white and ice blue. The background is usually smooth, but some are faintly ribbed (see Figs. 388-390). Don Moore pictured a marigold Tornado vase with a pedestal base in his *Complete Guide to Carnival Glass Rarities* (p. 49), and several notes about them were published in ICGA's *Carnival Pump* in 1983.

Town Pump. This distinctive novelty immediately recalls the Pump and Trough made in opalescent glass by Northwood at Indiana, Pennsylvania, in the late 1890s (see *The Early Years*, p. 134). The Wheeling-era Pump was apparently made only in Carnival glass, and collectors report them in marigold, green and purple (Fig. 621). These typically carry the N-in-a-circle.

There is some evidence available to date the production of the Town Pump. The National Association held a Joint Conference (meeting of manufacturers and representatives of the AFGWU) in Pittsburgh on January 12, 1912. The participants agreed upon the move and wages for "a pump vase" at Northwood's plant. The skilled workers were required to produce 650 vases per

turn of 4 1/2 hours for which they were paid $1.30 to $2.00.

Tree Trunk vases. Northwood's production of "swung" vases goes back to the early opalescent production at Wheeling (c. 1904), so it is not surprising to find so many different sizes and shapes in Carnival glass Tree Trunk vases. These vary from 7" to over 18" in height, and the base diameter varies, too (see Figs. 576, 707, 712-713, 725, 728-729, and 733). The outer surface really does resemble rough tree bark, as the glass depicts various bumps, curved lines, and even some knots! When a vase has been swung to create considerable elongation, these knots take on the appearance of tadpoles.

The larger specimens are often called "funeral" vases by Carnival glass collectors. Tree Trunk vases occur in the full range of Northwood's Carnival glass colors: marigold, blue, green, purple, white, ice blue, ice green and aqua opalescent. The N-in-a-circle is present on most Tree Trunk vases. Custard glass collectors have reported several sizes of Tree Trunk vases with Northwood's characteristic pink stain. Care should be taken to distinguish unmarked examples of Northwood's Tree Trunk from the similar Fenton "Rustic" vases.

Valentine. This is Northwood's No. 14 pattern, which was offered in clear glass in the fall, 1906, catalog. In a HOACGA newsletter, Don Moore reported a marigold bowl bearing the N-in-a-circle, and sauce dishes are also mentioned in his *Carnival Glass* (p. 145).

Vintage. Like Northwood's Basketweave, this is an exterior or back pattern, used on the underside of bowls or plates. It is seen on Three Fruits articles and on the bowls in Octet and Star of David and Bows. Notley reported bowls in Three Fruits with the Basketweave exterior which also had "traces of a vintage grape design" (*Journal* 1, p. 8). See Heacock's *Fenton Glass: The First Twenty-five Years* for Fenton's Vintage pattern.

Wheat. Just two articles, a covered compote or sweetmeat (Fig. 579) and a covered bowl, are known in this scarce Carnival glass motif. Both are known in purple, and the compote, which resembles its counterpart in Grape and Cable, also occurs in green. All carry the N-in-a-circle.

Wide Panel Epergne. This spectacular piece follows in the footsteps of the similar opalescent epergnes shown in Northwood's 1906 catalog. Northwood's inspiration for these epergnes surely came from England (Barbara Morris shows a number of nineteenth century examples in her *Victorian Table Glass and Ornaments*).

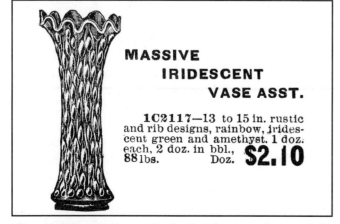

Tree Trunk vase from a Butler Brothers catalog, c. 1912.

Fall, 1909, Butler Brothers catalog.

The Wide Panel epergne was shown in Butler Brothers catalogs as early as the fall of 1909, when it was offered in "emerald green glass cleverly enriched with rainbow hued iridescent tones." This catalog cut remained unchanged for nearly three years until the epergne was offered in "crystal, blue and green glass [with] pearl iridescent finish." Northwood's Wide Panel epergne is known in marigold, amethyst, blue, green, ice blue, ice green and white as well as aqua opalescent. The N-in-a-circle may be found inside the base (see Figs. 355, 695 and 710-711).

Butler Brothers catalog (April, 1913).

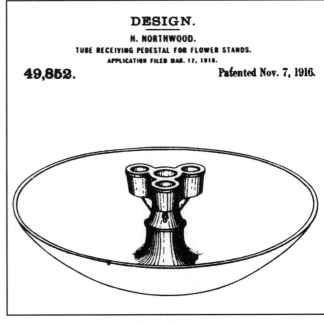

Detail from Northwood's design patent.

Harry Northwood patented a design for the "tube-receiving pedestal" apparatus in 1916, noting that "widely varying forms of bases ... may be employed" in addition to the plain one depicted in the patent drawing.

Wildflower. This motif is an exterior pattern, found on the outside of Northwood's Blossomtime compote (see Fig. 587).

Wild Rose (also called Shell and Wild Rose). This novelty was made in opalescent glass by Northwood about 1906, and the mould must have been used later for Carnival production (see Figs. 391-392). Two shapes, an open bowl and a candy dish made from it by flaring the rim, appear in a 1909 catalog issued by G. Sommers & Co. Neither article carries the N-in-a-circle. Incidentally, the openwork border is an unusual undertaking for Northwood, and Carnival glass collectors have noticed variations in feet and the marie, as well as stippling. Research continues into similar Dugan products.

Wild Strawberry. This pattern is much like Northwood's Strawberry, but Wild Strawberry features blossoms as well as berries. The Basketweave exterior is typically found on shallow bowls which are 9" to 9 1/2" in diameter. These are known in marigold, purple, green, ice green and white. The N-in-a-circle is on the outside of the marie.

Decorated Carnival Glass

In addition to the patterns listed earlier and the novelties detailed immediately above, mention should also be made of Northwood's many decorated Carnival glass pitchers and tumblers. Cecil Whitley has compiled a delightful study of the tumblers, *The World of Enameled Carnival Glass Tumblers*. Her book and materials from HOACGA were most valuable here.

Decorated tumblers were part and parcel of Northwood's abiding interest in lemonade sets, of course, so it is not surprising to find Carnival glass given treatments similar to Northwood's other decorated wares. The tumblers range from dark blue Carnival to marigold Carnival. The decoration typically appears just once on each tumbler.

The Apple Blossom tumbler appears on the cover of the Whitley book mentioned above. It is generally a straight-sided blue tumbler with 14 interior panels and good iridescence. The decora-

tion consists of a yellow flower overlapping a pink-white blossom. The accompanying pitcher, which is shown in the HOACGA booklet as number 128 in cobalt blue Carnival, appears to be like the pitcher shown as Fig. 300 in this book. The Anemone decoration is documented as number 127 in this same booklet.

Cherries and Little Flowers is found on a dark blue tumbler which has a ground bottom. These have the N-in-a-circle, and the iridescence is good both inside and outside (the underside of the bottom is not iridized). The pitcher with matching decoration is shaped like Fig. 402.

Both Cherries, Ground and Daisy and Little Flowers are on the same kinds of tumblers, which are dark cobalt blue with fine iridescence. There are a dozen panels inside, and the tumbler tapers gracefully to an attractive base. The Cherries,

Ground pitcher and tumbler appear in this book (see Figs. 309-310, and the Cherries and Little Flowers pitcher is the same shape as Fig. 402 (these are known in marigold, amethyst and blue Carnival glass).

A decoration called Cosmos (HOACGA booklet, number 136) is found in marigold Carnival on a pitcher shaped like Figs. 290 and 292. The Periwinkle tumbler, typically found in marigold Carnival, has ten interior panels, and the matching pitcher is shaped like Fig. 402, although the HOACGA booklet shows another Periwinkle decoration with a pitcher shaped like Figs. 290 and 292.

The Pretty Panels tumblers take their name from the decoration and the vertical panels, which are on the inside (there are 18, although Hartung first reported 20 in her book 8, p. 46). The panels, like the N-in-a-circle, are imparted by the plunger during the pressing process. The smooth exterior surface is often decorated with painted flowers, such as those in the Cara Nome style. These tumblers are also found in emerald green and satin-finished crystal (not iridized) as well as marigold and green Carnival hues. The non-Carnival tumblers will make up a water set with almost any one of Northwood's many decorated pitchers (see Figs. 301-314 for color photos of many of these). In Carnival glass, the Pretty Panels tumblers may have been grouped with the tall tankard pitcher called Wide Panel Variant in Edward's *Encyclopedia* (1989). This pitcher is known in marigold and in white, and it may be decorated with both gold and enamel paint in a myriad of styles.

In 1984, Don Moore sent Bill Heacock a photo of still another decorated pitcher with a set of

The "Connie" water set.

matching tumblers. Subsequently, the "Connie" tumbler was named for Don Moore's wife. It looks a lot like Pretty Panels decorated with blue and pink flowers in a style much like Cara Nome. At first, this water set was classified as Carnival in "white," but careful study suggests that the light iridescence on this set is due to satin-finishing with acid rather than to the spraying method typically used for Carnival glass.

These pieces do not exhibit the irregularities typically found on sprayed Carnival glass pieces—small droplets here and there, changes in thickness, differentiations in iridescence, etc. Furthermore, the Connie tumblers (like some green Pretty Panels tumblers) have no iridescence on their drinking rims, an effect that would have been difficult, if not impossible, to produce with spraying. In short, these pieces are a definitional quandry: they exhibit a measure of iridescence, but they are not, strictly speaking, Carnival glass.

The Jefferson Mould Mystery

Some of Northwood's Carnival wares have a great similarity to articles known to have been made in opalescent glass by the Jefferson Glass Company of Steubenville, Ohio. There is no doubt that Northwood bought some moulds from the Jefferson firm, probably when the latter relocated to West Virginia in 1906-07.

Connections between Harry Northwood and the Jefferson firm are many. When Northwood went to England in late 1899, the Jefferson firm was not yet formed. When it commenced in 1900, Harry Bastow, who had been a manager at

Northwood's Indiana plant, was its president. The January 5, 1901 issue of *Housefurnisher: China, Glass and Pottery Review* said the Jefferson had "the best talent obtainable" and added that "Mr. Bastow was formerly with the Northwood Co. and will have full scope for elaborating his ideas and improving on the fine effects he has already secured." Bastow's vice-president was George Mortimer, who had been a Northwood salesman at the Indiana, Pa., plant (Mortimer later joined Northwood's Wheeling firm in early 1905). George Pownall, a long-time friend who had been at Northwood's Martins Ferry, Ellwood City and Indiana plants, was the Jefferson's "chief decorator," according to the *Housefurnisher.*

Henry Findt, whose association with Northwood went back to the La Belle Glass Company in 1887, was a manager at Jefferson, and Frank Leslie Fenton, who was an apprentice decorator at Indiana in 1897, was also there, as were his brothers Robert and John. Bastow remained with the Jefferson concern until August, 1903, when he left for Coudersport, Pennsylvania, and refurbished a glass factory there. The Fenton brothers went with him. When that plant burned in late 1903, Frank Leslie Fenton found employment at the Northwood firm in Wheeling for a time before launching his own decorating business in Martins Ferry. Ironically, the Fenton enterprise was located in the old Northwood plant in Martins Ferry, which had been occupied by several tenants between late 1900 and 1905.

The Jefferson Glass Company made opalescent pattern lines and novelties between 1901 and 1906, and some of these were advertised in Butler Brothers assortments. Heacock traced several opalescent novelty pieces to Jefferson (Fine Cut and Roses, Meander, Ruffles and Rings, and Vintage); these were Jefferson's #249, #233, #208 and #245, respectively. Each of these occurs in Carnival glass also, sometimes with the distinctive N-in-a-circle.

In the second edition of his *Opalescent Glass from A to Z*, Heacock wondered "how the molds were transferred from Jefferson to Northwood." In *CG3* (p. 17), he suggested that Northwood purchased the Vintage mould from Jefferson. The correspondence files of the National Association of Manufacturers of Pressed and Blown Glassware provide the evidence. On August 5, 1909, Harry Northwood wrote to the National Association regarding the appropriate move and wages for a low foot comport, and he mentioned that his firm had purchased this mould "from the Jefferson Glass Company ...." By late 1906, the Jefferson firm had decided to move its operation from Steubenville to Follansbee, West Virginia, where a larger, more modern plant was constructed for them. Perhaps some moulds were sold at this time or shortly thereafter, when the new Jefferson firm was located just a few miles north of Wheeling. Northwood's sketch of the item, which accompanied his letter, shows no pattern, but the general shape of the item reminds one of the Meander pieces.

Despite the many popular stories about moulds moving from factory to factory, this Jefferson-Northwood transaction is one of a mere handful of such instances to be found in the National Association files. Nonetheless, the implications for glass collectors who value the history of their glass are significant. What conclusions can be drawn here? The unmarked opalescent items in these four motifs (Fine Cut and Roses, Meander, Ruffles and Rings, and Vintage) are probably Jefferson products, made at Steubenville. Any marked (N-in-a-circle) opalescent or carnival examples are, of course, Northwood-made, and they date from about 1908 and thereafter.

Northwood Carnival: In Conclusion

This chapter and the accompanying 360-plus color illustrations of Northwood Carnival glass cross-referenced in the text may be the most ambitious study yet undertaken of this remarkable glassware. Every effort has been made to provide details regarding pattern elements as well as colors known. Many dates of production can be inferred from trade journal advertising and/or Butler Brothers catalogs, bringing a chronology to much hitherto undated Carnival glass.

Nonetheless, nagging questions of description, attribution and color remain. Each issue of the various Carnival glass collector club newsletters brings forth both new information and questions to be answered. The frequent Carnival glass auctions and yearly club conventions offer more knowledge and further questions. At the 1991 convention of the American Carnival Glass Association in Parkersburg, West Virginia, an excited member displayed a Poppy and Scroll ruffled bowl in marigold Carnival (see Fig. 889 for a similar item in crystal), much to the amazement of fellow club members. The search continues. One wonders what Harry Northwood would think of it all!

CHAPTER FIVE
LIGHTING GOODS AND LUNA GLASS

Almost all previous writers on Northwood glass have concentrated on his production of tableware, ranging from the unique blown ware made at Martins Ferry in the early 1890s and the pressed custard (Ivory) glass produced at Indiana to the opalescent and carnival patterns and novelties from Wheeling. It may surprise some to know that Northwood was involved with lighting goods of one sort or another throughout most of his glassmaking career. In fact, the peak years of lighting goods production (1914-1920) were among the most profitable years in the history of Northwood's Wheeling plant.

This chapter will focus upon the lighting goods made at Wheeling (readers may also consult *Harry Northwood: The Early Years, 1881-1900,* esp. pp. 15-17, 29-30, 38, 45, 50-51, 55, 89, and 110-112) . When the Northwood plant commenced production in 1902, the United States was in the midst of an important technological change, namely, the shift away from kerosene illumination to electricity, which was being brought to every major city and to increasing numbers of households in rural areas as well. Harry Northwood must have been well aware of these developments, for the products of the Wheeling plant, especially his Luna glass, sought to meet the changing needs of consumers for lighting goods.

Lighting Goods 1903-1910
The first information about Northwood lighting goods is rather general. On June 12, 1903, the secretary of the National Association of Manufacturers of Pressed and Blown Glassware responded to a query from the Northwood firm regarding "opalescent stand lamps." These are the typical kerosene lamp consisting of a font (or bowl) and a base which come in various sizes ranging from hand lamps to tall table lamps.

In September, 1904, correspondence between the Northwood plant and the National Association mentioned "blown stand lamps with ribbed bowls," but no other specifics are given. One letter to Northwood, dated September 3, 1904, mentioned that similar lamps were being made at the Dugan Glass Company in Indiana, Pennsylvania, which had been formed in early 1904 and purchased the Northwood Glass Works from the National Glass Company, which had held title since 1900. Unfortunately, the correspondence includes no sketches or dimensions, so the exact nature of these lamps remains unknown.

The reference above to "opalescent stand lamps" probably refers to the kerosene lamp called "Primrose" in Thuro's *Oil Lamps* (p. 268). Lamps similar to Primrose, but which have a decorated bowl rather than an opalescent bowl, are pictured and described in the 1906 Northwood catalog. The bowl has "fired on Tinted Matt Ground and raised Enameled Decorations" which were obviously intended to simulate the commercial cameo wares produced in British factories, including the Stevens and Williams firm in Stourbridge where Harry Northwood's half-brother John was employed. The geometric-style decorations on these lamps are reminiscent of those on the #32 tableware line (Belladonna).

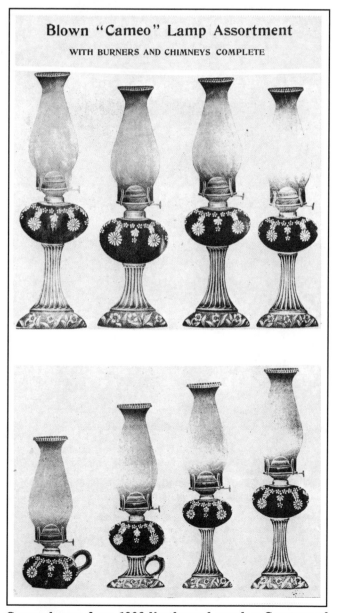

Cameo lamps from 1906 Northwood catalog. **Courtesy of Steve Jennings.**

Courtesy of Kerry Bachler.

The bases of some of these lamps were ruby-stained on the inside, but this decoration was not fired on and is subject to wear. Some have heavy, goofus-type gold on the inside of the lamp bases, too. All of these lamps have a threaded coupling that allows the bowls and stems to be interchangeable, so quite a variety of combinations is possible.

Undecorated hand lamps in Primrose with plain bowls are known with the characteristic Northwood N-in-a-circle mark on the underside of the base. Another lighting item which bears the

Courtesy of Kerry Bachler.

N-in-a-circle is an attractive hand lamp with a ribbed optic bowl and a grape and leaves motif on the inside of the base. The time of production is not known, but the design is certainly similar to Northwood's Grape and Cable pattern, which was in full swing in 1910.

In a brief note about Northwood's 1904 products, the October, 1904, issue of *Glass and Pottery World* mentioned "electric globes" without elaboration. The 1906 Northwood catalog illustrates several "crystal gas shades." All had 4 inch fitters (the approximate diameter of the collar), and some were available in either round or crimped styles.

The shade designated No. 8 appears to be that which is known as Astral to collectors today. A similar shade is credited to the Imperial Glass Co. (see Greguire, p. 20), but Hartung (10, p. 11) reports Astral shades in Carnival glass which have "Northwood" in block letters moulded into the glass in the fitter area which is normally covered by some part of the light fixture. The shade designated No. 5 is surely Hartung's Olympus (7, p. 60; see also 10, p. 26 for another Olympus). The No. 2 shade is similar to Hartung's Daisy Chain (7, p. 45).

These shades shown in the 1906 Northwood catalog probably remained in production for quite some time, as four of them appeared in Butler

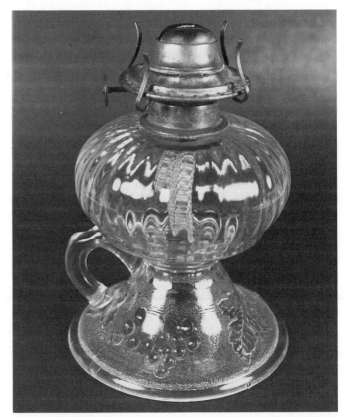

Note the similarity of the pattern on this lamp to Northwood's Grape and Cable.

Crystal Gas Shades

4 INCH FITTER

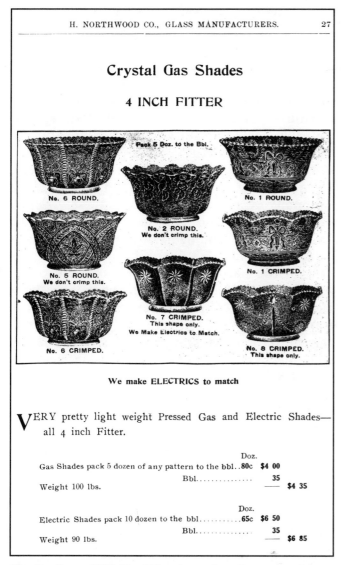

Pack 5 Doz. to the Bbl.

No. 6 ROUND.

No. 1 ROUND.

No. 2 ROUND.
We don't crimp this.

No. 5 ROUND.
We don't crimp this.

No. 1 CRIMPED.

No. 7 CRIMPED.
This shape only.
We Make Electrics to Match.

No. 6 CRIMPED.

No. 8 CRIMPED.
This shape only.

We make ELECTRICS to match

VERY pretty light weight Pressed Gas and Electric Shades—all 4 inch Fitter.

	Doz.		
Gas Shades pack 5 dozen of any pattern to the bbl..80c	$4 00		
Weight 100 lbs.	Bbl..............	35	$4 35

	Doz.		
Electric Shades pack 10 dozen to the bbl...........65c	$6 50		
Weight 90 lbs.	Bbl..............	35	$6 85

Shades from 1906 Northwood catalog. **Courtesy of Steve Jennings.**

Sketch by Harry Northwood, c. 1907.

Brothers catalogs throughout most of 1909 as the "Crystal Star Gas Shade Assortment." Another Northwood shade, the "Star Panel Gas Shade," also appears in a few Butler Brothers catalogs, again in 1909 (this shade is like No. 7 in the 1906 Northwood catalog).

Both Presznick (2, pl. 289) and Greguire credit Northwood with the production of a kerosene lamp in marigold Carnival glass. It's called Northwood "Wild Rose," and there is a fine illustration in Greguire's book, *Carnival in Lights* (p. 11). Northwood's Grape and Cable candlelamp (candlestick base plus matching shade) is known in three Carnival glass colors: marigold, green and purple (see Figs. 650 and 656 and Greguire, p. 13, for an excellent close-up of the fixture which holds the shade). Some other Carnival glass shades are discussed in the "Luna Glass" section below.

Correspondence between the National Association and Northwood during 1912-14 mentions pressed gas and electric shades which have 4" or 5" fitters. On April 2, 1914, Northwood sent samples of three electric shades—Numbers 1, 48 and 49—to the National Association office, but no further information is revealed in this or any other letter. In 1918, more correspondence discussed "opalescent" shades, but no ware numbers or other specifications were given. It seems probable that these shades were Northwood's Luna glass.

Luna Glass

In 1911-12, Harry Northwood made many experimental batches of an alabaster-like, opaque white glass. His notebooks detail dozens of trials, all focused upon developing a unique opaque white glass especially suitable for electric light shades, including large ceiling fixtures which could be drilled easily so that chains for hanging could be attached. Later, as an alternative to drilling, special clamps were developed.

A brief entry dated November, 1911, in Northwood's notebook discusses "a dense alabaster for Electric light shades and globes" (this entry is located just a page or two away from discussions of alabaster batches used at Northwood's Ellwood City plant in July, 1894). A separate notebook, devoted almost exclusively to Luna batches between 1912 and 1914, recounts the trials which led to success. A Luna batch dated March 18, 1913, was highlighted as the "Standard Batch" in one of Northwood's notebooks, and he noted that it was a "good working soft glass." Apparently, an August 25,

1913, Luna batch proved superior, as Northwood called it "excellent," adding "drills fine," and concluding that it was the "Best glass we ever made. Good for blown balls. Dense and no specks." An additional note reveals that this was the standard batch as of "this writing, Sept. 15th [1913]."

The earliest mention of Luna in the glass trade publications may be a brief note in the September 26, 1912, issue of *Pottery, Glass and Brass Salesman* which mentions longtime Northwood representative Frank Miller of New York: The H. Northwood Co., of Wheeling, W. Va., have just sent to their New York representative, Frank M. Miller, at 25 West Broadway, samples of a new line of lighting glassware which they have just brought out. One of the features of this new line is the "Luna" glass. This has a pearly white appearance and is well adapted to use in electric shades, etc. Its attractive nature will doubtless make a strong appeal to many. The samples thus far received include various sizes and shapes of shades for shower and other fixtures, as well as some large bowls for lighting large rooms." This account also calls attention to "shades made of iridescent glass in a broad range of colors, by means of which some unusual illumination effects are produced." Since Carnival glass was in production at this time, these shades could be the effects called "pearl" and "lustre" in the Luna catalog discussed below.

In addition to his own experimentation, Northwood also corresponded with other glassmakers, and he probably tried glass batches obtained from others. A short letter, dated October 3, 1910, from Northwood to A. H. Heisey in Newark, Ohio, reads as follows: "Re Alabaster. Formula calls for Salt Peter (Nitrate of Potassium). I'm afraid you are using Nitrate of Soda. Yours very truly, Harry Northwood." One notebook entry for "Luna Moonstone" credits a formula to H. Findt of the Jefferson Glass Company at nearby Follansbee, West Virginia. Northwood and Findt had been colleagues at the La Belle in 1887, and he made a trial pot of Findt's formula on August 23, 1915, observing that it was "rather too hard & costs more than our own." Another trial, "from John [Harry's half-brother], December, 1912," looked "exactly like Alba but too thin [and] full of particles." The use of the term Alba may be significant, as this was the trade name for lighting glassware being made by one of Northwood's major competitors, Macbeth-Evans.

The Rakow Library at Corning has a sixty-page catalog entitled "Illuminating Glassware Luna," which was issued by the Northwood company. The catalog's cover bears the stamp of a New England firm, Stuart-Howland of Boston, who were probably one of the Northwood's representatives. The catalog is undated, but it was issued sometime after February, 1913, since

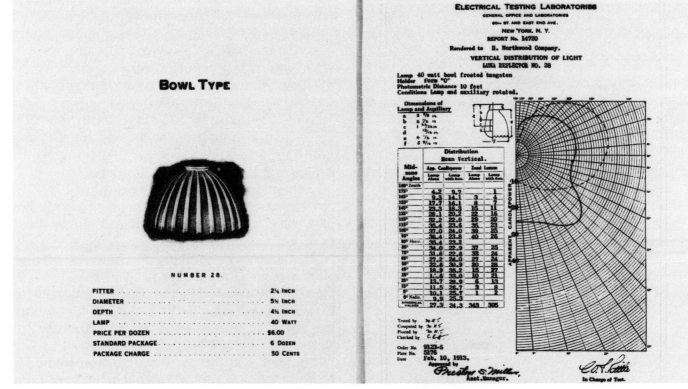

Courtesy of the Corning Museum of Glass.

SPHERES

10 INCH. GLASS ONLY. EACH	$ 3.00
12 INCH. GLASS ONLY. EACH	5.00
14 INCH. GLASS ONLY. EACH	10.00
16 INCH. GLASS ONLY. EACH	20.00
10 INCH. COMPLETE AS SHOWN. EACH	$ 6.50
12 INCH. COMPLETE AS SHOWN. EACH	10.00
14 INCH. COMPLETE AS SHOWN. EACH	15.00
16 INCH. COMPLETE AS SHOWN. EACH	25.00

PACKED AS DESIRED

Courtesy of the Corning Museum of Glass.

information from Electric Testing Laboratories of New York is cited throughout, and the tests were certified on February 10, 1913.

At the outset of the catalog, the virtues of Luna are extolled: "A perfect alabaster glass, free from specks and streaks. Made in correct shapes for diffusing, concentrating and distributing white light. No glare, soft as moonlight, restful to the eyes, and in every way the most up-to-the-minute lighting glass made." At the bottom of many catalog pages, the qualities of Luna are reiterated in brief phrases such as "restful vision," "no fire color," "smooth as satin," "efficient," and "artistic."

The catalog illustrates a variety of typical shades: four sizes of "semi-flared" type; five sizes of "flat" type, the largest of which is 11" in diameter; and five sizes of "bowl" type. Each of these is touted with an elaborate graph on the facing page which reports testing data on the vertical distribution of light for the shade in question. At least some of these shades have a two-digit number and the word "Luna" in block letters moulded into the glass in the fitter (the shade in Fig. 813 has "10 Luna" in the fitter).

A "Louis XIV Bowl" light fixture is shown, and four sizes are listed, ranging from 14" to 23" in diameter; the largest sold for $36.00 each (see Fig. 784). A few hemispheres, spheres and semi-indirect bowls are also illustrated, as are some gas shades. Among the more distinctive products are the 16" Gothic Bowl and the 16" Number 516 bowl, both of which are electric shades, and two electric shades called Sheffield and Venetian. The Sheffield and Venetian shades may have "Northwood" in block letters moulded into the glass in the fitter area which is normally covered by some part of the light fixture. Both the plain Sheffield and the distinctive Venetian were available in Luna glass as well as an iridized Luna called "pearl," which has the character of white Carnival glass; collectors often refer to Sheffield and Venetian, respectively, as Flared Panel and Pillar and Drape (or Square Pillar and Drape).

A third finish, called "lustre," was also available; this is illustrated in color in the catalog, so there can be no doubt that the term "lustre" refers to that which Carnival collectors today call marigold iridescence. The marigold iridescence

Venetian (Pillar and Drape) and Sheffield (Flared Panel) shades with Northwood's "lustre" finish (marigold Carnival).

Detail of fitter with distinctive Northwood marking.

163

Sheffield shade with Northwood's "pearl" finish.

covers up the white Luna glass to a great extent, of course, and some collectors refer to the total effect as "peach opalescent" (see Greguire, pp. 28-29). Greguire (p. 72) reports a shade with the lettering "Northwood No. 37," and another with the number 38 is known.

It is interesting to note that some of Northwood's Luna batch trials from his half-brother John's formula in February and March, 1913, were deemed suitable for the lustre iridescent finish, but not for regular Luna production. Northwood's comments are as follows: "No good for Luna but did for Luster ... Did well enough for Electrics with Luster ... Very smooth good working glass, but not dense enough. Would do fine for Luster shades." Obviously, the addition of the marigold iridescent finish made an otherwise unsuitable batch of glass acceptable.

Both the pearl and the lustre finishes were obtained by spraying the hot glass with a metallic salt solution, of course, and it is instructive to compare some of the wholesale prices given in this catalog for these shades. The Number 2 Sheffield shade, designed for 40 watt electric bulbs, was $4.00 per dozen in Luna plain, but twice that amount in pearl or lustre. Venetian type shades for 60 watt bulbs were $6.00 per dozen in Luna plain, but $10.00 per dozen in pearl or lustre. These sorts of iridescent shades may be those mentioned in the quote from *Pottery, Glass* *and Brass Salesman's* story of September 26, 1912, which described "shades made of iridescent glass in a broad range of colors, by means of which some unusual illumination effects are produced."

Macbeth-Evans vs. H. Northwood and Co.

The Northwood's most formidable competitor in the lighting goods line was probably the Macbeth-Evans Glass Company. Headquartered in Pittsburgh, this relatively young firm was brought about in 1889 by the merger of the separate Macbeth and Evans interests, each of which was a well-established organization in the glassmaking business. By 1915, the Macbeth-Evans organization embraced several large plants in Pennsylvania, Ohio, and Indiana, the most noteworthy being the huge factory at Charleroi, Pennsylvania.

Other glass companies were also making glass similar to Luna, often using it for lighting shades. The Jefferson Glass Company at Follansbee had its Moonstone line, and somewhat similar wares were offered by the Haskins Glass Company, which called its glass Lucida. Harry Northwood's brother-in-law, Percy J. Beaumont, operated the Union Stopper Company in Morgantown, West Virginia, and a Luna-like formula from him, dated October, 1913, is preserved in Northwood's notebook. The Beaumont firm called its lighting glass "Fer Lux."

Both George A. Macbeth and Thomas Evans had been deeply involved in lighting glassware since the days of kerosene lamps and chimneys, and the firm's publication *Fifty Years of Glass Making 1869-1919* details its interest in illuminating glass, although no mention is made of competitors' wares. A white glass called Alba was manufactured by Macbeth-Evans for both commercial and household applications, and two lines—Thebian and Decora—were developed especially for home use. These wares were protected by U. S. Patent #1,097,600 and by Reissue #13,766, which had been granted to George Macbeth on May 19 and July 7, 1914, respectively.

In November and December, 1914, Harry Northwood and Percy Beaumont corresponded about the likelihood of legal action against Northwood by Macbeth-Evans. On November 16, Northwood wrote that "it looks as if Macbeth-Evans Company is going to sue some of us for infringement of their Patent. I don't think the Patent valid, but hardly like the trouble and expense of a suit." The patent to which Northwood referred was, of course, Macbeth's formula for Alba glass. In his response, dated

November 18, 1914, Percy Beaumont suggested that "it would be to the advantage of all manufacturers making this kind of glass to pool together and help defend the suits brought by Macbeth-Evans."

In a subsequent letter to Beaumont, dated December 2, 1914, Northwood lamented that "the courts have been sustaining any inventor ... against piracy," but he acknowledged that the Macbeth-Evans firm was "the first to exploit this Glass for Lighting purposes; advertised it largely and spent lots of money to introduce it." The possibility of legal action apparently moved Harry Northwood to agree to pay Macbeth-Evans a royalty or fee which would allow his firm to make Luna glass, although Northwood's tone seems reluctant: "After much thought, we concluded to accept License for awhile, and will determine later what our future policy will be." Beaumont, in a reply to Northwood dated December 3, 1914, said he was "quite surprised to learn that you [Northwood] have accepted license yourself, but suppose that you have investigated thoroughly and have decided that this was the best plan for you to persue [sic]." Northwood's reply, dated December 4, 1914, revealed that "We are advised that the owner of a Patent can License others and make a Price Maintenance Agreement without violating the law."

A temporary licensing agreement with Macbeth-Evans had been signed on November 25, 1914, and Harry Northwood was the signator for H. Northwood and Co. This arrangement was extended several times, ceasing on December 31, 1915. A permanent licensing agreement was signed at that time. Both the temporary and the permanent agreement (which was to run until January 1, 1918) provided that Macbeth-Evans would receive royalty payments equal to 10% of Northwood's sales of Luna lighting glassware. During the term of the temporary agreement, this amounted to about $8500. The H. Northwood Co. paid Macbeth-Evans $3000 in cash, and promissory notes were signed for the $5500 balance.

Shortly after the permanent licensing agreement was signed, the Macbeth-Evans firm brought suit against the General Electric Company, alleging that lighting glassware produced in a GE plant at Fostoria, Ohio, infringed upon the Macbeth-Evans patents. Since the permanent licensing agreement between Northwood and Macbeth-Evans contained a clause which dissolved the contract if the Macbeth-Evans patents were invalidated, the Northwood firm ceased paying royalties to Macbeth-Evans, pending the outcome of the case involving General Electric. Northwood also refused to honor the promissory notes made during the temporary licensing agreement. Nonetheless, the Northwood firm continued to make monthly reports of the volume of its Luna glassware sales to Macbeth-Evans.

On September 21, 1917, the Macbeth-Evans Co. filed suit against H. Northwood and Co. in the United States District Court at Wheeling. The case seemed straightforward: Macbeth-Evans sought to enforce the terms of the permanent licensing agreement, asking that H. Northwood and Co. pay the royalty called for in the contract. Since the Northwood's monthly reports were a matter of undisputed record, the dollar amount was never in question, although Macbeth-Evans asked the court that interest be added, praying for about $36,000.

Lawyers for the Northwood firm first argued that the licensing agreement between Macbeth-Evans and Northwood should be set aside because it had been signed under duress. They charged that the prosperous Macbeth-Evans firm had, during November, 1914, threatened all makers of semi-translucent lighting goods with litigation for patent infringement unless these manufacturers agreed to pay royalties on their lighting glassware, even though they did not use the batch ingredients or procedures in the Macbeth-Evans patents.

Northwood's attorneys also said that the licensing agreement itself was a subterfuge to escape the Sherman Anti-Trust Act, which prohibited monopolies and price-fixing. They argued that the licensing agreement allowed Macbeth-Evans to set a "Schedule of Prices" on lighting glassware and that all manufacturers adhered to this listing lest they be sued by Macbeth-Evans for patent infringement. Evidence and the testimony of witnesses regarding the chemical differences between Macbeth-Evans' Alba glass and Northwood's Luna ware was ruled not admissible by the court during the trial, which began on November 24, 1919.

The court's verdict a day later was in favor of Macbeth-Evans, and a judgment of about $42,500 for damages and accrued interest was entered against H. Northwood and Co. Nonetheless, documents from the trial, which was heard at Wheeling, and a subsequent unsuccessful appeal by Northwood to the United States Circuit Court of Appeals at Phillipi, West Virginia, reveal much about the nature of the lighting glassware industry. According to Northwood's attorneys,

Macbeth-Evans had made its semi-translucent glass since about 1903, and the formula was a carefully-guarded secret. A former employee at the Macbeth-Evans Charleroi, Pennsylvania, plant joined the Jefferson Glass Company in 1910 and revealed the formula, enabling Jefferson to enter the lighting glassware market. The Macbeth-Evans firm obtained a permanent restraining order against both its former employee and the Jefferson Glass Company. By 1913-14, however, more than a dozen companies were making lighting glassware using many different formulas, and the resultant keen competition and price-cutting led to reduced profits for all concerned.

A mysterious man from New York with the surname Benjamin was engaged by Macbeth-Evans to effect pricing agreements among lighting glassware manufacturers which would not violate the terms of the Sherman Anti-Trust Act. The crux of the agreements was to be the patent rights for Alba glass secured by Macbeth-Evans in 1914, long after this firm had begun to make lighting glassware. The patent holder would then license the other manufacturers, provided that the latter pay royalties and adhere to a price schedule of lighting glassware items established by Macbeth-Evans. The price schedule, of course, would benefit all manufacturers, since it reflected an across-the-board rise in all prices. The royalty paid to Macbeth-Evans was, in effect, a *quid pro quo* for effecting the pricing schedule and lessening competition for the manufacturers of lighting glassware.

The plan faltered when General Electric refused to take part, and it came undone when the Macbeth-Evans firm could not sustain its patent rights in court against General Electric. Nonetheless, the Northwood firm was obligated to meet its royalty payment agreement under the temporary and permanent licensing agreements for the time during which the Macbeth-Evans patent was valid. Damages and interest totaled about $42,500, and this amount was entered as a loss on the Federal tax return for H. Northwood and Co. for 1918. When the Northwood firm went into receivership in 1925, problems over the tax status of the claimed loss were revealed.

The litigation over Luna glass certainly had no discernible effect upon Northwood's production and sales. The damages awarded to Macbeth-Evans, calculated at 10% of Northwood's gross sales of Luna glassware, would indicate that Northwood sold about $360,000 worth between December, 1914, and September, 1917. The 1916-

1920 period showed H. Northwood and Co.'s overall profits as follows: 1916 ($38,000); 1917 ($39,000); 1918 ($39,000); 1919 ($52,000); and 1920 ($53,000 on gross sales of $723,815.47). Luna did not account for all the profit, of course, but there seems little doubt that this glassware was responsible for a considerable measure of the firm's financial success.

Production and Patents

Correspondence from the Northwood firm in the files of the National Association of Manufacturers of Pressed and Blown Glassware and U. S. Patent Office documents provide some additional insights into the history of Luna and similar kinds of glassware. Luna was considered "special" glass in the agreements between the union glassworkers and the manufacturers, so somewhat different work rules governed its production.

On January 9, 1914, Harry Northwood reported that workers pressing Luna ware were being paid "piece work on all sizes up to 13 inch, and turn work from 13 to 24 inch." Those working the smaller sizes were required to produce a set number of pieces (the "move") during each 4 1/2 hour turn; those producing larger sizes were paid a set wage per shift, regardless of the number of pieces made. This differential recognizes the inherent difficulty in producing some of the larger pressed pieces due to bad glass or other conditions beyond the workers' control. At the annual conference of union representatives and members of the National Association in August, 1915, a motion was passed that "H. Northwood Co. shall work their semi-translucent turn work the same as all other factories."

In March, 1917, Harry Northwood wrote to the National Association for advice regarding the moves and wages for a gas or electric shade, and he enclosed a "rough sketch" of the item in question. The sketch is similar to a "Sanitary Fixture" in the c. 1913 Luna catalog, so these rather plain shades were probably in production for quite some time.

After the annual wage conference in 1917, the National Association's secretary, John Kunzler, and AFGWU President William P. Clarke undertook a joint project to gather information about pressed ceiling bowls. A printed questionnaire was sent to all manufacturers in the lighting goods field. The Northwood firm responded with a list of seven hemispheres, ranging from a 3-pound bowl (10" diameter) to a thirty-five pound

Louis XIV shade.

bowl (24" diameter) requiring six gatherers on the shop. These hemispheres were designated with numbers as follows: #82 (10" d.); #97 (12" d.); #920 (14" d.); #514 (16" d.); #516 (18" d.) #518 (20" d.) and #520 (24" d.). A line of "shallow" ceiling bowls ranging from 14" to 23" in diameter was also mentioned. The #516 ceiling bowl had been designated "Louis XIV" in the 1913 Luna catalog, and it was shown in the June 3, 1915, issue of *Crockery and Glass Journal.* Just a few weeks earlier, *China, Glass and Lamps* had illustrated another Northwood Luna shade (May 3, 1915).

Northwood's Luna glass was not, however, confined solely to lighting fixtures. An extraordinary glass bookend in the likeness of a standing bear was produced in 1916, as this quote from the May 25, 1916, issue of *Pottery, Glass and Brass Salesman* reveals: "Kelly & Reasner have received from the H. Northwood Company two attractive glass book ends, representing bears with brilliants for eyes, done in old ivory and dull black glass. The book ends are heavy enough for door stops if it is desired to use them for that purpose." The heavy bookends stand about 9" tall, and the base is nearly 7" at its widest point. A miniature version is far too light to function as a bookend or doorstop, but it makes a delightful paperweight.

Closely related to Northwood's Luna line are those lighting fixtures in a pale custard hue,

Northwood Luna shade (original name not known).

Bear paperweight.

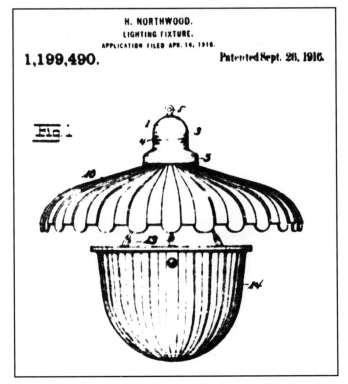

H. NORTHWOOD.
LIGHTING FIXTURE.
APPLICATION FILED APR. 14, 1916.

1,199,490.

Patented Sept. 26, 1916.

Fig. 1

Detail from patent drawing.

which was called Luna Ivory in Northwood's notebook. These fixtures (see Fig. 784) are often decorated with the brownish stain called "nutmeg" by today's collectors who have seen it on various Northwood novelty items. The stain was also used on tableware and novelties in a line called Antique Ivory, which was put on the market in 1914. One of Northwood's notebooks records good success with Luna Ivory batches during April-May, 1914, so these pieces may have been in production about this time.

Northwood's No. 42 shade in Luna Ivory (No. 45 was a larger version of this design).

Harry Northwood held several patents related to lighting goods generally and, often, to Luna glass specifically. These ranged from designs for various lighting fixtures to manufacturing processes. The large Luna and Luna Ivory bowls were designed to be hanging light fixtures, and Northwood patented a method for drilling holes in the glass so that threaded metal pins could be used to secure the bowls to chains or cords. This was U. S. patent #1,276,683, issued to Harry Northwood on August 20, 1918. Northwood's notebooks mention drilling Luna glass as early as 1913, so this patent may have been secured to protect some longstanding invention.

A suspension device for lighting fixtures was patented in September, 1916 (U. S. patent #1,199,490), and the illustrations accompanying Northwood's application show a bowl and reflector shade which are similar to articles depicted in the 1913 Luna catalog. Northwood also patented socket covers in February and May, 1917 (U. S. patents #1,217,489 and #1,225,649), but these devices were not made of glass and the patent drawings do not show any glass fixtures. A lighting fixture patented in November, 1917 (U. S. patent #1,247,445), was illustrated with line drawings of a bowl and reflector shade which were probably made in Luna glass. Shortly after Harry Northwood's death in 1919, a design patent for a lighting fixture (#53,538) was registered to Dent A. Taylor and assigned to H. Northwood and

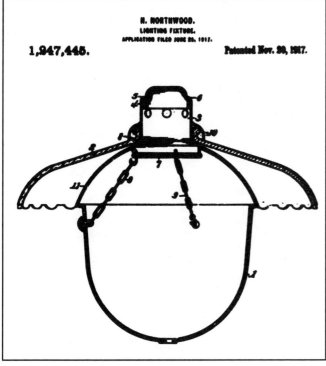

H. NORTHWOOD.
LIGHTING FIXTURE.
APPLICATION FILED JUNE 25, 1917.

1,947,445.   Patented Nov. 20, 1917.

Detail from patent drawing.

Northwood lamp part disk.

Co., of which Taylor was then general manager. The fixture was probably designed by Harry Northwood at some earlier time, and the firm registered the design in April, 1919, to guard against imitations.

Another Northwood lighting device seems not to have been patented, although the firm may have contemplated or attempted to secure a patent. The device is a glass disk about 4 1/8" in diameter which is open in the center. The disks, which are known in satin-finished crystal and both pale pink and pale yellow-orange hues,

tyically have raised letters near the edge which read "Northwood-Patent-Pending," and sometimes the number "141" or "155" precedes this.

The disks are designed to fit together with tapered shades which are held in place by a raised circle near the outermost edge of the disk. The shades are not marked in any way, but it seems safe to assume that the Northwood firm made them to accompany the disks. The shades may be plain satin-finished crystal, pale pink or pale yellow-orange glass to match the disks, and they may be reverse-painted with simple geometric designs or elaborate outdoor scenes.

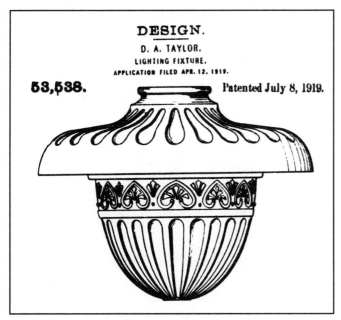

DESIGN.

D. A. TAYLOR.
LIGHTING FIXTURE.
APPLICATION FILED APR. 12, 1919.

53,538.   Patented July 8, 1919.

Detail from design patent.

Northwood reverse painted shade.

Northwood reverse painted shade.

Northwood reverse painted shade.

A variety of Northwood reverse painted shades, supported by disks and mounted on a candleabra (not an original fixture).

The shades often have a textured feel to the glass, as if covered with a thin layer of finely-crinkled paper. The illuminating effect is quite pleasant, as the shades diffuse and soften the light. One trade report, in the April 26, 1917, issue of *Pottery, Glass and Brass Salesman,* mentions "frosted glass" and "designs ... fired on the inside of the shade."

The importance of lighting goods generally and Luna glass particularly to the Northwood firm is clearly reflected in changes in the company letterhead. The familiar N-in-a-circle letterhead, which had been in use since 1906, was replaced about 1915 by new stationery featuring

GEO. E. HOUSE
PRESIDENT

HARRY NORTHWOOD
VICE PREST. & GEN'L. MGR.

D. A. TAYLOR
SECRETARY & TRE

H. NORTHWOOD COMPANY

ILLUMINATING GLASSWARE

WHEELING, WEST VA.

C. J. DELA CROIX
19 MADISON AVENUE
NEW YORK

the phrase "Luna Illuminating Glassware," and no mention was made of tableware or other products. This letterhead continued to be used at least until 1922 or 1923, when the references to Luna were dropped and the simple term "glassware" was employed.

Conclusion

Lighting fixtures were surely an important feature of the history of H. Northwood and Co.,

although little previous research has explored this area. There is little doubt that lighting goods generally and Luna glass particularly were important to the economic health of the Northwood factory. The chemistry of Luna glass remained of vital interest to Harry Northwood for some time, and his later creations in Brecciated Marble, Mottled Agate and Etruscan were probably extensions of his experimentation with various batches used for Luna glass. These are detailed in the next chapter.

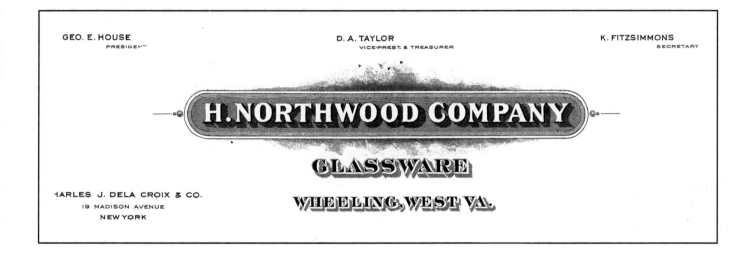

The relative success of Carnival glass in 1909-12 and the introduction of Luna lighting ware a year or so later were not to be the last of Harry Northwood's innovations in glassmaking. A new line in Ivory ware was unveiled in early 1914, and several interesting decorating treatments kept this line in the marketplace for about two years. In 1917, Northwood re-introduced iridescent glass, this time in a wide variety of shapes and colors which collectors call "stretch" glass today. About the same time, Northwood patented several unique effects (Brecciated Marble and Mottled Agate), and he continued to develop decorating treatments. This five year period in the history of H. Northwood and Co. was brought to a sudden and unfortunate close by the untimely deaths of Carl and Harry Northwood in January, 1918, and February, 1919, respectively.

Ivory Glass, Again!

Northwood first developed Ivory (custard) glassware at Indiana, Pa., in the 1890s, and he returned to it in 1903-04 at Wheeling with his decorated Carnelian (Everglades) line. In both instances, Northwood probably designed patterns with production in Ivory ware in mind, although the moulds were also used for opalescent effects and, in some cases, opaque colors such as "Mosaic" (purple slag). The first Ivory articles in 1914 may have been gold-decorated, but a brown stain was introduced within a few months, and blue and pink backgrounds were available somewhat later.

In early 1914, Ivory glass made its return appearance among the Northwood products displayed at Pittsburgh and featured in its New York showroom. The January 15, 1914, issue of *Pottery, Glass and Brass Salesman* had the initial details: "The H. Northwood Co., of Wheeling, W. Va., from whose factory have come many excellent lines of iridescent and crystal tableware, has brought out for 1914 a striking new glass which has been named the Ivory line, samples of which have just been put on display at the showrooms of Miller & Inge, 25 West Broadway. The Ivory line is so called because of the rich ivory color of the glass, which has a faint iridescence and a broad edge band of gold. There is a full assortment of tableware items in the showing, which includes several different raised designs. Included among the patterns are a

peacock design, a grape design and several conventionalized floral effects."

The peacock design mentioned above was, of course, Peacocks on the Fence, and the grape motif was probably Grape and Cable (see Figs. 740-763 and 766-771), although both Grape Arbor and Grape and Gothic Arches are also known in Ivory glass (see Figs. 764-765, 772-779, and 782-783). In previous years, these moulds had been

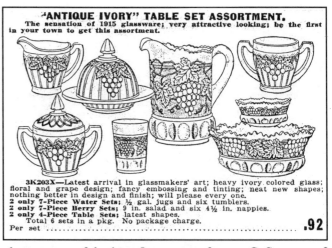

Assortment of Antique Ivory ware from a G. Sommers & Co. 1915 catalog. The reference to "tinting" probably denoted the "nutmeg" stain.

used for Carnival production, of course, and Grape and Gothic Arches also occurs in transparent emerald green, so Northwood's new Ivory line was essentially a well-known glass color reborn in established patterns. The Grape and Gothic Arches pieces typically have some iridescence to them, and a few collectors have called this "pearl Carnival glass," a name that probably ought to be discarded in view of potential confusion with Northwood's later use of the term Pearl.

Within a few months, more decorated Ivory ware made its debut. The first effect, which today's collectors call "nutmeg," was reported in the October 1, 1914, issue of *Pottery, Glass and Brass Salesman:* "Miller & Inge, New York representatives of the H. Northwood Co., of Wheeling, W. Va., have just received from the concern samples of a new line of fancy table glassware that is quite different from anything else in the showing. This line consists in an ivory yellow ware, tinged with a flat light brown, and is best described by its name, Antique Ivory. The effect is at once unusual and attractive, and is

Assortment of Northwood's Antique Ivory line from a Butler Brothers (Spring, 1915) catalog.

particularly pleasing in a classic design, having a conventionalized grape motif. Other patterns include grape and other fruit designs in various forms. Among the items now shown are fruit baskets, jardinieres, fern dishes, footed compotes, bowls, etc., and the line is to include a full assortment of tableware pieces, such as jugs, tumblers, sugars and creams, butter dishes, plates, trays, etc."

The January 11, 1915, issue of *China, Glass and Lamps* described salesman Carl Northwood as "busy as the proverbial bee" and called Northwood's Antique Ivory "the big feature of his company's exhibit." Although some iridescent wares were also displayed along with Luna articles, "Mr. Northwood never fails to revert to the Antique Ivory ware, in which he betrays most pardonable pride." The April 19, 1915, issue of *China, Glass and Lamps,* under the headline "Affairs at the Northwood Factory," said that Antique Ivory "met with immediate favor among buyers" and that the line "has assuredly been one of this season's hits."

The Antique Ivory line soon extended beyond the patterns mentioned above and into motifs as well as novelties which had had previous production in opalescent or Carnival glass (or both). Among the patterns reborn are these: Double Loop (Figs. 780-781); Three Fruits (Figs. 785 and 797-798); Poinsettia Lattice (Fig. 788); Singing Birds (Fig. 789); and Poppy (Fig. 799). The novelties include the Good Luck bowl, the Drapery vase, the Dandelion mug, the Bushel Basket, and rose bowls in Finecut and Roses and Beaded Cable (see Figs. 786-787 and 790-793).

Perhaps the most spectacular item made in Northwood's Antique Ivory is the Dancing Ladies covered urn (Fig. 922). This item is also known in Northwood's opaque Luna glass. A hanging light fixture in the Dancing Ladies motif has also been

reported. The exact production dates of these articles are not known for certain, but the manufacture of both Luna ware and Antique Ivory would have been a strong feature of the Northwood plant in 1915-1916. Entries in Northwood notebooks detail trials with "Luna Ivory" as early as April-May, 1914.

The mould for the Dancing Ladies urn was acquired by the Fenton Art Glass Company, probably after the Northwood firm closed in late 1925, and Fenton made this piece in a color called Chinese Yellow in the early 1930s. With the Northwood's Dancing Ladies as inspiration, the Fenton firm also made its own moulds, eliminating the handles and the pattern on the base. The result was a smaller covered urn and vases in a variety of shapes (see Heacock's *Fenton Glass: The First Twenty-Five Years,* pp. 25, 112 and 114 and *Fenton Glass: The Second Twenty-Five Years,* front cover and pp. 8, 29, 31, 68 and 86). Frank M. Fenton recalls hearing from longtime Fenton employee Francis O. Lehew (who first joined the Fenton firm as a mouldmaker in 1924) that the Dancing Ladies urn mould purchased from Northwood eventually made its way to Sapulpa, Oklahoma, where John Fenton envisaged a glassmaking venture sometime in the 1930s.

The success of Northwood's Ivory ware and the brown-tinged Antique Ivory stimulated further decorating innovations. The results were background decorations in two additional colors—blue and pink. These were applied to the backgrounds of items in Grape and Cable and other patterns (see Figs. 764-765, 767-768, 788, and 805-806). The new treatments were described in *Pottery, Glass and Brass Salesman* (July 15,

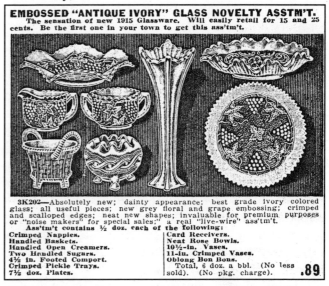

Antique Ivory assortment (G. Sommers & Co., 1915); note the Bushel Basket, Beaded Cable rose bowl and the Poppy pickle dish.

1915): "Some new effects in ivory glass tableware have just been sent by the H. Northwood Company, of Wheeling, W. Va., to C. J. Dela Croix, its New York representative, at 19 Madison Avenue. The ivory ware, which has been one of the most successful lines in the Northwood showing of tableware specialties is, as heretofore, shown in various relief designs, but the new showing differs from the old in that the ware is tinted in several new tones. A clear light blue and an old rose tint are used, throwing into relief the designs on the ware."

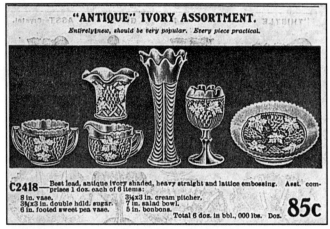

Assortment of Northwood's Antique Ivory line from a Butler Brothers (Spring, 1915) catalog.

The Ivory and Antique Ivory lines soon made their way into Butler Brothers catalogs as well as those issued by G. Sommers and Co. of St. Paul, Minnesota, a wholesaler who served accounts in the northern Great Plains area. Grape and Cable items are shown with pieces in Grape and Gothic Arches, and the Poppy oval bowl appears. A few novelties are also depicted, such as the Bushel Basket, the Beaded Cable rose bowl and vases in Drapery and Four Pillar.

Colored and Decorated Wares, 1915-1919

Unfortunately for today's glass history researchers, information on glass production during World War I is sparse indeed. As the nation's collective attention was turned to the war effort, the tableware industry experienced a general slowdown in trade. Many glassworkers, both skilled and unskilled, saw military service, of course, and some chemicals may have been in short supply. Advertising dropped sharply in the glass tableware trade journals, and the few editorial mentions of Northwood glass often pose more questions than answers.

Nonetheless, a few new lines can be attributed to Northwood and some dates of production can be established. A brief report in the November 25,

1915, issue of *Pottery, Glass and Brass Salesman* details some Northwood products:

"Several new additions have recently been made to the line of table glassware of the H. Northwood Company, of Wheeling, W. Va., who are represented in the East by Chas. Dela Croix, 19 Madison Avenue, New York. One of the most interesting of these, owing to the immense popularity of the design applied to the ware, is a short line of articles in a new bluebird pattern. The line includes jugs and tumblers, bowls, covered jars, trays, sugar and creams, footed compotes, etc., and a novel footed compote with cover. The shapes are colonial, and the decoration consists in bluebirds in different attitudes, perched on flowered twigs. The entire design is embossed, and the birds and twigs are attractively colored. Another addition to the showing is a short line of tri-footed nappies, bowls, sugars and creams, trays, etc., besides tray, sugars and creams and other articles not footed, in a pattern designated as No. 42. This ware is crystal and the design is a pressed ribbon and diamond effect that is very pleasing."

The colonial-style articles with bird decoration is the Singing Birds design in crystal glass, featuring careful hand-painting of the low-relief bluebirds and twigs which are, of course, part of the pattern when pressed. This line had been made in iridescent Carnival glass as early as mid-1911, and the few Ivory pieces probably date from about 1914 or 1915. Singing Birds pieces in crystal with decorated bluebirds are now hard to find in today's antiques marketplace, and most bear the N-in-a-circle, as did their predecessors in Carnival and Ivory. The No. 42 line, described above as "pressed ribbon and diamond effect" has yet to be identified.

In early 1916, *China, Glass and Lamps* mentioned the Singing Birds line and described other Northwood wares being shown as part of an abbreviated Pittsburgh exhibit: "A line of Vintage ware in ivory glass with grape and vine decoration, and a new Bluebird tableware line are among the features shown by the H. Northwood Co., Wheeling, W. Va., whose exhibit in Room 712 is presided over by Carl Northwood. A line of pressed ware in black and white is also shown. Other items include new lines of vases in crystal, ruby and green, also bluebird decoration, bonbons, puff boxes, jewel boxes, coasters, etc. Lemonade and wine sets, plain and decorated, are also on display, including a number of new shapes."

The "black and white" line remains a mystery

today, as does an assortment of black glass items described as "flat edge deep finger bowls ... in plain and pretty enamel decorations" in the March 30, 1916, issue of *China, Glass and Lamps*. About two months later, *Pottery, Glass and Brass Salesman* carried this lengthy report, in which a number of colored and decorated articles are described:

"Chas. J. Dela Croix, Easter sales agent for the H. Northwood Company, of Wheeling, W. Va., with showrooms at 19 Madison Avenue, is showing a new line of colored and decorated glass flower holders of various kinds, in numerous colors and patterns. The Northwood concern, well known as it is for its line of decorated table glassware, has outdone itself in this new line, which is made up of shallow flower bowls, vases, rose bowls, table centers and other pieces in numerous attractive shapes, many of which come in several sizes. These articles are made in black, light green, ruby, pink and crystal glass, plain and decorated. The black glass, comprising an unusually large assortment of items, is ornamented with coin gold rim treatments as well as flower patterns in

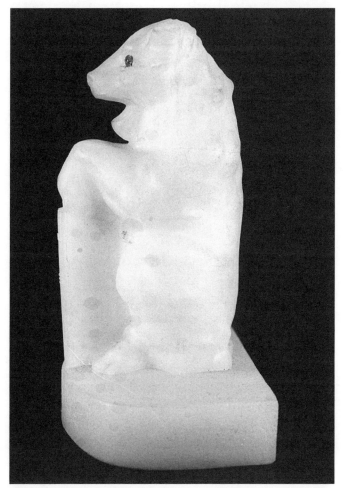

This Northwood Bear bookend or doorstop, which has tiny pieces of cut glass for eyes, stands 9" tall (see Fig. 817). Courtesy of Miss Robb.

enamel colors. The green glass is decorated with clusters of violets, the crystal glass with bluebirds and gold, violets, and other patterns, and the pink glass with bluebirds. Many of the articles are equipped with wire mesh flower holders, with which they are sold complete when desired. The line is especially attractive, and has won the admiration of numerous buyers, many of whom have been strongly impressed by the novel decorative pieces in black glass" (June 30, 1916).

The Northwood bear made its debut in May, 1916, and the May 25, 1916, issue of *Pottery, Glass and Brass Salesman* had the full particulars: "Kelly & Reasner have received from the H. Northwood Company two attractive glass book ends, representing bears with brilliants for eyes, done in old ivory and dull black glass. The book ends are heavy enough for door stops if it is desired to use them for that purpose." In addition to the large bear, which is known in Luna glass (see Fig. 817), a smaller version, perhaps for use as a paperweight, was also produced.

Imitation Marble Glass

Northwood's Luna formula, which had been developed in 1912 for use as illuminating glassware, was the basis for an unusual series of products introduced in 1917 with such bizarre names as Brecciated Marble, Mottled Agate and Etruscan. Although the glass has the look and feel of authentic marble, the color variations and vein-like effects were produced using various patented processes which had been developed by Harry Northwood and his brother Carl Northwood.

The first mention of the Northwood's new line came in the September 7, 1916, issue of *Crockery and Glass Journal:* "Chas. J. Dela Croix, representative for the H. Northwood Co., is showing a marble-effect glass beautifully veined in deep orange and brown coloring, some of the latter shading to almost a black. The items are in both glazed and matt finishes, and a feature that will add to their attractiveness to buyers for the exclusive shops is that no two pieces are alike. Some good shapes in flower centers and several styles in bowls, vases and novelties are displayed."

The January 4, 1917, issue of *Crockery and Glass Journal* provides some names for the new imitation marble glass and adds some vital information about it, namely, that the imitation marble was not a tableware line: "The H. Northwood Co. is showing a line of glass-ware unlike any other exhibited. Not one piece of table glassware, as the term is commonly known, is

Brecciated Marble two-piece compote (see Fig. 815-816). This piece was probably intended as a decorative rather than as a functional piece, and there may be small birds to perch on the rim! **Courtesy of the Oglebay Institute, Wheeling, WV.**

being offered. Ware known as "Grecian," "Marble," "Blood Agate," "Mooresque" and "El Ruscan" [*sic*, should be Etruscan] are the main novelties. These pieces consist of bird founts, Vatican urns, vases, etc. and are made for the department store trade. To go with the founts, birds and doves are to be had. The line is the most original of its character ever displayed here." A subsequent issue of *Crockery and Glass Journal* (January 18, 1917) noted that the glass "has the same peculiarly fascinating finish as real marble, with dark irregular veins running through ...."

This line was called Brecciated Marble in Northwood's advertising throughout 1917. The ware is a dense opaque white glass with a slight satin finish, but the most distinguishing features are the dark veins. Harry Northwood patented this glassware on June 12, 1917 (U. S. Patent #1,229,315), although his application for a patent had been filed almost six months earlier on January 30, 1917. The patent was for a "process of producing glassware presenting brecciated-marble effects." Both the patent specifications and Northwood's notebooks describe treating opaque white glass (probably made from the Luna formula) with acid to produce a "dull and lusterless ... surface texture similar to that of carved or sculptured statuary marble." The glass was then hand decorated with a mixture of black enamel and matt white to create "a network of irregular fine lines" when the ware was fired in a decorating lehr. Northwood's patent included a rendering of a tall vase which is identical to the Brecciated Marble vase shown in this book (see Fig. 816).

This ad appeared in the February 8, 1917, issue of **Pottery, Glass and Brass Salesman.**

Closely related to Northwood's Brecciated Marble line was the production of 'Etruscan," which was described as "a fine reproduction of alabaster in mottled brown effect made in both matt and polished finish" in the January 25, 1917, issue of *Pottery, Glass and Brass Salesman*. Like Brecciated Marble, Northwood's Etruscan was protected by a patent (U. S. Patent #1,217,490), which was granted on February 27, 1917. The ware began as the same dense opaque white used for Brecciated Marble, but it was first stained with a solution of copper sulphate and fired, followed by "a coating or partial coating of a silver salt solution and finally refiring the ware" (*National Glass Budget*, March 3, 1917).

Harry Northwood's notebook mentions "Agate mixtures ... from Carl's memo book," so this curious decoration may have been developed by Carl Northwood in his capacity as foreman of the firm's decorating room. The only piece of Northwood's Etruscan shown in this book (Fig. 814) exhibits a dark orange-brown decoration, which may explain a mysterious reference to "mahogany glass" in the January 24, 1918, issue of *China, Glass and Lamps.*

If an article in the May 17, 1917, issue of *Pottery, Glass and Brass Salesman* is correct, the Brecciated Marble, Etruscan and Mottled Agate wares were apparently used for a line of lamps

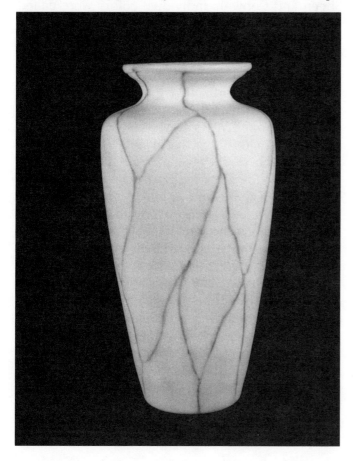

with silk shades: "The H. Northwood Company, well known through their handsome lighting glassware lines, have gone into the manufacture of portables and electric candlesticks, which are now shown by C. J. Dela Croix, 19 Madison Avenue. The bases are in two pieces—a neat stand and the base proper. Brecciated marble, agate and etruscan finishes have been used for the bases, which are neatly fitted with solid brass electrical fittings with sockets for two lights. The shades are made of silk in colors of rose, yellow and blue with silk fringe. The candlesticks are in the same marble glass effects, with dainty silk shades and electric converters. The line is one of real beauty, and should prove a popular addition to the Northwood line of lighting specialties."

The January 18, 1917, issue of *Crockery and Glass Journal* also refers to the Mooresque line, "a Moorish decorative treatment in gold on blue and purple glass in all sorts of articles." Unfortunately, neither the other trade publications nor the Northwood's advertising add anything to this frustratingly brief account. An advertisement in the February 8, 1917, issue of *Pottery, Glass and Brass Salesman* mentions Royal Purple and Venetian Blue as "All That the Names Imply" without any further description. These colors might be related to a new line of iridescent ware called Satin Sheen, which was also introduced in early 1917 concurrently with Brecciated Marble and the other patented effects.

Iridescent Wares, Again!

The Northwood firm began to market iridescent glass in earnest once more during the first few months of 1917. Dubbed Satin Sheen, the line was unveiled in mid-1916, but it was nearly overshadowed in the trade press by the imitation marble lines. The July 20, 1916, issue of *Crockery and Glass Journal* referred briefly to the Northwood's "assortment of Tiffany finish glass," but offered no details. The January 18, 1917, issue of *China, Glass and Lamps* mentioned "iridescent glass in rich new pearl effects [which] comes in flower centers, fruit bowls, bonbons, comports and vases," but the February 8, 1917, issue of *Pottery, Glass and Brass Salesman* had many important specifics:

"A brilliant new line of iridescent glassware called Satin Sheen, produced by the H. Northwood Company, is shown by C. J. Dela Croix at 19 Madison Avenue. The iridescence is brought out in an exquisite blue, purple and a rarely beautiful pearl. The shapes are classic reproductions of old antiques in bowls, vases in wide variety, flared vases, lipped bowls and many other quaint effects. The colorings are truly marvelous and different from anything ever before shown, while the shapes are truly classic and unique. Another solid blue iridescent line is shown in plain, gracefully shaped vases and lily pans with a gold checkered decoration enhancing the brilliant effect. Mr. Dela Croix is also showing a fine display of royal blue and purple in optic. Included in this line are vases in profusion, bowls, and in fact, a great variety of beautiful home ornaments suitable to the high-grade trade."

The Northwood's advertising in February-March, 1917, called Satin Sheen "a new iridescent glass of rich and delicate coloring." In contrast to Carnival glass, the Satin Sheen line lacked the bright, metallic iridescent quality usually present on Northwood's wares.

The articles in Satin Sheen were typically made from glass in crystal or rather pale colors—such as light purple or blue (called Royal Purple and Venetian Blue, respectively)—and the shapes are generally quite plain, unlike the elaborate patterns found in most of Northwood's Carnival glass lines. A purple vase with optic interior is illustrated in this book (Fig. 886), and this article could be Northwood's Royal Purple color (see also Figs. 857-858). The Pearl line was iridized crystal (see Fig. 859).

Within a few years, Northwood's iridescent lines also included "Cobweb," a form of iridescent glass called "stretch" by collectors today. Several colors, particularly blue and topaz, were made. Stretch

Few of Northwood's post-1915 articles are found with the N-in-a-circle mark, but this small comport has it on the center of the bowl as well as the inside of the stemmed base.

glass, like its predecessor Carnival glass, obtains its iridescence through spraying the hot glass with various metallic salt solutions. Unlike carnival glass, however, stretch glass typically undergoes finishing by a skilled worker who changes the shape of a pressed or blown article after the spray has been applied. The finishing process (and perhaps the application of several different sprays) causes the microscopically-thin iridescent layer upon the glass to pull apart slightly, and the resultant onion skin-like effect is distinctive.

Harry Northwood's notebooks contain a number of references to Iris trials" in early 1917. Northwood described a "good Matt Iris" on purple glass made by three separate sprayings and warmings-in. The solutions had varying results on different colored glasses, and Northwood's notebook records these. Similar wares were made by a number of other factories, including the Imperial Glass Corporation of Bellaire, Ohio, and the Westmoreland Specialty Company of Grapeville, Pa., as well as the Fenton Art Glass Company and the Diamond Glass-Ware Company, which had succeeded the Dugan Glass Company in Indiana, Pa., in 1913.

Eventually, the term Iris (the Greek word for "rainbow") was used in the advertising for this glassware in *Pottery, Glass and Brass Salesman* during February, 1917, replacing the earlier Satin Sheen and Cobweb. Individual colors were called Topaz Iris and Blue Iris. Later, the term Rainbow was used synonymously with Iris. The topaz hue was mentioned prominently in the August 2, 1917, issue of *Pottery, Glass and Brass Salesman:* "C. J. Dela Croix, 19 Madison Avenue, New York agent for the H. Northwood Company, has just received from the concern its new Topaz line of fancy glassware. The name accurately describes the ware, which possesses a beautiful iridescent lustre and shows a green that is a perfect topaz in color. The Topaz ware is shown in a full line of table pieces and is moderate in price." A few weeks later, a trade journal mentioned iridescent crystal ware with the stretch effect, calling it "Pearl" (*China, Glass and Lamps*, August 30, 1917).

Northwood's Blue Iridescent pieces can be found in many different articles today (see Figs. 818-833). Likewise, topaz pieces are known in a wide variety of shapes (see Figs. 834-850). These two colors were probably the most commercially successful of the Northwood iridescent lines between 1917 and late 1925, for blue and topaz are mentioned in both the trade press and Northwood's own catalog brochures throughout this period.

Northwood's iridescent lines from 1917-1919 contain several examples of articles produced initially from a single mould which could then be fashioned into different final shapes. A small folder from about 1920, entitled "Rainbow and Cobweb," shows the full selection of glassware then available, and most of these articles had probably been on the market for at least a short time. Two different styles of comports are designated No. 637. The No. 605 bowl was the basis for both the No. 609 bowl and the No. 807 bowl, and one can readily see the same relationship among these groups: Nos. 616 and 617; Nos. 640/641/642; Nos. 644/645/646; and Nos. 647/648/649. The term "Rainbow" was synonymous with Iris, of course, and simply denoted iridescent ware, but "Cobweb" may have referred specifically to the stretch effect.

The March 6, 1919, issue of *Crockery and Glass Journal* revealed that the Northwood firm had "a new creation ... called Sateena—a deep toned amber with rich iridescent effect." Unfortunately, this is the fullest description to be found of these wares, which were introduced just a month after Harry Northwood's death. The color certainly sounds interesting, and several candy jars shown in this book (see Figs. 869, 900 and 902) might well be from the Sateena line, for they display both amber tones and a pronounced iridescent effect.

Although most of the shapes shown in the "Rainbow and Cobweb" folder remained staples in the Northwood's line through 1925, quite a few additional items were developed, too. The larger bowls were accompanied by various styles of candlesticks to form the popular console sets of the early 1920s. These are discussed in the next chapter, and most, if not all, of the new shapes are shown in illustrations from original Northwood catalogs. As mentioned above, iridescent blue and topaz remained popular.

Glass researcher Berry Wiggins has made a close study of the various black bases made by Northwood and other firms. The Northwood-made bases are distinctive in shape (three concentric circles of diminishing size), and they have three feet (see Figs. 854, 860-861, and 864 for various sizes). There may be designations on the underside ("616" or "301-8 in NAP"), and the medium-sized base may read "638 NAP & 647" [the N in NAP is typographically backwards]. These bases were also made in opal glass by the Northwood firm to be used with the Jade Green line.

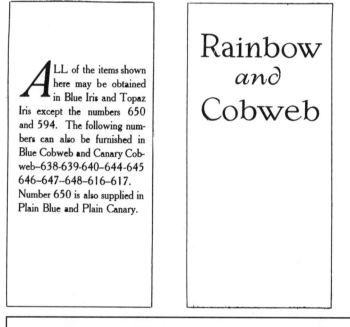

ALL of the items shown here may be obtained in Blue Iris and Topaz Iris except the numbers 650 and 594. The following numbers can also be furnished in Blue Cobweb and Canary Cobweb—638-639-640-644-645 646-647--648-616-617. Number 650 is also supplied in Plain Blue and Plain Canary.

Rainbow and Cobweb

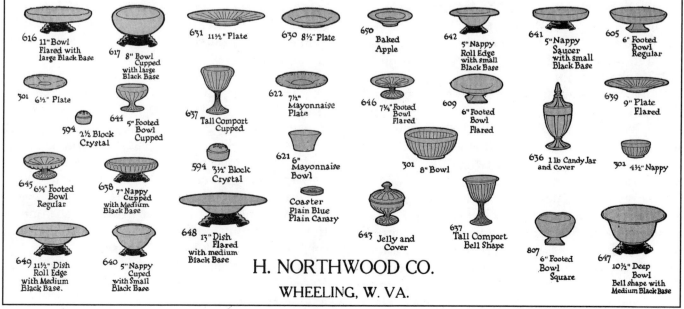

616 11" Bowl Flared with large Black Base

617 8" Bowl Cupped with large Black Base

631 11½" Plate

630 8½" Plate

650 Baked Apple

642 5" Nappy Roll Edge with small Black Base

641 5" Nappy Saucer with small Black Base

605 6" Footed Bowl Regular

301 6½" Plate

594 2½ Block Crystal

644 5" Footed Bowl Cupped

637 Tall Comport Cupped

622 7½" Mayonnaise Plate

646 7¼" Footed Bowl Flared

609 6" Footed Bowl Flared

639 9" Plate Flared

645 6¼" Footed Bowl Regular

638 7" Nappy Cupped with Medium Black Base

594 3½" Block Crystal

621 6" Mayonnaise Bowl

301 8" Bowl

636 1 lb Candy Jar and Cover

301 4½" Nappy

649 11½" Dish Roll Edge with Medium Black Base.

640 5" Nappy Cuped with Small Black Base

648 13" Dish Flared with medium Black Base

Coaster Plain Blue Plain Canary

643 Jelly and Cover

637 Tall Comport Bell Shape

807 6" Footed Bowl Square

647 10½" Deep Bowl Bell shape with Medium Black Base

H. NORTHWOOD CO.
WHEELING, W. VA.

179

Death of Carl Northwood

When the January, 1918, glass exhibit opened at Pittsburgh's Fort Pitt hotel, Carl Northwood was present to preside over the display of H. Northwood and Company. Born in England in 1872, Carl Northwood had emigrated to the United States in 1892, although he probably had visited in prior years. Thus, he was at his brother Harry's side during the last year of the Martins Ferry plant and throughout the times at Ellwood City and Indiana, Pa. In an 1894 ad from the Ellwood City plant, Carl is listed as salesman for the "east and south." A year or so later, after additional salesmen had been engaged, his territory was confined to the South.

Ads from the first few months of Northwood's Indiana, Pennsylvania, operation list Carl Northwood as salesman for the West, and he was mentioned by the trade periodicals in conjunction with the Pittsburgh exhibitions as early as 1898. Both Harry and Carl journeyed to England during their father's illness in the spring of 1898, and Carl married Rose Overton there on June 25, 1898, shortly before they returned to the United States with Harry Northwood. Carl continued to be listed as Western Salesman, and he may have assumed some responsibilities in the decorating department in early 1899. He became an American citizen on March 9, 1899.

When the Indiana factory became part of the National Glass Company in late 1899, both Harry and Carl Northwood returned to England, where they had charge of the National's London showroom. The employees at Indiana presented Carl Northwood with a gold-headed cane.

At Wheeling, Carl continued to be involved with sales, but there is evidence to suggest that he also had a strong role in the factory's decorating innovations. Several of the June, 1906, photographs taken inside the plant show Carl Northwood in the decorating shop. Harry Northwood's notebooks contain references to mixtures and techniques gleaned from notes kept by Carl, and the January 16, 1911, issue of *China, Glass and Lamps* noted that "the decorating department is well taken care of by Carl Northwood."

Apparently, Carl Northwood was a bit indisposed with a cold about ten days after the Pittsburgh exhibit opened in early January, 1918, at the Fort Pitt hotel. He took to his bed for a day or so, but soon felt better and was seen "chatting with friends in the lobby," according to *Crockery and Glass Journal*. His condition quickly became worse, however, and attending physicians diagnosed pneumonia. An ambulance was called on January 15, but Carl Northwood passed away en route to the hospital. His wife, accompanied by the company's secretary-treasurer Dent A. Taylor, was on her way to Pittsburgh when Carl Northwood died.

The glass exhibit was closed on Wednesday, January 16, 1918, and a large group of glassware salesmen and manufacturers "accompanied the body to the Pennsylvania station ... when it was taken to his late home in Wheeling" (*Crockery and Glass Journal,* January 17, 1918). The Wheeling *Register* called Carl Northwood "one of the best known glass manufacturers in the country," noting further that his role as the Northwood firm's salesman "gained a wide acquaintance with men in the trade." The funeral was held in his family's home at 518 S. Penn St. on Friday, January 18, 1918. The pallbearers included his brother Harry as well as Sam Stafford, Harry White Jr., Harry Robb, Thomas Dugan and Alfred Dugan.

Death of Harry Northwood

On February 4, 1919, Harry Northwood, age 58, passed away at his home (310 S. Front St.) in Wheeling. The death certificate lists the cause of death as "liver trouble." He was taken ill in mid-summer, 1918, but the November 28, 1918, issue of *Crockery and Glass Journal* reported that he was "making satisfactory progress toward recovery." A month later, however, this same publication said that "his condition is not as favorable as might be wished" (December 26, 1918). He was not able to attend the annual January glass exhibition in Pittsburgh, of course, but his notebooks contain records of telephone conversations about glassmaking with factory manager James Haden as late as mid-January, 1919. His condition became critical in late January, and a nurse was engaged to assist with in-home care.

This headline from a Wheeling newspaper told all: "HARRY NORTHWOOD, FOREMOST GLASS MANUFACTURER, IS DEAD." An obituary in the *Wheeling Register* called Harry Northwood "one of the pillars in Wheeling's great industrial growth" and said "he held prestige as one of the vigorous and representative business men of the West Virginia metropolis." *Pottery, Glass and Brass Salesman* eulogized Harry Northwood as "one of the most popular men in the glass business and one of the best known" (February 13, 1919). Under the headline "Trade Mourns the Death of Harry Northwood," this same publication carried a poignant story:

"In the death of Harry Northwood, who passed away at his home in Wheeling, W. Va., last week, the glass trade lost one of its most popular members. Mr. Northwood was a big-hearted, whole-souled man, with legions of friends in the pottery and glass trade. His death, however, did not come as a surprise to those near him. Last summer he was attacked with dropsy, and long before the year was out he knew his end was near. During December he remarked to a friend that he hoped to "spend Christmas in heaven with his brother Carl." The remark was characteristic of his simple and beautiful faith. Carl Northwood died just a year ago, while he was exhibiting the concern's line during the January glass show at the Fort Pitt Hotel, Pittsburgh. Harry Northwood came of a fine old Staffordshire family that for generations had been prominent in that part of England and long identified with the glass industry. His father was a wonderful glassmaker, and produced certain pieces of glass manufacture, such as the Birmingham Vase, a replica of the Portland Vase and others, which were considered the greatest achievement in glass manufacture since the Roman era."

The bold headline above the *National Glass Budget's* front page obituary captured the effect of Harry Northwood's death in four short words: "A BRILLIANT CAREER ENDED." The *Budget's* story is a lengthy (and generally accurate) account of Northwood's life and glassmaking experience:

"Surrounded by his family, Harry Northwood, one of the foremost glass manufacturers in the world, died at his home in Wheeling, W. Va., at 10:50 last Tuesday evening. He was vice-president and general manager of the H. Northwood Co., and affiliated in smaller ways with other concerns in the Ohio Valley. When he felt the first tinge of the disease late last summer that ended his career, he reduced his working hours at his office, but early in the winter took to his bed. The physicians pronounced his malady dropsy, which made serious inroads and gradually undermined his rugged construction. He was the scion of the staunchest of English stock, the name Northwood having long been identified with the annals of Staffordshire, England. He was born at Wordsley, that country, on June 30, 1860, being the son of John and Elizabeth (Duggins) Northwood, both of whom were likewise born in Staffordshire. His father was actively concerned in the practical manufacturing of glass, being an artist in the manufacture of cameo glass, and produced, after years of close application, the masterpieces known as "The Birmingham Vase," "The Dennis

Vase" and also an exact copy of the famous "Portland Vase," considered to be the greatest work of art in glass reproduction since the Roman era.

"Mr. Northwood gained his early education training in schools of Stourbridge, Worcestershire, England, the center of the glass industry in that country. He began an apprenticeship to the trade of glassworker when he was 14 years of age, and received specially careful instruction under his distinguished father. He was continually identified with the manufacturing and decorating of glassware during his entire career and his skill and technical knowledge was of the highest order. His early training in all the details of glass manufacturing admirably fortified him for the management of the splendid enterprise with which he was so prominently connected. In 1881, shortly after attaining his legal majority, Mr. Northwood severed the ties that bound him to home and native land and came to America. He made Wheeling his destination and accepted

HARRY C. NORTHWOOD
General Manager H. Northwood Glass Co.
Wheeling, W. Va.

This caricature of Harry Northwood probably appeared in a Wheeling publication about 1916, perhaps one put out by the Wheeling Board of Trade. The object in his right hand is surely a Luna shade, but the other items are mysteries. **Courtesy of Miss Robb.**

181

employment as a designer and etcher for the firm of Hobbs, Brockunier & Co. The original plant of this concern, established in 1836, is now part of the fine factory of which he was the general manager at the time of his death. From 1883 to 1887 Mr. Northwood was manager of the LaBelle Glass Works at Bridgeport, O., and thereafter he was vice-president and general manager of the Northwood Glass Co., at Martins Ferry, until 1892, when the base of operation was transferred to Ellwood City, Pa., where he continued the incumbent of the same official positions, under the original corporate title of the company until 1896. Thereafter he was managing partner of the Northwood Co. at Indiana, Pa., until 1899, when he returned to his native country and assumed the position of manager of the London office of the National Glass Co. In 1901 he returned to the United States and soon afterward effected the organization of the H. Northwood Co., of Wheeling.

"Mr. Northwood was an authority in regards to all details of the manufacturing of glassware, in connection with which he invested and successfully introduced various original methods and devices. He came of a family that has been concerned with the manufacturing of glass in England for many generations and, in fact, it may be stated that no family on that island takes precedence of the Northwoods in the matter of continuous associations with this industry, from which it may be inferred that the subject of this review had an inherent as well as an acquired talent for the important business in which he held so much prestige as one of the chief executive officers in one of the foremost concerns of its kind in the United States.

"Mr. Northwood was an enthusiastic advocate of the upbuilding of the larger and greater Wheeling and held prestige as one of the vigorous and representative business men of the city. Politically he was a Republican. He was a member of Ellwood City Lodge, No. 599, Ancient Free and Accepted Masons, and besides held a membership in Cyrene Commandery No. 7, Knights Templars, Wheeling. He was reared in the faith of the established Church of England and continued as a communicant of the Protestant Episcopal church after coming to this country.

"On May 27, 1882, was solemnized the marriage of Mr. Northwood to Miss Clara Elizabeth Beaumont of Handsworth, Staffordshire, England, to whom two children were born. He is survived by his widow and the son and daughter. The son is H. Clarence Northwood, of Cincinnati,

This may be the last formal portrait of Harry Northwood, ca. mid-1918 (note the photographer's "ocean" backdrop). **Courtesy of Miss Robb.**

and Mrs. H. W. Robb, of Wheeling, is the daughter. His only brother, Carl, died in January, 1918."

Harry Northwood's funeral took place from the family home, 310 S. Front St. (Wheeling Island), on Friday, February 7, 1919. Services were conducted by the Rev. J. Logan Fish of St. Andrew's Episcopal Church. Company president George E. House was among the pallbearers, as was mould room foreman George Matheny. Other pallbearers were longtime neighbor and family friend George Lutz, Wheeling insurance agent Dave Morgan, William Tibbett of East Liverpool, and Sam Stafford of Pittsburgh. Harry White, Jr. and Alfred Dugan of Indiana, Pa., were in attendance, and the *Indiana Progress* newspaper recalled Harry Northwood as "a successful businessman [who] had many friends" (February 12, 1919).

At its May, 1919, meeting the members of the National Association of Manufacturers of Pressed and Blown Glassware appointed a committee of three (C. B. Roe, C. R. Harmon, and Victor Wicke) to draft a memorial resolution in honor of Harry Northwood. On May 27, 1919, a letter was sent to Clara Northwood:

"In the passing of Mr. Northwood this Association has lost a proven and tried friend, one who was loyal at all times to the Association, and, moreover, kind to each individual member whenever the opportunity presented itself to show kindness. Everyone was his friend.

"The National Association of Manufacturers of Pressed and Blown Glassware has lost one of its most efficient and meritorious representatives, one who also introduced into the industry new ideas and methods, many of which will continue to bear fruit in the future.

"While a copy of this letter will be incorporated in the minutes of the National Association of Manufacturers of Pressed & Blown Glassware, such a reminder will not be necessary to keep Harry's memory green in the minds of our members. We shall miss his congenial personality and sound advice when we meet in the future, and often in the years to come we shall speak of him and he shall not be forgotten."

Clara Northwood's handwritten reply, dated June 21, 1919, on black-bordered stationery, said, in part: "The kind letter was a great comfort to me, and I shall always treasure it, for it brings assurance that it comes from life long friends who really knew him and his worth."

310 SOUTH FRONT ST.
WHEELING, W. VA.

June 21st/19.

Mr C. B. Roe
" C. R. Harmon,
" Victor G. Wicke.

Dear Friends:-
Will you please convey to the "National Association of Manufacturers" my many thanks for the "Memorial Tribute" to my Late Husband. The kind letter was a great comfort to me, and I shall always treasure it, for it brings assurance that it comes from life long friends who really knew him and his worth.

Yours very Sincerely
C. E. Northwood

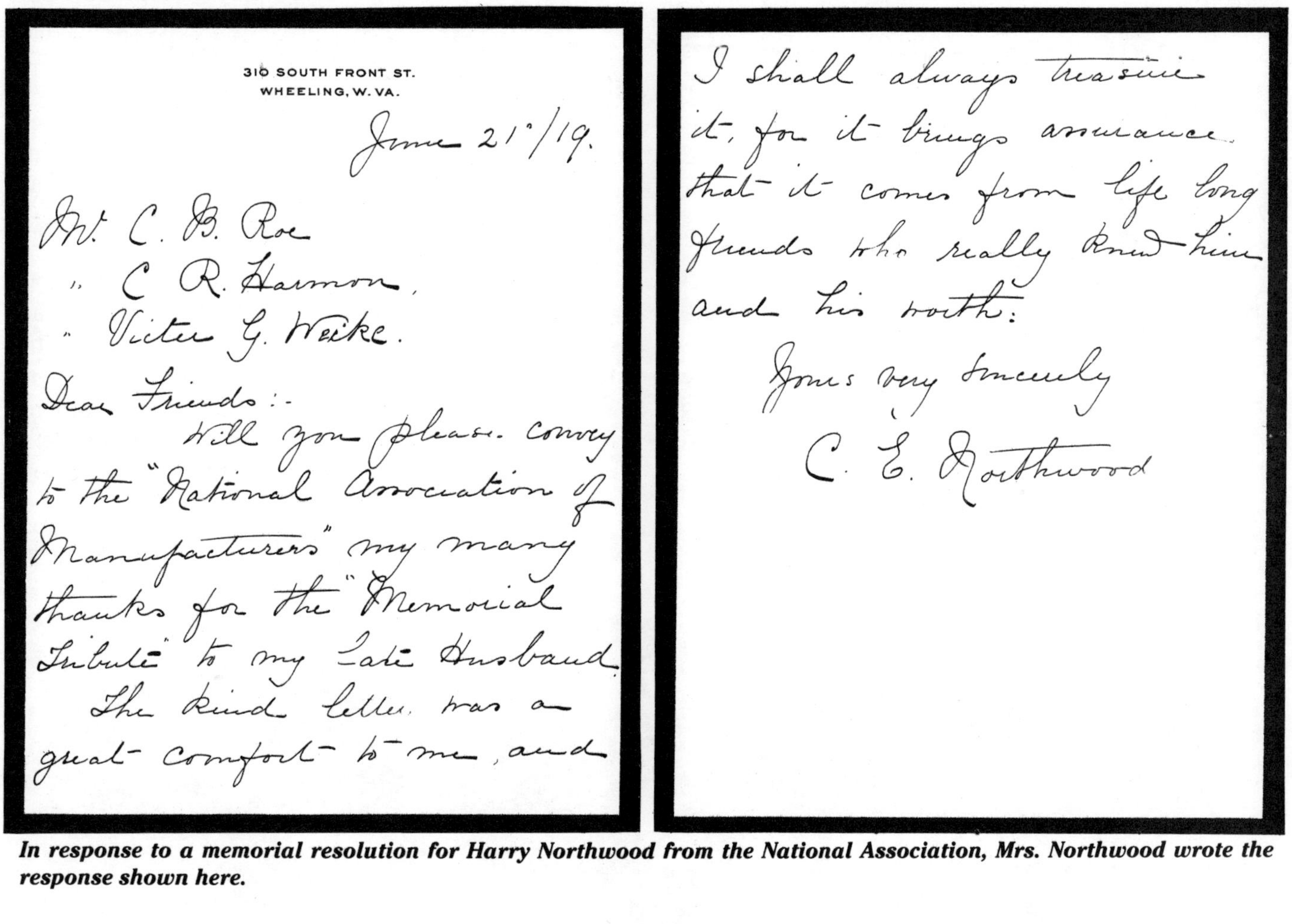

In response to a memorial resolution for Harry Northwood from the National Association, Mrs. Northwood wrote the response shown here.

After Harry Northwood's death in February, 1919, the firm of H. Northwood and Co. was reorganized. George House continued as president, and treasurer Dent A. Taylor, who had been with the firm since 1907, took charge of day-to-day operations in the office, assisted by his son Morgan Taylor, a former U. S. consular service employee who had no previous experience in the glass business, and by secretary Katherine Fitzsimmons. Clarence Northwood remained as salesman for the firm's western territory; he lived in Cincinnati, Ohio, and was not connected with the plant's day-to-day operations. Factory manager James Haden, who may have been with the firm since its inception in 1902, was an experienced glassmaker, and he produced several new colors between 1919 and 1924, but the Northwood firm struggled financially.

Competition in glass tableware and lighting goods was always keen, of course, but the Northwood's tableware was similar in colors and shapes to that being offered by Imperial, Westmoreland, Fenton, and the Diamond Glass-Ware Company of Indiana, Pa. Ironically, the Fenton firm was headed by Frank L. Fenton, who had been an apprentice decorator at Northwood's plant in the late 1890s and later worked briefly at the Wheeling plant in 1903-04. A Northwood cousin, Alfred Dugan, was involved with the Diamond concern.

The Northwood enterprise was unable to match its sales successes of earlier years, and debts arising from factory renovations in 1921-22, the MacBeth-Evans lawsuit, and an IRS tax investigation were substantial. Ultimately, the struggle proved too much for the company, which went into receivership in late September, 1925, and ceased production in December of that year. Despite rumors of possible re-openings, the venerable H. Northwood and Company slipped into history.

Northwood Family Matters

The deaths of Carl and Harry Northwood had profound effects upon their immediate families as well as upon the glass business. Carl's widow, the former Rose Overton, returned to England. Daughters Amy (b. 1899 in Indiana, Pa.) and Mildred (b. 1900 in England) stayed in Wheeling where they married and had families. Amy Northwood Hamilton died in 1983, and Mildred Northwood Gilleland in 1984.

Harry Northwood had not died a wealthy man, although his monthly income of $600 had certainly provided a comfortable lifestyle. The family home at 310 South Front Street on Wheeling Island was free from mortgage and he left an automobile and a gold watch, but the bulk of his estate was stock in H. Northwood and Co. It

Northwood's No. 643 covered bon bon (left) has counterparts from the Diamond Glass Co. of Indiana, PA (center), and the Fenton Art Glass Co. of Williamstown, WV (right). Fenton also used the 643 designation. Notice the differences in height as well as the thickness of the stems and design of the finials.

had considerable worth on paper, of course, but without the benefit of Northwood the glassmaker, its potential value and liquidity soon dwindled. The company had had a $25,000 life insurance policy on Harry Northwood, but money could neither replace nor purchase the necessary knowledge. Even this cash caused problems, as the IRS contended that the firm had not treated it properly on the corporation's 1919 income tax return.

Harry Northwood's widow, Clara Elizabeth Beaumont Northwood, who preferred to be called "Lil," remained in Wheeling, although she took no active interest in the company. The Northwoods' daughter, Mabel Virginia (b. 1884), had married Harry M. Robb in 1909. The Robb family's home was also on S. Front St., across the street from the Northwood residence. Robb worked at the Whitaker mill in Wheeling and in a family business, Greer and Laing. Later, he became a partner in the Lukens Jewelry Store on Market Street; the couple's only child, Elizabeth Northwood Robb, was born in 1913.

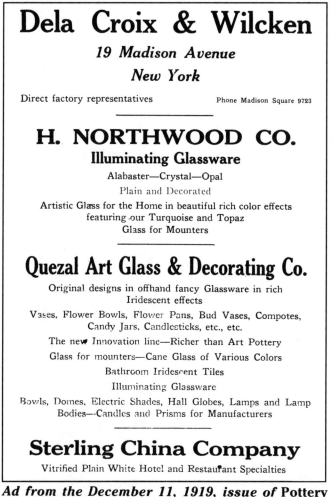

Ad from the December 11, 1919, issue of **Pottery Glass and Brass Salesman.** *Although "Illuminating Glassware" is featured, Luna is not mentioned, perhaps because of the lawsuit between Macbeth-Evans and Northwood.*

Clara Elizabeth Northwood decided to build a home on Rockledge Road in Wheeling, and it was completed in the early 1920s. The deepening financial difficulties encountered by the glass company sometimes made it difficult for her to meet the mortgage payments, and she was assisted by her son-in-law Harry Robb and by her brother Percy Beaumont, who was then in charge of the Beaumont Glass Company at Morgantown. The Northwood, Robb and Beaumont families were close knit, visiting frequently and vacationing together in the summer at Parry Sound, Ontario. In 1920-21, Clara Elizabeth Northwood accompanied George House and his wife on an automobile trip across the United States to California. While there, they visited with friends, including Mr. and Mrs. C. M. Rodefer, who owned a glass plant in Bellaire, Ohio. Clara Elizabeth Northwood died in 1937.

Clarence Northwood, the only son of Clara Elizabeth Beaumont Northwood and the late Harry Northwood, passed away at age 40 in early December, 1923. His name had been connected with the Wheeling firm since early 1904, when a glass trade journal called him "an enthusiastic factor in the general sales department." He was pictured in a photograph taken inside the factory in June, 1906. The December 6, 1923, issue of *China, Glass and Lamps* carried this obituary: "News of the death on Tuesday, at his home in Cincinnati, of Clarence Northwood ... was received the same day at the offices of Chas. J. Dela Croix, New York representative for the Northwood factory. Mr. Northwood traveled from Ohio south for the company and was well known and well liked in the trade. He was operated on recently for appendicitis and following the operation he developed pneumonia from which he died. ... A wife, his mother and sister survive him."

New Colors for the Roaring 20s

Northwood's light blue and topaz iridescent hues remained popular, and an opaque blue was introduced in 1921. During the early 1920s, the Northwood firm sought to regain a foothold in the glass tableware industry. To this end, it continued its line of glass in Blue Iris or Blue Iridescent (see Figs. 818-833) and Topaz Iris (see Figs. 834-850). In 1922, a distinctive new transparent color called Russet (see Figs. 851-856 and 860-865) was added to join the opaque blue, which was then called Jade Blue (see Figs. 872-881). There is one interesting note about an iridescent "white" with black decoration in a 1923 journal (see Fig. 890).

No. 705 comport.

Later, two more opaque colors—Jade Green (see Figs. 904-916) and Chinese Coral (see Figs. 935-964)—were placed on the market. Rosita Amber, a transparent glass which was not iridized, was developed in 1925 (see Figs. 867-868, 870-871, 925, and 932-933). Unfortunately for the Northwood firm, several of these hues, especially the opaque colors, competed with similar wares being marketed by other firms, including Fenton and Diamond, all of whom were becoming increasingly successful by the mid-1920s.

The various articles in which the Northwood's colors were made are shown in promotional materials put out by the firm in the 1920s. The first of these is a folder entitled "The Lure of Rainbow," which contains a price list dated March 1, 1924. By this time, the term Rainbow was being applied to the entire line of colors, both iridescent (Blue, Topaz and Russet) and opaque (Jade Green and Chinese Coral). A quick comparison of this folder with the "Rainbow and Cobweb" folder (see Chapter Six) will reveal the substantial number of new articles which had been added to the lines, as follows: candlesticks; vases; bulb bowls; comports; fruit bowls; nut bowls; and water and iced tea sets.

Another catalog devoted to "The Rainbow Line" was issued later in 1924 or early in 1925; neither Russet nor Jade Blue is mentioned, but Blue and Topaz continue as the line's iridescent colors. The opaque colors (Jade Green and

Chinese Coral) remain present, and the transparent Rosita Amber, which was first noted by the trade press in December, 1924, is listed for the first time. Each hue in the Rainbow line was illustrated in color and many articles were shown in black and white (see the last page in the color section of this book and the five pages which follow it).

Among the new articles listed in "The Rainbow Line" catalog was the No. 724-725 console set, which consisted of a large two-handled oval bowl and an interesting pair of candlesticks (see Figs. 908-909). A twisted vase, No. 727, was also shown, and it was available in several sizes (see Figs. 819, 867, 932 and 935). Various "Lamp Vases," designated Nos. 1000-1006, were illustrated (see Figs. 882-883 and 926), and these were available in four colors—Blue, Canary, Jade Green and Chinese Coral—as well as black. This is the first mention of black glass since the World War I era, although Northwood had made its line of black bases throughout the 1920s. Several new black bases were also shown, the High Black Stand (see Fig. 905) and those to be used with the aquariums. Incidentally, the aquariums represented a completely new departure for the Northwood firm, away from tableware and novelty items.

As one might suspect, the glass tableware trade publications often greeted each new Northwood color of the 1920s with the customary fanfare. Blue Iris and Topaz Iris were mentioned in the June 9, 1921, issue of *China, Glass and Lamps,* but the January 19, 1922, issue of *Pottery, Glass and Brass Salesman* had a full description of Northwood's new Jade Blue and Russet: "The H. Northwood Company, of Wheeling, W. Va., has just sent some very attractive novelties to Dela Croix & Wilcken, 19 Madison Avenue. These include two very pleasing new colors, both applied to a variety of fancy articles. One is termed "Jade blue" and the other a "russet," and both are in iridescent effect and most charming. The jade blue is ... a rich luster much after the order of a turquoise and somewhat suggestive of a robin's egg. The russet is transparent and, as the name would indicate, strongly suggests a rich russet apple color. Both of these are applied to a full line of fancy articles, including bowls, candlesticks, etc."

The lone reference to be found to Northwood's white iridescent is in the August 9, 1923, issue of *Pottery, Glass and Brass Salesman:* "Kelly & Reasner, with showrooms in the Shops Building, 17 North Wabash Avenue [Chicago], have recently

The Lure of Rainbow

RAINBOW

The very name is suggestive. The radiance and colorings of this Ware are among the most beautiful ever achieved by skilled artists in the decorative glassworker's craft.

Rainbow Ware is subject to imitation from many sources, yet its beauty of shape and design, and its originality of colors remain unequaled. Its appeal is instant and universal to those who appreciate beautiful glassware, and wish to use it in decorating and beautifying the home.

The Rainbow Line

is offered in a variety of unusually beautiful colors. Three of these, Blue, Topaz and Russet, are transparent and iridescent, reflecting from their specially treated surfaces all the values of light in the vari-colored hues of the rainbow. The other two colors are opaque and include the popular Jade Green, and a new shade known as Chinese Coral. This new color is a distinctly novel introduction in colored glass but its vividness of coloring has led to wide acceptance where a bizarre decorative note is desirable.

The entire Rainbow line is obtainable either in plain colors or decorated with a band of coin gold. This produces a striking effect, adding appreciably to the beauty of any of the colors with which it may be used.

The universal recognition accorded the Northwood name wherever quality glassware is known has come only with the knowledge gained through many years close association with the glass working industry. Established as one of the pioneer glass factories on the American continent, Northwood leadership in design and manufacture has been consistently maintained.

Northwood designs are created by artists of traditional talent and long experience and are carried out by workers who spring from generations of skilled artisans in the glassworking craft.

Thus it is that a piece of glassware, known to be of Northwood origin, carries with it the fullest assurance of originality, novelty and inherent quality.

PRICE LIST

MARCH 1, 1924

	List, Colors	List. Gold Band
Nos. 616-617-660-661-718 (Roll Edge) Bowl and Base	$16.80	$23.00
Nos. 647-648-649-673-697-717 Bowl and Base	20.00	26.00
No. 662 Bowl and Base (same shape and size as No. 617)	16.00	22.00
No. 663 Bowl and Base (same shape and size as No. 660)	16.00	22.00
No. 669—8" Bowl and Base (same shape as No. 620)	14.00	18.00
Nos. 692-693-694 Bowl and Base	11.50	15.00
No. 620 Bowl and Base	21.00	27.00
No. 638 Bowl and Base	12.00	16.00
Nos. 640-641-642 Bowl and Base	11.25	15.00
No. 658—7" Candle-stick	9.00	12.00
No. 657—8" Candle-stick	10.50	13.75
No. 651—10½" Candle-stick	30.00	35.00
No. 659 Candy Jar and Cover	13.50	18.50
No. 636 Candy Jar and Cover	17.50	22.75
No. 643 Candy Jar and Cover	13.50	18.50
Nos. 644-645-646 Ftd. Bon Bon	8.00	10.50
Nos. 652-653-654-655-656 Ftd. Comport	8.00	11.50
No. 666 Ftd. Comport	16.00	19.50
No. 637 Ftd. Comport	8.00	10.50
No. 650 Baked Apple Dish	6.00	9.00
No. 301—4½" Nappy	3.00	4.50
Nos. 613-618 Vase	12.00	17.00
No. 569 Sweet Pea Vase (Rolled or Flat Top)	8.00	11.50

	List, Colors	List. Gold Band
No. 668 Wall Vase	16.00	22.00
No. 559 Jug and Tumbler	15.00	20.00
No. 621 Mayonnaise Bowl	8.00	10.50
No. 670 Finger Bowl	6.00	8.50
Nos. 671-672 Bulb Bowl	6.00	8.50
Nos. 301-701—6" Butter Plate	4.00	6.50
No. 622 Salad Plate	8.00	11.50
No. 630—8½" Luncheon Plate	12.00	15.50
No. 639 Service Plate	8.00	13.50
No. 631 Cake Plate	12.00	17.50
No. 703—11" Plate	8.00	13.50
No. 595 Turtles	7.50	....
No. 594—2½" Flower Block	3.60	....
No. 594—3½" Flower Block	5.00	....
No. 5 Crystal Coaster	1.30	....
No. 5 Colored Coaster	1.60	3.25
No. 640 (Small) Black Base	4.00	....
No. 638 (Medium) Black Base	5.00	....
No. 616 (Large) Black Base	6.00	....
No. 669 (Special) Black Base	5.00	....
No. 620 (Special) Black Base	6.00	....
No. 674 Plate	6.00	8.50
No. 685 Sherbet	4.50	6.50
No. 675 Handled Candle-sticks	8.00	12.00
No. 676 Candle-stick	7.00	10.50
No. 989—11" Swung Vase	6.00	8.00
No. 816—11" Swung Vase	6.00	8.00
No. 930—15" Swung Vase	12.00	15.00

	List, Colors	List. Gold Band
No. 576 Flower Pot and Saucer	18.00	28.00
Nos. 677 to 684 Footed Bowls	24.00	30.00
With Black Foot	28.00	35.00
Nos. 713-714-715 Ftd. Bowls	18.00	22.50
With Black Foot	21.60	24.00
No. 688—8 Pc. Ice Tea Set— Hld. Tum.	36.00	60.00
No. 691 Covered Almond or Bon Bon	18.00	23.00
No. 695—8½" Candle-stick	10.50	13.75
No. 696—10" Candle-stick	12.00	16.00
No. 698 Handled Tray	14.00	20.75
No. 699 Cheese and Cracker Set	22.50	30.00
No. 700—7 Pc. Water Set	30.00	45.00
No. 704 Deep or Roll Edge Mayonnaise	8.00	11.50
No. 705 Tall Comport	12.00	17.00
No. 706—Ash Tray	4.00	8.00
No. 707—3 Ft. Bowl Reg.— Cupd.—Fld.	7.00	10.50
No. 708—8½" Candle-stick	10.50	13.75
No. 709 Black Stand for No. 647	10.00	....
No. 710 Black Stand for No. 640	8.00	....
No. 711 Black Stand for No. 692	8.00	
No. 712 Black Stand for No. 616	10.00	
Nos. 716/695 Console Set (11½" Roll Edge Bowl)	36.50 Special	
Nos. 692/695 Console Set	30.00 Special	

This price list for the Rainbow line from 1924 tells us that all of these articles (over 75 pieces) were made in five different colors—Blue Iris, Topaz Iris, Russet, Jade Green and Chinese Coral.

received a collection of novelties in fancy glassware from the H. Northwood Company, of Wheeling, W. Va. One of these has a white iridescent body and is decorated with a black lattice which takes the form of a border decoration. This is shown in a complete range of tableware." This description may reflect a rebirth of the Pearl color introduced as part of the original Satin Sheen line in 1917 or it may refer to an opaque white (i. e., opal) glass. (see Fig. 890).

A new color called Jade Green was slated for introduction in early 1924. This preliminary report appeared in the November 8, 1923, issue of *Pottery, Glass and Brass Salesman:* "The latest

production of fancy glassware of the H. Northwood Company, Wheeling, W. Va., is a line of jade-colored glassware, samples of which have just been received at the office of the C. J. Dela Croix Company, 19 Madison Avenue, local representative of the concern. The jade is remarkable for its true simulation to the genuine Chinese jade. Placing a piece of the former in proximity to the latter, it is difficult to tell which is which. Certain of the items, such as candlesticks, bowls and other footed pieces, may be obtained with the base in opal—if desired-or else the whole article can be had in the same color. The two-tone effect is very striking. The line includes console

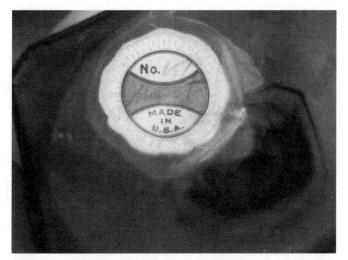

Original label on the underside of a No. 651 candlestick in Russet. Courtesy of Kitty and Russell Umbraco.

RAINBOW IRIDESCENT
FRUIT BOWL
With Attached Stand

Your customers won't be able to resist when they see this fruit bowl—attractively displayed under a knockout price.

1C2405—2 styles, rolled edge and belled, 11½ in. diam., extra deep shape, allover rainbow iridescent colorings, 6½ in. jet base. 3 pcs. each style. 6 in bbl., wt. 40 lbs.
Each **$1.10**
(Total $6.60)

Butler Brothers catalog (May, 1924).

IRIDESCENT ART GLASS
FRUIT BOWL
With Stand
One of our best offerings

1C2400—12 in., mammoth deep bowl, allover iridescent hand decorated golden and rainbow colors, 6½ in. jet base. 1 in carton, wt. 6 lbs............Each **$1.20**

STAR VALUE

Butler Brothers catalog (August, 1924).

sets, cracker and cheese dishes, handled sandwich trays, bowls in great variety, flower blocks and punch sets."

Some Jade Green articles may be found today with gold banding or other similar gold decor. These might have been done in the Northwood's own decorating shops, of course, but the Lotus Glass Company of nearby Barnesville, Ohio, is known to have marketed Northwood's Jade Green decorated with its own gold band motifs (see the color page between Fig. 919 and Fig. 920).

The Northwood firm made arrangements to market an extensive assortment of its Jade Green items through Carson Pirie Scott, a department store chain headquartered in Chicago. Carson Pirie Scott also contracted for additional jade articles from other glassmaking firms and prepared a special flyer which illustrated the entire offering (see overleaf). Most of the items shown are Northwood products, but the "thin blown glassware" articles near the upper left were made by some other firm. This Carson Pirie Scott flyer was shown in color by Stout (*Depression Glass III,* pp. 42-43), but the glassware was mistakenly attributed to Fenton, probably because Stout borrowed the flyer from the Fenton archives. Frank M. Fenton is sure that these particular Jade Green articles are not Fenton products, although Fenton did make other items in its jade hue for Carson Pirie Scott.

Chinese Coral, an opaque color sometimes called red, was also slated for introduction in early 1924. *China, Glass and Lamps* (January 7, 1924) pictured a "console set which can be had in five colors—blue, topaz, and russet iridescent, jade green and Chinese red." The set consisted of a bowl and "candlesticks ... marked by a series of raised rings on the stick and by a hollow foot."

NEW COLORED ART GLASS ASSORTMENT.
Just the assortment to tone up your glassware stock. Very popular.

K262X—New colors and shapes; high grade glass; most popular selling pieces only; blue iris, russet, topaz and jade blue colors; all pieces, with exception of candlesticks, with black footed separate bases; an assortment that will give you a good profit. 1 doz. pieces in assortment.
Per assortment **17.50**
A pair of candlesticks counts as 1 piece in the assortment.

Assortment of Northwood glassware from a 1922 catalog issued by G. Sommers & Co. Note the specific references to Northwood colors, including Russet.

This attractive jade green glassware is one of the most successful lines brought ou
table decoration.   Shipped direct fr

Thin blown glassware.

6270   Goblets.   Tall Sherbets.   Footed Tumblers.   Coasters.

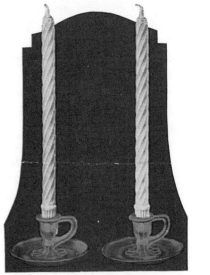

6253   Handled Candlesticks.

6246   Flower Holder.   **6248**   8¾ in. Bowl and Stand-   **6238**   7½ in. Bowl and Stand-
2½ in.   3½ in.   ard.   ard.

6252   Candlesti

6254   8½ in. Plate.   **6285**   6¼ in. Bon Bon.   **625**   7½ in. Comport.

6256   8¼ in. Bowl and Standard.

624   13 in. Bowl and Standard and 3½ in.
Flower Block.

6257   11 in. Bowl and Standard.

6265   Console Set wi
Does not inclu

62   10½ in. Bowl and Standard.

6251   Console Set.   Does not include candles or fruit.

6258   1 lb. Candy Jar.   62

he soft coloring of the various pieces give it complete harmony with any
'actory, at factory prices.

626   Cheese and Cracker Plate.   **6261**   Sandwich Plate.

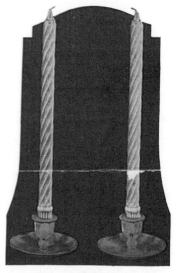

6262   7½ in. Bon Bon.   **6263**   7 in. Comport.   **6264**   Mayonnaise and Plate.   **6255**   Candlesticks.

in. high.

6289   9½ in. Bowl and Standard.

6245   Handle Candlestick.   **6247**   8½ in. Comport.   **6291**   Sweetmeat

6243   11½ in. Footed Bowl.

, Flower Block.
s or flowers.

6260   10 in. Bowl and Standard.

6283   Bon Bon.

6244   Bowl and Standard.

6249   Console Set.   Does not include candles or fruit.

191

DELA CROIX & WILCKEN

19 Madison Avenue, Madison Square, East - - New York

Phone Madison Square 9723

REPRESENTING

The H. E. Rainaud Company

MERIDEN, CONN.

1922 Line
Unique in Novel and Original
Ideas

Chicago Office:
IRA A. JONES CO.
17 No. Wabash Ave.

At the Shows:
PITTSBURGH
William Penn Hotel
Mr. Walter Bishop

CHICAGO
Morrison Hotel
Room 611

H. Northwood Company, Wheeling, W. Va.

New Lines for 1922:

Jade Blue Glass: A jewel of approved color.
Russet Glass: A new and pleasing color.
Blue and Topaz Iris: Always popular.
All made in Flower, Fruit and Salad Bowls, Comports, Covered Bowls, Candy Jars and Candlesticks.

Paste Mold Aquarium Bowls, Crystal and Colored.

Crystal Flower Blocks; Black Glass Stands; Coasters, Crystal, Blue and Canary. Glass for Mounting.

Lustre Art Glass Company, Maspeth, Long Island, N. Y.

Manufacturers of
Lead Blown Offhand Glassware
High grade—Exquisite color effects.

Specializing in
Artistic and Fancy Table Glassware
Exclusive Designs for Illumination

T. J. Callet Cut Glass Company, Johnstown, Pa.

Complete Line of High Grade Val St. Lambert and Bryce Bros. Blanks in Artistic and Original Designs.
Light and Heavy Cuttings. Table and Illuminating Glassware.

COMPLETE SAMPLE LINES ON DISPLAY
Visiting and Local Buyers Cordially Invited.

Dela Croix and Wilcken represented a number of American glass manufacturers. Note the Northwood's new color for 1922, Russet; Jade Blue is an "approved color" and Blue Iris and Topaz Iris are "always popular," indications that the latter three had been on the market for some time.

(Continued from page 189)

This description refers to Northwood's No. 708 candlesticks (see Figs. 937 and 951).

The January 17, 1924, issue of *Pottery, Glass and Brass Salesman* was enthusiastic about the new Chinese Coral, and the editor alluded to the previous success of Jade Green: "The H. Northwood Company, of Wheeling, W. Va., which has met with a conspicuous success in the production of colored glassware—notably its Chinese jade green—has just put on the market another new color which it calls a Chinese coral. This strongly suggests rouge flambe, so well known in Chinese art porcelains. It is indeed a beautiful tone and is shown on a full line of fancy tableware and other pieces, including several new numbers. The entire sample range is on display at the showrooms of the local representative, the C. J. Dela Croix Company, 19 Madison Avenue."

Like most red-orange glasses, Northwood's Chinese Coral varies a bit in color from batch to batch, so collectors cannot expect perfect harmony among all the articles in the line. Some pieces exhibit light brownish-orange tones (see Fig. 924). These are sometimes called "tan coral" by collectors, but there is no evidence to suggest that the Northwood firm placed them outside the realm of its Chinese Coral line. Incidentally, the Fenton Art Glass Company had its Venetian Red wares on the market in 1924, too, and there are some difficult questions of attribution to be solved on a few Grape and Cable articles which could be either Fenton- or Northwood-made (see Fig. 647 as well as Heacock's *Fenton Glass: The First Twenty-Five Years*, pp. 71 and 138).

The last color developed by the Northwood firm was a dark, transparent amber dubbed Rosita Amber (see Figs. 867-868, 870-871, 925, and 932-933). An interesting article in the December 11, 1924, issue of *Pottery, Glass and Brass Salesman* reflected upon the successful introduction of Jade Green before extolling the virtues of the new hue: "Somewhat over a year ago the H. Northwood Company, of Wheeling, W. Va., after considerable experimentation produced a jade green in glassware that so faithfully copied a piece of genuine Chinese jade that, so far as tone was concerned, it was impossible to tell the genuine jade from the glass; only the texture proclaimed the difference between the two. This made a great hit with the trade and spurred on the concern's chemists to produce a new color this year which would be equally beautiful as well

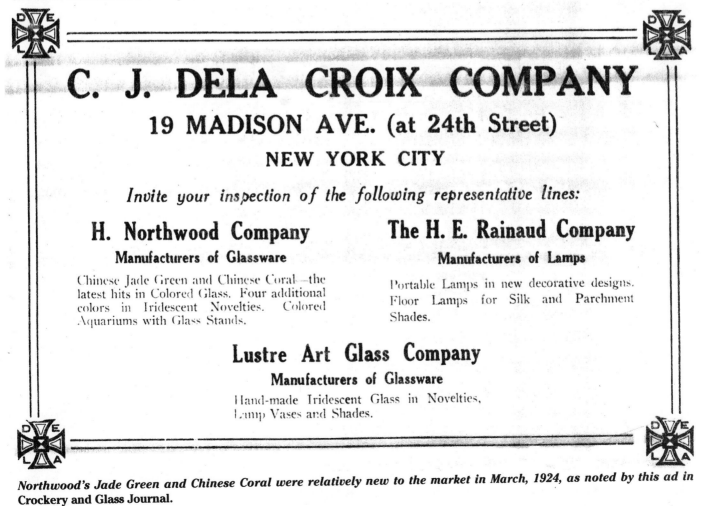

Northwood's Jade Green and Chinese Coral were relatively new to the market in March, 1924, as noted by this ad in Crockery and Glass Journal.

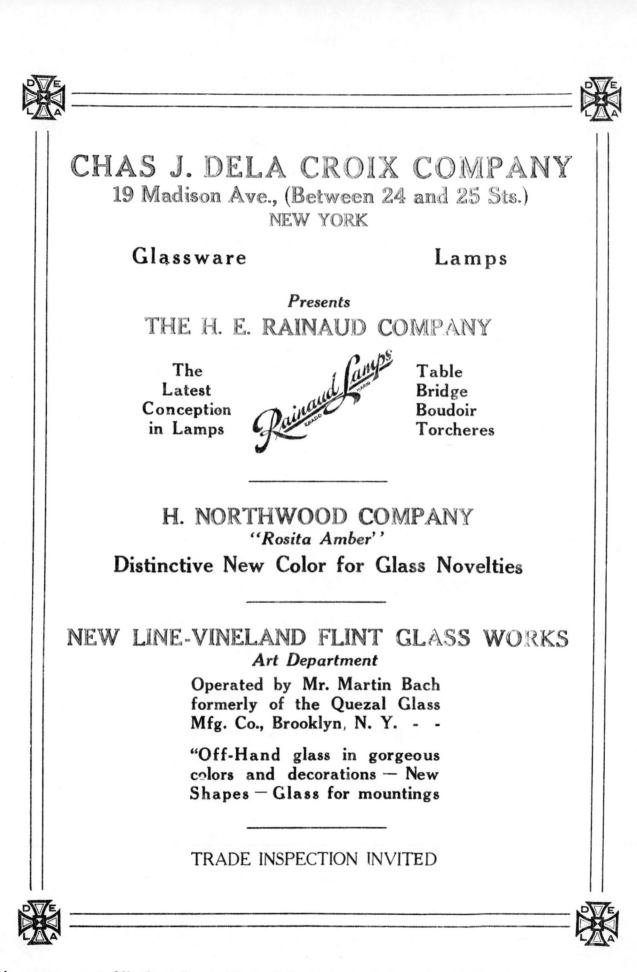

CHAS J. DELA CROIX COMPANY
19 Madison Ave., (Between 24 and 25 Sts.)
NEW YORK

Glassware   Lamps

Presents
THE H. E. RAINAUD COMPANY

The
Latest
Conception
in Lamps

Rainaud Lamps

Table
Bridge
Boudoir
Torcheres

H. NORTHWOOD COMPANY
"Rosita Amber"
Distinctive New Color for Glass Novelties

NEW LINE-VINELAND FLINT GLASS WORKS
Art Department
Operated by Mr. Martin Bach
formerly of the Quezal Glass
Mfg. Co., Brooklyn, N. Y. - -

"Off-Hand glass in gorgeous
colors and decorations — New
Shapes — Glass for mountings

TRADE INSPECTION INVITED

This announcement of Northwood's new "Rosita Amber" color in the December 18, 1924, issue of Crockery and Glass Journal *is one of the last major mentions of the firm's products.*

as excellent from a merchandising standpoint. This they believe they have done in a new tone they are pleased to call Rosita Amber. It has about it the rich scintilliancy of a glass of old sherry held to the light. It is an amber, but richer and deeper than most amber tones, and has the merit of being new as well as extremely attractive. It is applied to a full line of fancy ware. Samples have just been received at the offices of local agent Charles J. Dela Croix & Co., 19 Madison Avenue, where they make a fine display."

Despite the rainbow of new colors and the words of praise from trade journal editors, the Northwood firm gradually lost its ability to compete. The final drama began in the early fall of 1925.

The Northwood in Receivership

On September 23, 1925, George E. House, president of H. Northwood and Co., filed a bill of complaint (case in equity #122) in the United States District Court at Wheeling, asking the court to appoint a receiver to oversee the dissolution of the corporation and the disposition of its assets. The court immediately appointed H. Northwood Co.'s general manager, Dent A. Taylor, to act as receiver.

House's petition did not, however, paint a particularly bleak financial picture. The company had expended nearly $90,000 for factory improvements between 1919 and 1922. After five years of continuous profit (1916-20), the firm had suffered its largest single-year loss in 1921 ($37,000), followed by two years of only modest success (1922 showed a profit of $2,700 and 1923 slightly over $14,000). A loss of about $7,200 had occurred in 1924, but House's petition noted accounts receivable of over $30,000 and an inventory of glassware on hand of nearly $70,000. The firm apparently had no mortgages on its land or any other liens, but it was indebted to the Dollar Savings and Trust Company for about $58,000.

Nevertheless, there were both immediate and long-term concerns. The glassware inventory could not be liquidated quickly. A payroll of $4618.70 for about 150 workers and managers had to be met on Saturday, September 26, 1925 (a list of the individuals on this payroll appears in this chapter). The IRS had challenged the firm's 1918 and 1919 tax returns several years earlier, seeking more than $40,000 in additional taxes and interest. A letter of deficiency was issued on May 5, 1925; this ruling was appealed by the Northwood's lawyers. The firm's assets of $300,000 included $100,000 in capital stock, but its real value was, of course, suspect in view of slow sales and the rumors of shutdown. Corporate officers and stockholders, including Clara Elizabeth Northwood, had made personal loans of over $15,000 to the corporation to meet current expenses, probably weekly payrolls or pressing bills from suppliers.

As one might suspect, news of the Northwood's difficulties was closely followed both locally and in the glass trade publications. Articles appeared in the Wheeling *Intelligencer* as well as in *Pottery, Glass and Brass Salesman* (October 1, 1925) and, later, the *National Glass Budget* (January 2, 1926). The plant continued to operate through November, 1925. The receivership case file contains a ledger sheet from Harshaw, Fuller and Goodwin, a chemical company in Cleveland, which indicates that the Northwood firm continued to order glass coloring materials such as Uranium and Cadmium compounds through mid-September, 1925. Glassmaking operations probably took place only to fill orders in hand which could not be met through inventory. Decorators continued to report for work, and the melting furnaces were kept fired so that molten glass in the pots and tanks would not be lost.

Miss Bessie O. Kirsten was employed as a decorator at the Northwood plant for about eight years, and she was there when the plant closed. She does not recall any employees' worry over the firm's possible closure, so it probably happened quickly. Decorating room foreman Charles Facer gave her a decorated crystal comport and wished her well on her last day at the plant. She also owned a pair of Northwood's No. 708 candlesticks with unusual decoration; the top and base are painted bright yellow and black, and the rest of the candlesticks are decorated with gray/blue and brown paint (see Fig. 965). After the Northwood closed, she went briefly to the Central Glass Company and then to the Wheeling Tile Works for a time. She retired from the Stone and Thomas department store in Wheeling. The Kirsten family home at 3637 Wetzel was almost literally in the shadow of the Northwood plant; she lived there until 1988.

Despite some published local rumors to the contrary, no new investors emerged to bolster the financial position of H. Northwood Co. The plant ceased all operations on December 12, 1925, and the gas was shut off to the furnaces. This was the final blow. As subsequent reports by the court-appointed receiver would reveal, the Northwood's sales network deteriorated rapidly, as

These employees were on the H. Northwood and Co. payroll for the week ending September 26, 1925

General Help
James Haden
 (factory manager)
Harry Snyder
John Deakin
William Reinbold
Andy Morris
Chas. Gensche
Ed. Short
Dan Barnhart
Louis Rembach
Francis Jurezak
Chas. Beaver
John Reiver
Frank Kurenski
Harry Beaver
Ivan Lewis
Louis Rentner

Shipping & Packing
Dave Parkins
Albert St. Myers
Julius Montandon
William Spaar
Lloyd Yates
Grace St. Myers
Joseph Wilson
George Bischoff
Roy Earlewine
Edna Gesser
Albert Poole
Tillie O'Neil

Decorating Room
Chas. Facer
 (foreman)
John Petermann
Lizzie Mann
Eleanor Hannan
Abe Richards
Sim Johnson
Beatrice Rayl
Ida Klages
Bessie Kirsten
Fred Howell
Helen Reineke
William Lewis
Bertha West
Crilda Wieneke
Mary Rutherford
Thelma Nest
Rachel Davies
Emma Cope
Estella Blazier
Madelyn Muir
Margaret Montandon

Selecting Room
Harry Scarbrough
John Bromer
Rose Schweitzer
Mrs. Tamer Watson
Rose Shimek

Grinding Dept.
Jesse Broncircle
Carino DiEgidio
William Dittmar
Lester Werner
Irene Bugard
Sophie Demsick
John Oleska
Katheryn Coleman
Agnes Swesey
Eugene Keefe
Mae Cook
James Cook
Joseph Bero

Mold Shop
George L. Matheny
 (foreman)
Howard Smith
Edward Kratz
Jacob Bertschy
William Scherrer
Emma Brimson
Nellie Jefferson

Factory
Carl Anderson
Enoch Anderson
Ted Brannon
Ollie Cuproskey
Chas. Dusterdick
Chas. Frederick
Carl Fagerstrom
Ed. Haden
Werner Johnson
Arthur Kessmeir
David Klages
August Minkemeyer
Harry McCarthy
Ernest Orlofske
Ignaz Svach
Otto Stenberg
John Sweeney
Dan Schuler
Ed. Schlicher
Carl Weber
Chris Weneke
William White
Edwin Attwell

M. Bass
Eugene Burns
Earl Carlisse
Joseph Carrol
Edward Czerwinski
Walter Cole
William DeMuth
Chas. Dusterdick, Jr.
John Dolan
Stephen Granski
Stanley Gerlak
William Gary
Dell Hahle
Henry Hahle
Carl Hadam
Joseph Heil
Mike Harrish
Ed. Heller
Francis Jurezak
Sam Judge
Stanley Kaloszka
Joseph Loefler
Chas. Lynch
John Muzur
William Macklin
William Orlofske
John Parker
Ignatius Podeszwa
Howard Parker
Robert Rine
Edmond Sands
Bernard Schrebe
Amel Scheestel
Elmer Schnell
Andrew Scherrer
Atwood Smith
Robert Stanley
William Schrebe
Stephen Vargo
V. Wesolowski
Urban Yeager
John Yeager
John Zdonezyk
Vincent Zabo

Office
D. A. Taylor
M. O. Taylor
Thos. L. McGranahan
Frank Hissrich
Kate Fitzsimmons
Marian Rush
Mary Brown

representatives worried about their commissions and customers feared that orders would go unfilled. The unemployed glassworkers found jobs elsewhere in Wheeling or left the city.

The IRS proceedings against the H. Northwood Co. over tax returns from 1918 and 1919 dragged on, and several meetings of the creditors were postponed because of uncertainty over the company's tax liability. Finally, in May, 1926, the judge overseeing the receivership proceedings allowed the receiver to sell the plant and other company assets at auction, even though the tax matter with the IRS remained unsettled. The May 27, 1926, issue of *Pottery, Glass and Brass Salesman* had these details: "A contract to sell the plant, equipment and stock on hand of the bankrupt H. Northwood Company has been given to Gert's Realty Experts of New York and New Orleans. The contract is for thirty days and has been approved by the receiver, the creditors and the stockholders. The Northwood plant is reported to be in good condition and the stock of molds is said to be one of the largest in the country."

The only recorded appraisal of the real estate and the glass plant's fixtures was taken in late September, 1925, about two months before operations ceased. The land was valued at $30,000 and the buildings at about $45,000. The itemized valuation of machinery and equipment mentioned $51,000 worth of moulds for glassmaking, about $11,000 of which had been added since 1921, when a previous appraisal had been done. Unfortunately for today's researchers, no listing of moulds by shape or pattern was done. The firm's assets were valued at over $300,000 *in toto*, but over one-third of this consisted of accounts receivable and glassware in inventory. During the first half of 1926, receiver Dent A. Taylor filed monthly reports, detailing sales of glassware from inventory and attempts to collect on accounts.

An auction was scheduled for June 14, 1926 (*Pottery, Glass and Brass Salesman*, June 3, 1926), but it was postponed for a month. In the interim, *China, Glass and Lamps* (July 8, 1926) carried this ray of hope: "From Wheeling, W. Va., comes the report that certain business interests there are interested in the formation of a new corporation for the purpose of taking over and placing in operation the plant of the Northwood Glass Co., which has been listed for sale under a court order. That such preliminary steps as necessary have been taken is generally admitted at Wheeling, but definite proposals have not been divulged." A similar account in *Pottery, Glass and*

A snapshot of Harry Northwood near the factory, c. 1915. Courtesy of Miss Robb.

Brass Salesman (July 8, 1926) said that "several of the concern's large creditors" were behind the plans.

The auction went forward on June 14, 1926, and Robert Hazlett, representing the Dollar Savings and Trust, purchased the plant and its assets for $30,000. A July 15, 1926, report in a Wheeling newspaper included this reflective note:

"Originally the Hobbs-Brockunier plant, the Northwood plant, has had a most unusual and honorable career in the industrial life of Wheeling. The leading glass-makers of this valley had their training in the Hobbs-Brockunier factory; and for many years, it was conducted as a highly profitable institution.

"About 1904 [actually, 1902], the plant was taken over by the H. Northwood Co., being conducted very successfully under the management of the late Mr. Harry Northwood. It continued a prosperous career until about 1920 when industrial conditions changed, and the plant had two or three years of heavy losses. Due to competition and conditions, it was unable to recover from these losses, and a receivership was forced several weeks ago. The plant has been offered for sale a number of times, but no bidders

ONE OF WHEELING'S PIONEER GLASS PLANTS, THE NORTHWOOD

This photo appeared in the Wheeling Board of Trade's 1911 Yearbook *publication.* **Courtesy of Bill Carney.**

appeared until yesterday when Mr. Hazlett took the plant over."

In late September, 1926, Judge William E. Baker voided the sale of H. Northwood and Co.'s assets to the Dollar Savings and Trust (*Pottery, Glass and Brass Salesman,* September 30, 1926). The United States Board of Tax Appeals had finally rendered a judgment in the company's case relating to its 1918 and 1919 tax returns. The firm's liability was reduced from $40,000 to about $23,000, but the company was unsuccessful in both further appeals and an offer of compromise settlement. The Dollar Savings and Trust could not gain clear title to the property because of a tax lien, of course, so they asked that the terms of the sale be set aside, and Judge Baker concurred. On October 27, 1926, the Dollar Savings and Trust recorded the deed in Ohio County.

In November, 1927, local newspapers and glass trade periodicals alike carried reports that the J.R. Greenlee Co. of Bellaire, Ohio, would purchase and remodel the Northwood plant (*National Glass Budget,* November 19, 1927; *China, Glass and Lamps,* November 21, 1927; *American Flint,* December, 1927). The Greenlee firm, said the various accounts, had hired John Fenton to oversee the renovations and become general manager of the plant, which would manufacture "quality tableware, lighting fixtures and high-grade novelty goods." John Fenton was said to be "working on new moulds and coloring processes for making and decorating their new wares." A lengthy article from the Bellaire *Daily Leader,* quoted in the *National Glass Budget's* account, said that the Greenlee firm was aided "largely

through the efforts of the Dollar Savings and Trust Co., of Wheeling." This venture never materialized, and later reports that the factory would be sold to the Dooley Electrical Manufacturing Company (Wheeling *Intelligencer,* March 9, 1928) were likewise false.

Receiver Dent A. Taylor filed his final report in June, 1928. The lawyers who had argued the Northwood's unsuccessful tax case were paid, as were the expenses of the receiver himself. The IRS lien for about $23,000 in taxes took the remaining funds (about $6500), and the legal affairs of H. Northwood and Co. came to an end. The real estate, buildings and fixtures were ordered to be sold at auction. The auction was held over one year later, on August 27, 1929. The Dollar Savings and Trust bought everything for $21,500. The Great Depression forestalled any possibility of re-starting the glass factory, of course, and the Wheeling Dollar Savings and Trust finally disposed of the property in April, 1944, when it was sold to P. J. Gast and Sons, Inc.

Epilogue

Although the life of Harry Northwood and the affairs of the Wheeling firm he founded are now history, glass collectors today eagerly seek both Northwood glass and details about its namesake's life. This book, reflecting years of research by several authors and painstaking photography by several professionals, would not have been possible without the enthusiasm of those glass collectors for such a project. It is but a small tribute to a genuine genius in the history of American glassmaking—Harry Northwood.

BIBLIOGRAPHY

Addis, Wily P. *What's Behind Old Carnival: A Study of Patterns Seldom Seen*. Lakewood, OH: by author, 1971.

The American Flint, publication of the American Flint Glass Workers Union, Toledo, OH, various issues, 1910-26.

Asbury, Ray and Verda. "Burlington, Iowa—Our Home Town and Home of Fern Brand Chocolates," *The Carnival Pump* (December, 1986), p. 10.

Boultinghouse, Mark. *Art and Colored Glass Toothpick Holders*. N.p.: n. d.

Brahmer, Bonnie J. *Custard Glass*, second ed. N. p.: by author, 1967.

Butler Brothers catalogs, usually titled "Our Drummer," various issues (cited in text or photo credits), 1903-1926.

Callin's Wheeling Directory, various issues, 1881-1924.

Cambridge Glass Co. *1903 Catalog of Pressed and Blown Glass Ware.* (reprinted by NCC, Inc., 1976).

Charleston, R. J. *English Glass*. London: Allen and Unwin, 1984.

China, Glass and Lamps, various issues, 1900-1929.

Cosentino, Geraldine and Stewart, Regina. *Carnival Glass: A Guide for the Beginning Collector.* New York: Golden Press, 1976.

Crockery and Glass Journal, various issues, 1900-1929.

Dugan, Blanche Mock [Marshall]. "Samuel Dugan family history" (handwritten, 1960).

Edwards, Bill. *Northwood: King of Carnival Glass.* Paducah, KY: Collector Books, 1978.

Edwards, Bill. *The Standard Encyclopedia of Carnival Glass.* Paducah, KY: Collector Books, 1982; revised 2nd edition, Paducah, KY: Collector Books, 1988.

Eige, Eason. *A Century of Glassmaking in West Virginia.* Huntington: Huntington Galleries, 1980.

Ellwood City Historical Association. *A History of Ellwood City, Pennsylvania.* Ellwood City: privately printed, 1942.

Fenton Museum, archives and photos, Williamstown, WV.

Ferson, Regis and Mary. *Yesterday's Milk Glass Today.* Pittsburgh: privately printed, 1981.

Fish, Herb. "Rare Carnival Glass Lamps," *Glass Collector's Digest,* April/May, 1990, pp. 32-33.

Freeman, Larry. *Iridescent Glass*, enlarged second edition. Watkins Glen, NY: Century House, 1964.

Gilleland, Mildred Northwood. Interview with Jabe Tarter (recorded in August, 1978, at Indiana, PA).

Goldstein, Sidney M. and Leonard S. and Juliette K. Rakow. *Cameo Glass: Masterpieces from 2000 Years of Glassmaking.* Corning: Corning Museum of Glass, 1982.

Greguire, Helen. *Carnival in Lights*. N. p.: privately printed, 1975.

Grover, Ray and Lee Grover. *English Cameo Glass*. New York: Crown, 1980.

Hallam, Angela. *Carnival Glass*. Reisgate, England: Wise Books, 1981.

Hand, Sherman. *Colors in Carnival Glass* (four spiral-bound books). Scottsville, NY: by author, 1968-72.

Hand, Sherman. *The Collectors Encyclopedia of Carnival Glass*. Paducah, KY: Collector Books, 1978.

Hartung, Marion T. *Carnival Glass Series* (ten spiral-bound books, cited as Hartung 1, etc). Emporia, KS: by author, 1960-1973.

Hartung, Marion T. *Carnival Glass in Color: A Collector's Reference Book*. Emporia, KS: by author, 1967.

Hartung, Marion T. *Northwood Pattern Glass: Clear, Colored, Custard and Carnival*. Emporia, KS: by author, 1969.

Hartung, Marion T. *Opalescent Pattern Glass*. Des Moines: Wallace-Homestead, 1971.

Heacock, William. *Pattern Glass Preview* (abbreviated *PGP*).

Heacock, William. *The Glass Collector* (abbreviated *GC*).

Heacock, William. *Collecting Glass* (abbreviated *CG*).

Heacock, William. *Toothpick Holders from A to Z*. Marietta: Antique Publications, 1974; second edition, 1976.

Heacock, William. *Opalescent Glass from A to Z*. Marietta: Antique Publications, 1975; second edition, 1977.

Heacock, William. *Custard Glass from A to Z*. Marietta: Antique Publications, 1976.

Heacock, William. *Syrups, Sugar Shakers & Cruets from A to Z*. Marietta: Antique Publications, 1976.

Heacock, William. *1000 Toothpick Holders*. Marietta: Antique Publications, 1977.

Heacock, William and Bickenheuser, Fred. *U. S. Glass from A to Z*. Marietta: Antique Publications, 1978.

Heacock, William. *Oil Cruets from A to Z*. Marietta: Antique Publications, 1981.

Heacock, William. *Old Pattern Glass According to Heacock*. Marietta: Antique Publications, 1981.

Heacock, William. "Carnival Glass by Dugan and Diamond," *The Antique Trader Weekly*, February 25, 1981, pp. 78-81.

Heacock, William and Gamble, William. *Cranberry Opalescent Glass from A to Z*. Marietta: Antique Publications, 1987.

Heart of America Carnival Glass Association, *Educational Series I*. N. p.: Heart of America Carnival Glass Association, 1990.

House, George E., plaintiff, v. H. Northwood Co. *et al*. Case No. 162, District Court of the United States for the Northern District of West Virginia (records now stored at the National Archives, Mid-Atlantic Branch in Philadelphia).

Housefurnisher: China, Glass and Pottery Review, various issues, 1900-1907.

Husfloen, Kyle (ed.). *The Antique Trader Antiques and Collectibles Price Guide.* Dubuque, IA: Babka Publishing Co., 1990.

"John & Harry Northwood: A Family Tradition," exhibition catalog for the Mansion Museum prepared by Holly L. Hoover. Wheeling: Oglebay Institute, 1982.

Kamm, Minnie Watson. *Pattern Glass Pitchers.* Vols. I-VIII. Grosse Pointe, MI: by author, 1939-1954.

Klamkin, Marian. *The Collector's Guide to Carnival Glass.* New York: Hawthorn, 1976.

Klein, Dan and Lloyd, Ward. *The History of Glass.* London: Orbis, 1984.

Lagerberg, Ted and Vi. *Collectible Glass,* Books 1-4. New Port Richey, FL: privately printed, 1963-1968.

Lechner, Mildred and Ralph. *The World of Salt Shakers.* Paducah: Collector Books, 1976.

Lee, Ruth Webb. *Nineteenth-Century Art Glass.* New York: Barrows, 1952.

Lyon Brothers. *Spring and Summer Catalogue* (#453). Chicago: n. p., 1906.

MacBeth-Evans Co. v. H. Northwood Co. (records now stored at the National Archives, Mid-Atlantic Branch in Philadelphia).

Mackey, David. "New Interest Spurred in Old Wheeling Factory," Wheeling *News-Register,* September 5, 1965.

Manley, Cyril. *Decorative Victorian Glass.* New York: Van Nostrand Reinhold, 1981.

McDonald, Ann Gilbert. "Milk Glass Lamps and the Northwood-Dugan Connection," *Antique Trader,* February 27, 1985.

McKinley, Carolyn. *Goofus Glass.* Paducah, KY: Collector Books, 1984.

Markley, Lee. "Northwood's Bushel Baskets," *Glass Collector's Digest,* April/May, 1991, pp. 31-34.

Measell, James and Smith, Don E. *Findlay Glass: The Glass Tableware Manufacturers, 1886-1902.* Marietta: Antique Publications, 1986.

Moore, Donald E. *The Shape of Things in Carnival Glass.* Alameda, CA: by author, 1975.

Moore, Don. *Carnival Glass: A Collection of Writings.* Alameda, CA: by author, 1987.

Moore, Don. "Carnival Glass: Cinderella Comes of Age," *Glass Collector's Digest,* August/September, 1990, pp. 27-30.

Moore, Don. *The Complete Guide to Carnival Glass Rarities.* Alameda, CA: by author, n. d.

Mordini, Tom and Sharon. *Carnival Glass Auction Price Report.* Freeport, IL: by authors, yearly. All issues available (1984-85, 1986, 1988, 1989 and 1990) are $9.00 each, postpaid, from the authors at 36 N. Mernitz Ave., Freeport, IL 61032 (add $2.00 per volume, US funds, for overseas mailing).

Morris, Barbara. *Victorian Table Glass and Ornaments.* London: Barrie and Jenkins, 1978.

National Association of Manufacturers of Pressed and Blown Glassware. Archival materials, including minutes of local and national conferences between the assocation and the AFGWU (1902-1931), correspondence and other records relating to wage/move disputes, and various file folders and notebooks containing details of glassware items governed by agreements.

National Glass Budget, various issues, 1899-1927.

"90-Year-Old Tells Shiny Sliver of History," Wheeling *News-Register,* June 23, 1991.

Northwood, *John II. John Northwood: His Contribution to the Stourbridge Glass Industry, 1850-1902.* Stourbridge: Mark and Moody, 1958.

Northwood, Ken. Correspondence with James Measell (1989-90).

Notley, Raymond. *Carnival Glass.* Shire Publications, Ltd., 1983.

Notley, Raymond (editor). *Journal,* numbers 1-14. Published by the Carnival Glass Society [United Kingdom]. Issue 5 contains much excellent material on Northwood.

The Official Price Guide to Carnival Glass, second edition. New York: House of Collectibles, 1990.

Ohio County, WV. Public records, including deeds, births, deaths, and wills.

Owens, Richard E. *Carnival Glass Tumblers.* La Habra, CA: by author, 1975.

Peterson, Arthur G. *Glass Salt Shakers,* second printing. Des Moines: Wallace-Homestead, 1970.

Peterson, Arthur G. *Glass Patents and Patterns.* Sanford, FL: by author, 1973.

Presznick, Rose M. *Carnival and Iridescent Glass* (four spiral-bound books). Lodi, OH: by author, 1964-67.

Pullen, Anne Geffken. *Glass Signatures, Trademarks and Trade Names.* Lombard, IL: Wallace-Homestead, 1986.

Quinton-Baxendale, Marion. *Carnival Glass Worldwide.* Cornwall, England: Carnivalia Publications, 1983.

Resnik, John D. *The Encyclopedia of Carnival Glass Lettered Pieces.* Nevada City, CA: by author, 1989.

Revi, Albert Christian. *American Pressed Glass and Figure Bottles.* New York: Nelson, 1964.

Revi, Albert Christian. *American Art Nouveau Glass.* Exton, PA: Schiffer, 1968.

Revi, Albert Christian. *Nineteenth Century Glass: Its Genesis and Development,* revised edition. New York: Galahad Books, 1967.

Robb, Elizabeth Northwood. Correspondence and interviews with James Measell (1989-91).

Secrist, C. "Northwood Carnival Facts Are Explained," *Collector's Weekly,* August 13, 1974.

Smith, Frank R. and Ruth E. *Miniature Lamps.* New York: Nelson, 1968.

Sommers, G. & Co. catalogs, various issues (cited in text or photo credits), 1906-1926.

Spillman, Jane Shadel. *American and European Pressed Glass in the Corning Museum of Glass.* Corning: Corning Museum of Glass, 1981.

Spillman, Jane Shadel. *Glass Tableware, Bowls & Vases*. New York: Knopf, 1982.

Spillman, Jane Shadel. *Pressed Glass, 1825-1925*. Corning: Corning Museum of Glass, 1983.

Sprain, Thomas E. *Carnival Glass Tumblers: New and Reproduced, 1964-1984*. Millbrae, CA: by author, 1985.

Sprain, Tom. *Carnival Glass: Description and Price Guide*. Vacaville, CA: by author, 1991.

Taylor, Ardelle L. *Colored Glass Sugar Shakers and Syrup Pitchers*. N.p.: n. d.

United States Patent Office, various records pertaining to U. S. Patents and Designs.

Welker, John and Elizabeth. *Pressed Glass in America: Encyclopedia of the First Hundred Years, 1825-1925*. Ivyland, PA: Antique Acres Press, 1985.

Wheeling Board of Trade, *Manual of the Wheeling Board of Trade, 1900-01*. Wheeling: Daily Intelligencer Steam Job Press, 1901.

Wheeling Board of Trade, *First Annual Report ... Year Ending November 30, 1901*. Wheeling: Wheeling News Litho. Co., 1901.

Wheeling Board of Trade, *Year Book 1907*. Wheeling: Board of Trade, 1907 .

Wheeling Board of Trade, *Year Book 1911*. Wheeling: Board of Trade, 1911 .

Wheeling *Intelligencer*, various issues, 1902-1926.

Wheeling *Register*, various issues, 1902-1926.

Whitley, Cecil. *The World of Enameled Carnival Glass Tumblers*. Houston, TX: by author, 1985.

Wingerter, Charles A. *History of Greater Wheeling and Vicinity*. Chicago: Lewis Publishing, 1912.

INDEX